To Peggiann & Bob,

SCUBA DIVING
THE WRECKS AND SHORES OF LONG ISLAND, NY

See you on the USS San Diego!

David Rosenthal

David Rosenthal

3/29/08

The Wharves Project

New York, New York

Dedicated to
My Wife Lynda, my SCUBA buddy son Matthew, daughter Sophia,
and my Mother; Joan Leonard.

Thank you to Editor Justin Misik, Layout and Graphic Designer Elizabeth Heldrich

Acknowledgements to:

Steve Bielenda for advice, graphics and experiences on his dive boat the *RV Wahoo*
at the start of my diving career, Randi Eisen for advice and great training, Gary Gentile for
advice, graphics and the inspiration of his great book on the *USS San Diego*. Thanks also
to Dennis Anacker, Bill Cadden, Freddy and George Hughes, Pearl Miles, and Thomas
Savini for their thoughtful comments on the manuscript. Thanks to fellow author
Nili Gold for her inspiration in this project.

Thanks also to Stephen Edelstein from the NYC Sea Gypsies and Herb "Cap" Kaasmann
author of 'OREGON Greyhound of the Atlantic. ' for their assistance with graphics.

There are many great dive boats in the New York area; thanks to all their dedicated
Captains and Crews. Specifically thanks (in alphabetical order) to Dan Berg of the
Wreck Valley, Hank Garvin of the *RV Garloo*, John Gorman of the *Lock Ness*,
Howard Klein of the *Eagles Nest*, Frank Persico of the *Sea Hawk*, Bill Redden of the
Jeannie II and the late Captain Ken and Jean Marie Jastrzebski of the dive boat
Jean Marie. Also thanks to Captain Chuck Wade of the *Sea Turtle* out of Montauk who
provided excellent training to my son and I when we first started in this sport.

I am grateful for the professional service from all our local dive shops. Shops that
have played an integral part in my diving are (in alphabetical order) Hampton
Dive Center in Riverhead Long Island, Long Island Scuba in Lindenhurst Long Island,
Pan Aqua in Manhattan and especially my local shop; Stingray Dive Shop in Brooklyn.
I enjoy being a member of the Long Island Divers Association and am a past
president of the New York City Sea Gypsies dive club.

Thanks to all the divers I have dove with over the years and
others that have shared their experiences with me.

Finally, this book is also dedicated to the divers that have died while
exploring local wrecks.

Table of Contents

Filling the Lifeboat. Picture courtesy Herb Kaasmann,
OREGON, GREYHOUND OF THE ATLANTIC

FOREWORD

"If I have seen further it is by standing upon the shoulders of giants."

Sir Isaac Newton

Local diving would not be what it is today were it not for those who went before us. Amongst the many contributors to local diving over the years, there are two men who have been an integral part of the history of diving the waters of Long Island, New York. I asked Gary Gentile and Steve Bielenda to put a few thoughts to paper for this book and they kindly complied.

Steve Bielenda

My scuba diving career has spanned 48 years and to me, scuba diving is still one of the most exciting adventures anyone can participate in. My diving dreams started after reading of the exploits of the US Navy Underwater Demolition Teams in Popular Mechanics magazine in the 1950's. I wanted to experience the underwater world for myself and it launched my career in both sport and professional scuba diving.

I made my first dive in 1959 under the George Washington Bridge in the Hudson River. It was scary and exciting at the same time. Afterwards, a friend took me to Brooklyn's Garrison beach for a more controlled experience and I was hooked. I signed up for scuba lessons and after being certified wanted even more. I dedicated myself to diving, continued my education and became an Instructor Trainer for both the YMCA and PADI.

My passion for the sport had me diving five or six days a week. I spent a lot of hours diving Beach 8th street, Jones Inlet, Montauk and making many trips to other Long Island shore dive sites.

In 1961 I dove the wreck of the *USS San Diego*. That convinced me I only wanted to be a wreck diver. I spent the next several years diving and crewing aboard the Jess Lu fishing fleet out of Freeport Long Island and also ran my own 21 ft dive boat eventually serving as President of the Eastern Dive Boat Association for eleven years.

Becoming a licensed Merchant Marine officer allowed me to dive *and* make money bringing divers to many shipwrecks ranging from the *Black Warrior* to the *Andrea Doria*. I was an instructor on the Holland America Line's *New Amsterdam* traveling and diving throughout the Caribbean. I dove the Florida Keys many times and organized several expeditions diving Florida caves in the late 1960's through the 1990's. In the 80's and 90's I led several expeditions in the Pacific diving Truk Lagoon's sunken warships. My career included opening the *Andrea Doria* to divers, involvement in the discovery of the *SS Republic*, and I was an expert witness in the controversial case to allow diver access to the wreck of the *USS Monitor*.

I owned and ran several dive boats over the years but building *RV WAHOO* was one of the most rewarding and challenging endeavors of my life.

I met David on the *WAHOO* in 2001. It was to be his first dive on the USS *San Diego*; some 40 years after my first dive on her. David's excitement at diving shipwrecks and exploring many shore dive sites has mirrored my own early feelings of how I felt when starting my exploration of the underwater world.

I have made hundred of dives on the *San Diego*, *Oregon* and many other shipwrecks. A particularly challenging project was my involvement in the recovery of the fine art panels created by Guido Gambone from the *Andrea Doria*. Participation in that project was one of my many contributions to diving history; we all contribute in our own ways.

David's ability to relate his experiences in the printed word is his contribution and is a valuable tool to encourage others into joining him in diving our local waters.

By including his early diving career along with frank self-analysis there are lessons to be learned as we join David under water. This book is an enjoyable read for both divers and non-divers. If you're planning to dive any of these wrecks or shore sites you will find the shared experiences and anecdotal information in this book informative and entertaining.

Captain Steve Bielenda
Diver/Owner/Operator R.V.
WAHOO
Long Island, New York
December 2007

Gary Gentile
The spirit of adventure is alive and well.

This fact may not be apparent to people whose only view of events emanates from newspapers or television: media that thrive on murder and mayhem. As David's book clearly demonstrates, the instinctive drive that led mankind to leave his cave to search far and wide, to sail tempestuous seas, to cross vast forests and plains, to climb tall mountains, and to venture into the ocean's depths, is still a motivating force in certain individuals.

Whereas some people are merely passing through life, David and others like him are embracing the unknown experiences that make life exciting. His adventures in deep waters, and in long-distance penetrations into the cavernous hull of the *San Diego*, are only the obvious parts of the story that his book relates: the sweet icing on a rich cake that is multi-layered and made from many esoteric ingredients.

Certainly this book is about exploration. But it is about more than the investigation of sunken and collapsing shipwrecks: it is about the examination of the inner self. On the surface, the narrative hook appears to be about problems that are encountered, confronted, and overcome in a hostile environment in which death is literally only a breath away. In a broader sense, the book probes the subtle determination of people who seek somewhat risky activities not because they enjoy the feeling of fear and the rush of adrenaline, but because they possess an unquenchable desire to learn about their reactions to situations of stress. They can then be better prepared to anticipate and modify those reactions when similar circumstances recur during future emergencies.

If this analogy sounds tautological – like pursuing danger for the sake of pursuing more danger – then you are misreading my intent. An encounter with the unknown will strengthen the soul when the person takes the trouble to analyze the encounter. Honest analysis makes a person stronger than he was before the encounter. Additional encounters enable a person to flex and exercise his intellectual might – in short, to grow emotionally. Facing perils and overcoming them is a way to build character and self-confidence.

Because bottom time is limited by air supply, a diver needs to heighten his powers of observation and perception. Learning to think quickly and to retain fleeting images are essential. The deeper one descends into the dark abyss, the quicker one must be able to react "under pressure."

People dive – and dive deep – for different reasons. For me the reasons are the challenges that are presented and the adventures that ensue. After reading David's book, I suspect that he and I have similar philosophies. The following book is about people who dare to do what others only dream about.

Gary Gentile
Philadelphia, PA
November 2007

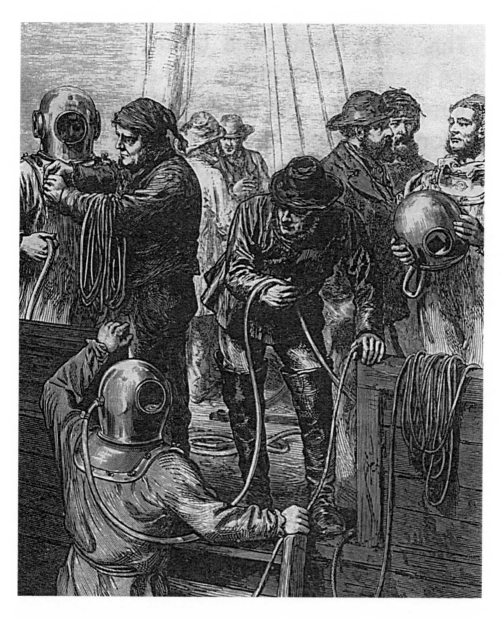

Divers Preparing for Work. Picture courtesy Herb Kaasmann,
OREGON,GREYHOUND OF THE ATLANTIC

Warning from the Author

SCUBA Diving is an inherently dangerous sport and almost every year a number of divers lose their lives in the waters off of Long Island, New York. This book reports my personal experiences and is intended as entertainment for the reader. It is not in any way meant to be a guide to techniques, dive sites or a how-to manual on diving. Conditions change and drawings and maps of dive sites are not intended for use by the reader as a guide to current conditions. There are practices described in these stories including solo diving, wreck penetration, decompression diving, diving in high currents, diving in cold and ice that require specialized training and support. You need to stay within your training and comfort level and have the common sense to call off your planned dive if you feel uncomfortable about it or do not have the proper training for any aspect of it.

Diver's hood

Mask

Dry Suit Inflator Valve

BC Harness

Dry Suit Exhaust Valve

Breathing regulator

'Weights

Dive Computer

Dive reel

Additional Weights and Rock Boots

A SCUBA diver (me!) wearing a Dry Suit and in full gear at the Ponquogue Bridge, Long Island, NY

INTRODUCTION

What is SCUBA Diving?
Equipment, Dangers, and Pleasure

"I check my air. I still have a lot, so I decide to try squeezing into a small entrance that was once a hatch when this wrecked naval vessel sailed almost one hundred years ago. I barely fit through the cramped passage. My light illuminates the narrow hallway. Silt, dislodged by my bubbles, gently falls from the ceiling, caught in the powerful light. A large blue eel slithers across the floor and through a rip in the wall that must have been caused by the explosion that sank this great ship. I follow, my heart pounding, into this dark shipwreck 110 feet beneath the Atlantic off the coast of Long Island. The only other sounds are that of my own heavy breathing and the escaping bubbles as I exhale. Wriggling through the opening, I gasp. Suddenly I am in an open room, its floor a tumble of wooden crates. Some have been opened by the explosion. A hint of gold glimmers in my light..."

The above could have been part of a description of any one of my dives on local shipwrecks. I haven't yet found gold, but I have caught glimpses of a history that previously I knew only from books and television shows such as National Geographic. The following real-life adventures were originally written for myself and for other SCUBA divers; they include terms that a non-diver may not understand. I have greatly simplified my explanations, and in fact I've omitted important items that are not relevant to my SCUBA stories. If you're interested in learning how to SCUBA dive, please get formal training from one of the dive-certification organizations, such as the Professional Association of Diving Instructors, also known as PADI. This introduction defines some basic terms and concepts and gives background and context for the stories that follow.

SCUBA stands for **S**elf **C**ontained **U**nderwater **B**reathing **A**pparatus, and the sport of SCUBA has relied upon equipment similar to that used by modern divers since about the 1950's. When I was a kid, I wanted to be an "underwater scientist." Shows like The *Undersea World of Jacques Cousteau* (Cousteau developed the modern SCUBA air regulator) and National Geographic introduced me to a world that was interesting, beautiful, and with conditions intrinsically hostile to human life. In many respects, SCUBA diving is as dangerous as the vacuum of space to the human body. In space, the body has to be protected against a more-or-less constant vacuum. A SCUBA diver, though, is increasingly *compressed* the deeper he or she goes. At sea level, the body must cope with about fifteen pounds of air pressure per square inch. To visualize, you can imagine a square-inch column of air extending all the way up to the outer edge of the atmosphere. For every 33 feet of water depth, pressure increases by another 15 pounds per square inch. At 132 feet deep, pressure is now at 75 pounds per square inch. This is still within the range of traditional recreational SCUBA diving. More advanced technical divers—still sport divers—regularly go down deeper than that. Dives of 200 feet are fairly common, even with over 90 pounds pressing on every square inch of the body.

Luxfer Gas Cylinder

Not only the SCUBA diver is compressed—all of his equipment gets compressed as well. At depth, a neoprene rubber wet suit may be squeezed to only one-quarter of its thickness, with a corresponding loss of the suit's thermal insulating characteristics. Even the diver's air becomes further compressed at depth. If a SCUBA diver goes deeper than 60 feet, it is questionable as to whether he will make it to the surface should there be a critical equipment failure. Look at a six-story building, assuming that each floor is 10 feet high. Imagine trying to swim that distance without air or in an emergency.

Now for the first lesson in SCUBA diving. Never hold your breath while breathing SCUBA compressed air—your lungs will rupture and explode if you ascend even just a few feet. That will kill you, by the way.

So now, imagine trying to make it the distance of that six-story building without air, keeping in mind that you'll need to be exhaling while you ascend in order to expel all the air from your lungs!

The reason you can't hold your breath is that the air you're breathing from the air tank is compressed, and the deeper you are, the more compressed it is. So let's say that you take a breath of this compressed air at about 30 feet deep and then you start going up. As you go up, the air is becoming less compressed in your lungs and is expanding. By the time you reach the surface, the air requires twice the volume or space it required at 30 feet. If you're not holding your breath on the way up, great, because all you have to do is exhale and inhale normally and you will be fine. The air expands, comes out of your open lungs, and escapes. But if you are holding your breath, then like a balloon popping your lungs will rupture because they cannot expand enough. So while trying to make that swim to the surface from 60 feet down, you must be exhaling constantly, even if your air tank is empty. I had to do this once from only 25 feet deep and it was very uncomfortable, to say the least. Forcing yourself to exhale when your body is screaming for air: not a pleasant experience.

This is one of the reasons a SCUBA diver needs training and practice. The ability to keep one's wits in an emergency and to avoid instinctively holding his or her breath is something a new diver simply must learn. There are other hazards that a diver must deal with as well, but before discussing them, let's take a closer look at training, types of diving, and the equipment required.

About nine years ago, I decided to get SCUBA training with my son Matthew, who was 14 at the time. We both got a kind of basic training called *Open Water Certification*, which would prepare us for dives up to 60 feet deep. I had been viewing this as a way to bond with and stay close to my son as he entered his teenage years.

We both enjoyed SCUBA diving at local shore sites on Long Island. Matthew displayed an aptitude for the sport, and I became almost obsessed with it, diving any chance I could get. The next year, the two of us signed on for training in *Advanced Open Water,* for deeper dives up to 130 feet. That same year, we both took a medic first-aid course and a course in the use of oxygen for treatment of diving injuries, and we finished that dive season with training and certification in *Dive Rescue.* Meanwhile, I was diving every week, all year round, with special equipment for the winter. Matthew gravitated towards diving in the warmer months. To each his own! The following year, we took a course in *Nitrox,* learning to dive using a gas with a higher oxygen content than what is found in regular air. This past year, while continuing to dive every weekend, I took a course in *Advanced Nitrox,* which teaches techniques for using pure oxygen as well as other skills needed for deeper, longer dives.

Common Types of Diving in the New York City Area

Lake and Quarry Diving: Diving in lakes (such as Candlewood Lake in Connecticut) and abandoned quarries (such as Dutch Springs in Pennsylvania) is good for training and for testing new equipment, because in lakes there are no currents and the water clarity— also known as visibility or vis—is generally decent. When I say decent, I mean that perhaps you can see 15 feet or so underwater. (By contrast, the Caribbean typically boasts a vis of over 70 feet.)

One of the considerations when diving these types of sites is that they typically have silt or mud bottoms: if you kick your fins too close to the bottom, your visibility can drop to zero in an instant. As with all diving, while descending you must periodically equalize the pressure in your ears to prevent them from being injured by the increasing pressure. This is usually done by holding your nose and carefully blowing very gently through it. You feel the ears "clear." Sometimes this has to be done a few times as you are making your descent.

Basic SCUBA Diving Equipment

- **Mask and fins** so the diver can see and move underwater.

Mask   Fins

- **Air tank, hoses, and regulators** to deliver the air to the diver underwater.

Diving regulator

- **Lead weights,** either on a belt or as integrated weights contained in special Velcro pockets on the buoyancy compensator vest. Weights are necessary to make sure that the diver can sink underwater. Some of a diver's other equipment—like a neoprene foam-rubber wet suit—would otherwise cause him to

Weight belt

float. Sudden unplanned loss of weights underwater can be a life-threatening situation: the diver can suddenly get so buoyant that he is uncontrollably shot to the surface. Ascents that are not gradual can kill the diver.

- **A *buoyancy compensator,* or BC.** This device, either in the form of a vest or a harness that the diver wears, is what the tank attaches to. It also contains a bladder that is connected to the air tank with a hose. The diver can control how much air enters the bladder from the tank, thus controlling trim and buoyancy. Uncontrolled inflation of the air bladder can result in a life-threatening rapid ascent.

Buoyancy Compensator Vest (BC)

- **Dive computer.** An electronic gadget that tells the diver how deep he is, how long he's been there, and other important information. The dive computer is sometimes combined with a compass or with an air gauge that reports how much air is left in the tank.

Dive computer

Shore Diving: The Long Island Sound and the Atlantic Ocean are accessible from many locations all around the New York City area. Typically the diver walks into the water from a beach. This diving is more challenging than lake and quarry diving because of the tides and currents. Most of the ocean shore dive sites have strong currents which force the diver to plan to dive near high tide, when the current stops or "slackens" for some time—usually for about 30-60 minutes. We don't want to get washed out to sea, now do we? The waters of the Long Island Sound generally have much less of a tide or current issue than you'll find in the ocean, and they make for a somewhat easier dive. Another potential hazard with all diving is that years of fishing have left countless monofilament fishing lines underwater.

They are hard to see, and you will at some point get snagged by "mono." This is why you have a dive knife, by the way. Not to do battle with a shark, but so you can free yourself if you get caught. I carry a knife and a set of underwater shears just in case.

Popular Shore-diving Sites:

- Bayville (Long Island Sound)

* Secret Beach (Long Island Sound)

- Garvies Point Jetty (Long Island Sound)

- Rockaway Beach 9th Street (South Shore Queens, Long Island; tidal current issues need to be planned for).

- Ponquogue Bridge (South Shore Suffolk County, Long Island; tidal current issues).

People have been throwing things into the water ever since man developed arms and the capacity to throw. For some reason, people think that when they throw something into a lake or into the ocean, it vanishes forever. Actually, it lays there on the bottom. Sometimes an object ends up buried and sometimes it gets washed to another location, but if it's non-biodegradable it's always there to be discovered in the future. Items ranging from antique bottles to ancient stone age artifacts and all sorts of other things are down there waiting to be found.

Apollo underwater Scooter

Some divers like to bring a spear gun with them. There are lots of edible fish in the New York area, including bass, flounder, fluke, blackfish, and eel. I suppose that if you really love sushi, you could take a couple of bites underwater! But personally, I like to look for artifacts. I carry a small red canvas bag with a gardener's shovel to help me dig. There are also underwater scooters (like in a James Bond movie) that you can hold backwards so that the prop wash quickly digs a hole in the sea floor, helping you to recover some buried item. Bringing a metal detector underwater can also be fun.

Many of the shore dive sites are in channels or near inlets. It is very easy to get confused underwater and to surface on the opposite side of the channel, or to get otherwise lost. Especially in lower-vis situations, it can all look the same down there. That is why an underwater compass is worn on all dives, but particularly on shore and lake dives. Be aware that you are sharing the waterways with boats too! A surfaced diver is almost impossible for a boat to see, and he or she runs a serious risk of being run over.

Visibility on shore dives varies from site to site and even from day to day. Storms far out at sea can stir things up. It is not always predictable. More than a few times, I've lugged all of my equipment out to the car and drove to the dive site only to peer down into the water and decide that it was too murky to dive. Still, days like that are rare, and usually you end up having lunch with your dive buddy, swapping stories in some diner or restaurant. Hopefully it's a seafood place!

Wreck Diving: Yes! Now we get to what is considered by many to be the ultimate in northeast U.S. diving: taking any one of a number of dive boats that leave early in the morning and going to visit local shipwrecks.

The basic idea is that you wake up at 3:00 a.m. Take an anti-seasickness medicine, like Dramamine or Bonine. Load your gear in the car. Drive to a dock where one of the local dive boats berth. Put your gear on the boat. Leave the dock about 5:30 a.m. or so. Ride on the boat for maybe an hour along with perhaps 10 other divers to one of the many shipwrecks that are off the coast of Long Island. One of my favorites is the *USS San Diego*, a 500-foot-long naval cruiser that was sunk about 12 miles or so out in the ocean in 110 feet of water by a German mine in 1918.

Wrecks will either be marked with a small float—perhaps a Clorox bottle with a line going down to the sunken ship—or else the captain will use GPS coordinates to generally locate the wreck and will then drop a grapnel into the water to snag the wreck. The dive boat sends one of the crew down to attach the anchor line to the wreck. Then divers jump into the water, descending along the anchor line to get down to the wreck. They explore the wreck and its rich complement of sea life. Then they find the anchor line again and slowly ascend along it back to the dive boat. Visibility on these offshore shipwrecks can vary—on excellent days it can be over 40 feet. After resting a couple of hours on the dive boat, many divers then go back down a second time to visit the shipwreck.

Where allowed, many wreck divers try to bring back a souvenir such as a porthole from the wreck. This is exciting but potentially dangerous diving. If you actually go into the shipwreck, it is easy to get lost. In a metal ship, your compass will be useless. You only have a limited amount of gas to breathe in your tank. If you can't find your way out of the wreck, you will die. For various reasons—including getting lost and running out of air—at least eight divers have died while exploring the *USS San Diego*. Wreck divers carry a reel of string or line that they can tie to something near the entrance, unreeling the line as they go deeper into the wreck. Even if conditions

Diver's reel

deteriorate to zero vis, the diver hopefully can follow that line back out to exit the wreck. Another potential problem is entanglement: if a diver gets caught on something and cannot extricate himself, a buddy can be a life saver.

In addition to a reel of line and a powerful underwater light, wreck divers usually take an additional air tank down with them. This tank, sometimes called a *pony tank* or a *safety bottle*, is to provide extra air in case of an emergency. Some divers dive with a single tank on their backs, along with one safety bottle. Other divers have two tanks, called *doubles*, on their backs as a bit of redundancy, so that if any piece of equipment fails underwater the diver will have some survival options. Remember my previous example of a six-story building? Well, the *USS San Diego*, at 110 feet deep, is as deep as an eleven-story building is tall.

This type of deeper diving brings some additional potential for danger. Previously we mentioned that everything is increasingly compressed the deeper underwater we go. So a breath taken at 130 feet has as much air in it as five lungfuls at the surface, with five times as much oxygen and five times as much nitrogen, the other major component of air. (Air is 21% oxygen, 78% nitrogen, and 1% other gasses, such as carbon dioxide.) The body is able to use the extra oxygen, but the excess nitrogen accumulates in the tissues of the body. It continues building up throughout the dive. The deeper you go—and/or the longer you stay—the more nitrogen your body will sequester.

Now the diver has so much nitrogen in his tissues that if he comes up too fast, the excess nitrogen will bubble out of the tissues like soda fizzing when shaken. These bubbles can cause extreme pain if they lodge in bone and muscle. If the bubble forms in the bloodstream, it can block blood to the brain, causing a fatal aneurysm or stroke. If it forms elsewhere, such as near the spinal cord, it can cause paralysis or numbness in an extremity. Called *decompression sickness* or *the bends*, it is a very serious, sometimes fatal problem.

Treating the bends involves having the victim breathe pure oxygen to flush the excess nitrogen out of his system. He may then be transported to a *hyperbaric chamber* at a hospital, where he is put back under pressure in a controlled environment in order to shrink the bubbles back down. The pressure is then very gradually reduced over hours or days, allowing the nitrogen to come out a tiny bit at a time.

You can avoid the bends by ascending very slowly from your dive. Most recreational dive-training organizations, such as PADI, produce computed tables that tell the diver how long he can stay down at a specific depth. The diver is supposed to consult these tables before the dive and avoid staying down longer or deeper than planned. He should come up slowly, but the tables are designed to avoid depth/time combinations that would expose the diver to high risk of the bends.

More advanced wreck divers, called *technical divers*, often want to stay down longer than these no-decompression limits allow. These divers will have to put substantially more planning into their dives. For example, let's suppose that the PADI table says that if you are doing a dive at 110 feet, you must start coming up after only 16 minutes. That is not a really long time to explore a wreck. Normally you would also wait underwater, hanging on the anchor line at about 15 feet for three minutes on the way up. That is an extra precaution called a *safety stop*. It allows more time for the accumulated nitrogen to come out of your tissues safely.

Some more advanced divers might consult the U.S. Navy Decompression Dive Tables instead of the PADI table. The U.S. Navy tables say that if you stay down at 110 feet for 50 minutes instead of 16 minutes, you must not come right back up to the surface. You have to ascend to 20 feet deep, hang on to the anchor line for eight minutes, then go up another 10 feet so that you are 10 feet deep, and then *stay there for an additional 26 minutes, underwater.* You better have planned to have enough air to breathe for all this hanging around, because if you run out of air and surface before putting in your decompression or *deco time*, you will almost certainly end up in the hospital with the bends. This type of diving takes a lot of planning and additional equipment.

Divers also have a dive computer that they wear on their equipment. It tells them how long they have been in the water, how deep they are, the water temperature, and other information, including how long they'll need to take to ascend in order to decompress properly. Used in conjunction with good planning before the dive, the dive computer is a valuable tool for any diver.

Now just to give you a bit more info. You can dive while breathing air, the same stuff you are breathing now. That is 21% oxygen and about 79% nitrogen. You can also get other mixtures of gases. For example, if you are breathing a gas that has 36% oxygen and only 64% nitrogen, you can stay at 110 feet for 29 minutes instead of the 16 minutes you'd be limited to if you were breathing regular air. These gas mixtures are sometimes called nitrox and are available in different percentages of oxygen.

Just to keep you on your toes, though, too much oxygen becomes toxic as you go deeper, and it can cause convulsions and drowning. For example, breathing pure oxygen can kill you at depths below 20 feet. Different gas mixes have different allowable maximum depths. So you have to factor that all in too!

Sometimes a diver has a few bottles of gas with different percentages of oxygen in each. These are called *stage bottles*, and the diver switches between them as per his pre-arranged plan.

All of this is advanced technical diving stuff. Many divers elect to stay within the recommendations for no-decompression limits so that they don't have to deal with all this tech stuff—and they are having a great time.

Cold Water and Ice Diving

To some divers, any northeast diving is cold water diving. Water temperatures for shore dives may get up to just 70 degrees at the height of the season. The deep water wrecks don't get much warmer than 55 degrees at their warmest. According to the U.S. Navy, diving in waters 40 degrees or less constitutes cold water diving. I enjoy cold water diving and I dive year round, generally at least once a week, even in water temperatures as low as 31 degrees. The vis is usually at its best during the cold season, as all of the microscopic plankton and algae die off from the cold. There is not a lot of sea life in the winter months, but if you are an artifact hunter like me, conditions couldn't be better.

Now is a good time to talk about wet suits and dry suits. Most recreational divers use a wet suit, a neoprene suit that allows water into it and then traps the water in the suit. This trapped water and the thickness of the suit are what keeps the diver warm. One problem is that water, possibly really cold water, enters the suit. Another problem, mentioned earlier, is that if you dive deep, the suit gets compressed and loses much of its thermal insulating ability. Most wreck divers and cold water divers use a different kind of diving suit—a dry suit. Basically, this is a suit that keeps all of the water out, allowing you to wear heavy thermal underwear which can be varied according to the temperature.

wet suit

In the summer I wear a fleece undergarment. I call this a "Smurf Suit" because with my belly I look just like an ill green Smurf when wearing it. In the winter, I wear an undergarment that is as thick as a sleeping bag. Booties are attached to the dry suit so that your feet do not get wet, and my suit also has attached gloves. Your head sticks out through a latex rubber neck seal, as do your hands if you don't have the attached glove system. A hose, snaking from your air tank to a valve on the dry suit, lets you add air to the suit as you go deeper and as the suit becomes more compressed. Adding a small amount of air allows the insulating material in the undergarment to fluff up a bit, keeping you toasty-warm. Uncontrolled inflation of the dry suit can result in a life-threatening rapid ascent.

It is important that you stay well hydrated while diving to decrease your risk of the bends. That means drinking a liberal amount of water all day. One potential issue with a dry suit is having to pee. It's not too big a deal on a shore or ice dive; actually, it's more of an issue on a deep wreck dive where you may have to "hang for deco" for a substantial amount of time in order to prevent the bends. Some divers wear adult diapers. Other divers install a gadget called a "pee valve", which allows male divers to urinate while in the suit: the urine passes through a condom-like catheter and thence via a hose to the ocean outside. Just like an astronaut, right?

Cold water diving and ice diving require some awareness that equipment may freeze up. The regulators—the equipment that delivers air to the diver from the tank—can "free flow" or get stuck, the air gushing out uncontrollably. Usually this can be dealt with easily by a trained diver, but you might have to end your dive early if you lose a lot of air.

The stories that follow are all true. Many of them describe a problem I had, or one which I narrowly avoided, and most contain some kind of lesson. But the most important lesson is that constant awareness is needed to maintain safety in this extreme sport. No matter how many dives you may do, you must never get complacent about safety.

Enjoy the Stories...

David Rosenthal

In the photo of me at the beginning of the Introduction I am wearing a DUI Drysuit with attached dry gloves.

Thanks to the following equipment vendors for the use of photos of their equipment.

Luxfer Gas Cylinders

Apollo Sports, USA - scooter

Reef Scuba Accessories, Inc. - reel

Aeris, Inc. - dive computer

Aqua Lung - BC, regulators, fins, mask

O'Neill Dive - wet suit

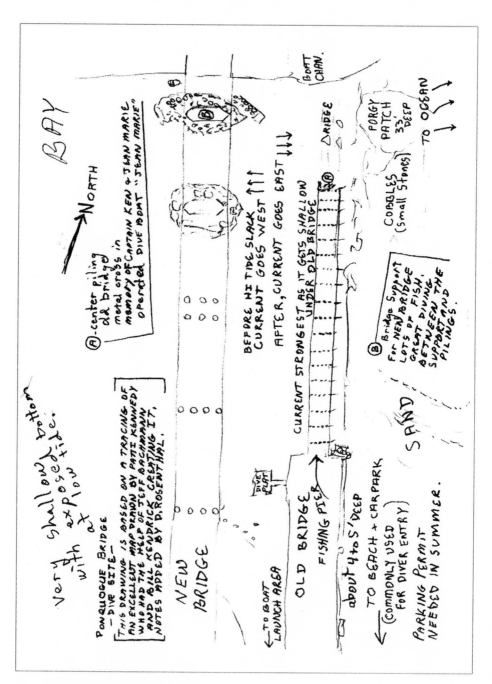

Ponquogue Bridge, Hampton Bays Dive Site

CHAPTER ONE

The first seasons; where I learn I love SCUBA diving even though I am prone to seasickness, the 'bends' and inexperience.

In the summer of 2000, I discovered a fascinating artifact in the waters of Long Island's Shinnecock Bay.

I do a lot of diving in our sometimes — murky local waters — much of it on the South Shore of Long Island at the Ponquogue Bridge. The bridge connects mainland Long Island with the barrier beach island immediately south of the town of Hampton Bays. This is a good shore dive with blackfish, bass, flounder and other local flora and fauna in abundance. Visibility can range from a couple of feet to over 20 feet, and due to the very strong tidal currents it can be a challenge. Shinnecock Bay, named after the local Shinnecock Indians, fills and empties with the tides. The current is too strong to combat, so diving the bridge must be done at the time of slack tide. At this location, that's the time right after high tide when the bay becomes briefly still before emptying back out into the sea again through narrow Shinnecock Inlet, about a mile east of the bridge. Once familiar with the bridge and the currents, you can get a good 45 minutes to over an hour of dive time, when the conditions are right.

Well, on this particular summer day, I was nearly out to the boat channel under the bridge when I spied an object just lying on the bay bottom, about 25 feet deep. It looked curious. Whatever it was, it was almost a foot long and was gently curved, ending in a point. It looked like it was made from wood. I tucked it into my buoyancy vest and continued my dive.

When I got out of the water, I examined it more closely. Now, in the light, it appeared to be bone. A carved bone. Furthermore, it came to a point on one end and near the other end were smooth grooves running across it. These polished—looking grooves, stained a brownish hue, seemed to be from something—perhaps a leather cord—that had once tightly tied this object to a longer stick of wood. With time and use, the grooves had worn into the object. It was in perfect condition. (The day I found it, I showed it to someone who snapped it in

two by accident. Aghh!!) I soaked it in fresh water for a day or so and then let it dry out and photographed it, as you can see in the picture accompanying this story.

I emailed the photos to a few museums, and to my surprise I got some responses. The horn-and-bone specialist at the Museum of Natural History in New York City asked me to bring it in. He examined it and declared it to be a real artifact, a bone spear like tool probably made from a seal rib bone and originally affixed to a wooden shaft for use as a fishing spear. As a diver that has seen many flatfish on the bottom bays, I could visualize an Indian standing very still in the shallow water and using such a weapon to catch his dinner. The scientist directed me to the local Native-American-oriented Garvies Point Museum on Long Island. I went down to the lab in the basement, where an archeologist examined my find under a microscope. He concurred with the opinion of the first expert, further stating that he thought the object was from the Archaic Indian period—over a thousand years ago!

It must have been buried for a long time; the fast tidal currents uncovering it for me to find that summer day. When I lose something, I get a little annoyed at myself. I wonder if that bay fisherman felt the same way so long ago, too. Did he just pull out another spear tip? Or was it his last? Did he go hungry that day?

USS San Diego 1915, Courtesy of US Navy Historical Center

My First Dive on the USS San Diego – April, 2001

I went to dinner tonight at the Milleridge Inn on Long Island and somehow got one of those dirty, very old pennies in my change. Once home, I placed the penny in vinegar to clean it, and you could just make out the year. 1918. What a coincidence! Just yesterday, I had my first dive on the famous USS *San Diego*, an armored cruiser that was sunk in 1918 by a German U-boat mine.

The ship lies totally upside down in about 110 feet of water, about 12 miles or so out of Fire Island Inlet. It's an hour-and-twenty-minute trip by dive boat from Captree, Long Island. My previous wreck dives had been in the Shinnecock Reef area—

boats such as the *Mandy Ray* (an intentionally sunk fishing trawler) and the *Panther*. The *Mandy Ray*, a recent wreck, was quite intact, but there was little left to the *Panther* aside from a boiler. The USS *San Diego* would be my first "serious wreck."

I was very excited and a little nervous. I had not been able to get anyone to come with me on this trip (impulsively, I booked myself for the trip and only then went looking for buddies). Although I told everyone who cared for my well-being that I was sure I'd pick up a buddy on the dive boat, I honestly hoped I'd be diving solo. I have a love of diving alone that will probably kill me one day! But I felt well-prepared for the *San Diego* dive. I would not go inside of the wreck today, because I was alone and had only one tank of air. But mostly, I had no idea how to do it safely. Although I am, at the time of this writing, in my third year of diving, I've only recently allowed myself to go into the helicopter at the flooded Dutch Springs Quarry. At the quarry I practiced some non-silting techniques that I had read about, and I experimented with going in and out of openings without getting caught. Still, I knew I was not ready to do any serious shipwreck penetration.

But I was in very good shape for this expedition. I was used to cold water diving, having done shore dives every weekend locally all winter. I had been to Dutch Springs Quarry and had recently done four deeper dives so as to get accustomed to my new equipment configuration and tanks. My new steel 104-cubic-foot tanks were pumped up, and I wore another 30-cubic-foot tank on my side. I was ready to go. The captain of the dive boat *RV WAHOO* wanted me on board at 5:30 a.m., and then we'd leave from Captree on Long Island's southern shore. Having had mixed experiences with seasickness on previous dive-boat excursions, I took a Bonine anti-sea sickness pill and arrived right on time.

The first thing I noticed was that I was the only one with a single-tank configuration. All the other divers had big double tanks and the standard "serious wreck diver" gear setups. My new little single-tank Halcyon harness looked puny next to these hi-tech configurations. But when I thought about it, I saw that my well-planned rig had pretty much the same things that the experienced technical divers had—the only real difference was that I only had half as much gas as everyone else. Minor detail? There was still much to learn by looking at the other gear. One diver had a compass epoxied to the back of a gauge; another had fixed a thick rope to his tank manifold and had slung it over his shoulder: a large D-ring at the end of the rope allowed him to attach additional equipment. In the future maybe I should take photos of other divers' gear as we journey out to a given wreck. Looking at the gear and trying to figure out why a diver has set it up a certain way is instructive. Of course, simply asking them helps too! I have found that when other technically oriented divers see that you are serious about diving, they are usually very helpful and love to talk about equipment, wrecks, real-life stories, near disasters, and unfortunate accidents involving other brave underwater explorers. For example, through the NYC Sea Gypsies dive club, I met Chris Gregory, a long-time diver who has given me some great advice on equipment configurations as well as other information that you just cannot get from any book. I must have interrupted his dinner 100 times with some silly telephone call about an obscure piece of equipment, but he always had the time to answer that question and to educate me about three other related things that I hadn't even considered!

My plan was to go down the anchor line—which was shackled to the wreck near the stern end of the bilge keel at about 85 feet deep—and to then drop over the side of the wreck and down to the sand, to a location beneath one of the large guns. I'd be able to use the gun as a landmark, in conjunction with a reel line that I would run. Then I'd spend about five minutes checking for any interesting artifacts in the sand (which could not be removed legally from this protected site). I figured that the seafloor would lie about 115 feet down, so I knew my time was limited. I also had to be aware of getting slightly narced from nitrogen narcosis. This is a drunken-like effect on the brain caused by a concentration of nitrogen, a component of the breathing gas, at depths beyond 100 feet. (Whew! between the bends and getting narced, that nitrogen causes all *sorts* of problems for divers!) I planned on ending the dive after using half my gas.

Well things didn't go exactly as planned! First of all, the entry point into the water from the boat was about 40 feet or so from the anchor line. I would have to follow the anchor line down to the wreck, but to get to the anchor I'd have to pull myself along a different yellow line. It seemed to go on forever, and I realized later that the depth of this line varied from some 30 feet to seven feet where it connected to the anchor line. So as I rapidly pulled myself along, I paid no attention to depth changes, violating every gradual-ascent rule I had ever learned. By the time I got to the anchor line, I had been down to 32 feet, then back up to seven feet, my dive computer's alarm complaining constantly about the fast ascent. I was also a little winded and excited, so before I even went down the anchor line I had used up more gas than I should have.

I love descending to a wreck through our murky, green, northeastern waters. As you move down the line, you have no idea what you are going to see. There is a point where you can no longer see the surface, yet there is no hint of what awaits you at the bottom of the line. Then suddenly there it is! The wreck, a dark and spooky but inviting mass. The greenish-brown colors, the cold, and the weight of all the water on top of you together make you feel the weight of history. Men once walked on this ship. Went to war in this ship. Died on this ship. The ship is upside down. The right side is the left side and the top is the bottom. For those who stop to think about it; it's a pretty awesome experience.

Once I touched down on the top of the keel of the upside down ship, I noted that the visibility was pretty good—maybe 30 feet. I could see down to the sand. I dropped over the side, taking care to stay even with the anchor line so I could find it easily on the way back up, and I found some large debris sticking out of the sand. A large gun protruded from the side of the warship above my head. I tied off my reel of line to some metal thing and went out into the debris field to find treasure. After a couple of minutes I checked my gauges and decided that I would go up a bit to the 90-foot level to look around.

I disconnected my reel and tried to clip it to the D-ring on my crotch strap. It wouldn't clip. Tried again, no good. I then realized that the waist strap for my harness was totally undone and my crotch strap was flapping behind me like a little tail. I must have been slightly narced because I remember thinking, "Oh this goes here and I have to put this through here," like I was dull witted and in slow motion. A few seconds later the strap was fixed. But because I didn't know why it had opened, I clipped my reel off to a chest D-ring so that it would not put any more weight on the harness waist strap. I now had only a bit over a third of my gas left. So much for my dive plan! I knew that I was using my gas much faster the deeper I was, so I headed up the side of the ship for the anchor line. Maintaining a conservative ascent rate, I headed up the line. While I wasn't too worried as I had my additional 30-cubic-foot safety bottle, I really did not want to have to touch it—especially on this first of two dives for today.

There was a crowd of four divers at 70 feet also slowly moving up the line. These guys had double tanks and a zillion other tanks. They probably could not identify with the concern I felt about my gas-usage rate. They were sure moving slow! I wanted to ascend at a conservative rate, but not quite as conservatively as they were ascending. I wanted to get to a depth where my gas usage would slow down. At 40 feet they stopped on the line. Having some kind of chat, I was sure.

I did not want to stop here. I was planning on stopping at 20 feet. I stopped with them and wondered if it was rude (in diver etiquette) to pass these guys. I was now at about 800 or 900 lbs of air and decided to go around them. They didn't hit me or anything. I continued ascending quite slowly, hand over hand, and did my safety stop at 20 feet as scheduled.

The plan for my second dive on the *San Diego* today was not to go to the sand, but to stay at about the level of the keels and head for the stern, about 40 feet away, using the hull and keel to navigate my way back to the ascent line. Over time the stern has broken up a lot into a jumble of collapsed metal plates. I was able to drop down a bit near the large propeller shafts into the opened wreck. Going inside a wreck, or penetrating, is considered one of the most dangerous things to do when diving. Divers can get snagged on debris or get lost. And this wreck is as long as a 50-story building. I saw rectangular openings where the rivets holding the steel plates had decayed and the entire plates had slid off the ship to the sand. I peeked into rooms that since 1918 had only been visited by those carrying their own air and wearing heavy suits as they braved the hostile, unforgiving environment of the sea. I resisted the urge to enter—it would have been so easy—and continued my tour.

I was back at the anchor shackle and down to half my gas. I decided that I would use my 30-cubic-foot safety bottle on my ascent in order to test how its regulator worked at this depth and also to determine how long, for ascent purposes, I could expect my small 30 cf tank to last. I decided that I could use 400 more psi of air from my main tank as long as I stayed within sight of the ascent line and toured a bit on the hull. Now I was back at the ascent line with about 1100 psi in my main tank. I switched to the safety bottle and began my ascent at a nice, slow rate. Did my three-minute stop and an extra two minutes at 20 feet and still had air to spare in the small bottle. I knew now that this bottle would work in an emergency. Of course,

I would be breathing faster when under stress, but I would probably make it out okay. I switched back to my main air for the swim to the back of the boat and ended the dive.

Back in the safety of my warm, dry home, I put the penny back in the vinegar. A little later I pulled it out. It was bright; just like new! What a contrast to the dark browns and greens enveloping the USS *San Diego* as the unrelenting sea reclaims the once great ship.

Seasick Problems Diving the Barge "Markland" off Shinnecock, Long Island – June, 2001

As I lay on the deck of the boat, drifting in and out of a fitful sleep, I could see the angry waves through the boat's window. Normally, a beautiful sky, the sun, and the occasional cloud would have been visible from my angle there on the floor of the boat. Now, I was forced to endure the pitching of the disabled 35-foot-long boat in the increasingly violent seas as we awaited Sea Tow some six miles out of Shinnecock Inlet. I'd never felt so miserable in my entire life. Death seemed a pleasant alternative to this incredible, debilitating seasickness that was passing over me in waves with the each lurch of the boat. How had I gotten here, and when would we ever get back to land?

Along with my 15-year-old son Matthew, also an experienced local diver, I had recently taken a nitrox course. That course taught us how to dive with breathing mixtures containing a higher percentage of oxygen than regular air's 21 percent, to decrease the risk of the bends. We had done well on the classroom side. It was now time for the two boat dives to complete the nitrox certification. We had agreed to go out on a private boat (as opposed to a professional dive vessel). Both my son and I were familiar with ocean dives up to 100 feet or so using air, and were looking forward to these nitrox dives, which we treated like a free bonus for taking the course.

This boat—older and not so well-kept—had been out only once so far this season and had experienced engine problems, but the captain assured us that it was ready to go now that he had fixed it up. He explained that as he had fixed one problem over the winter, he would find another and another, but that it was now all taken care of. I nodded with appropriate sympathy at all the work he had to do on the boat.

The plan was to go out to the *Markland*, a barge which had sunk many years ago. She'd been hauling a cargo of stone, and today little remains of the boat itself. But the dressed stones lying at about 105 feet are now home to lobster and other denizens of the deep. We knew that around noon the weather would start to turn sour, so we were going to go out and back, lickety split. If we encountered heavy fog, we would dive closer in on Shinnecock reef—perhaps we'd check out the sunken trawler *Mandy Ray* or something.

Normally I take Bonine to prevent seasickness before all boat dives, but I thought that because this dive would be fairly close to shore I would be okay. I had never been seriously seasick before and had not the slightest idea how truly miserable it is.

As we went out through Shinnecock Inlet and into a beautiful day, I took out my Irish tin whistle and played songs like "The Wreck of the Edmund Fitzgerald," with some of the others onboard singing along. What an idyllic scene. But after the inlet, BANG! We immediately plunged into heavy fog. The captain turned on the radar and reduced speed dramatically. We passed Shinnecock Reef, continuing out to sea. A few miles out, our port engine sputtered and died. I guess there was a moment when the captain must have considered turning back, now that we had lost half of our power. But I imagine he then would have thought of the *Markland* and how we were probably going to be the first divers to dive it this season. And the size of that lobster he was going to bring up.

We plodded ahead through the fog at an even more reduced speed. This slow speed allowed the engine exhaust to blow back onto the boat; there was no place on the boat to get away from it. At this point I was not playing the flute anymore. Those times were past—the next six hours would be the most nauseating of my life. I felt every wave. Finally, after spending about 30 minutes trying to secure the boat to the wreck of the *Markland* by dragging a grapnel, we stopped and I got sick. Very sick. I had never realized how incapacitating seasickness is. Had there been an emergency on the boat I would have been unable to assist, perhaps even unable to save myself. I was on my knees, head over the gunwales for what seemed like forever. But we were here to dive. I struggled with the equipment my son brought over to me, trying to look at the horizon to maintain some control over my breakfast. I even took a Bonine. But alas, it was all too late. Pulling on my dry suit and thermal undergarments took forever.

The captain said: "There are no women onboard. Take all that stuff off and jump in the water naked. You'll feel better!"

My son helped pull the half-donned underwear jumpsuit off of me and it dropped onto the deck of the heaving boat. I did a forward roll over the edge into the seven-foot swell. Now I was naked in the freezing water and rolling seas—and I was STILL sick! It was too cold to stay in the water like this, so I clambered back on board— shivering and naked as a rat's tail—and dried off. If you have ever tried to don a fleece garment with even the slightest amount of moisture on your legs, you can probably imagine that even though I'd dried off, I had some difficulty getting the suit dive underwear on easily. As sick as I was, I should have called off the dive right then. But I managed, somehow, to get my equipment on, even as I continued to be sick over the side of the boat. Finally, geared up again at last, I felt quieted down enough to roll into the water, where my son awaited me.

On the descent line to the wreck, I was okay. But I did notice that I had overlooked my flashlight, my backup light, and—worst of all—my reel of line. I couldn't bear the thought of going back up to the pitching seas, so my son and I descended to the Markland.

The dive itself was great. Seventeen minutes of no throwing up. Lots of eels, monkfish, hake, and zillions of lobster antenna teasing us from under the Markland's stone cargo. But this story is not about a great dive that had extended bottom time because of nitrox. It is about what happened before and after the dive.

We ascended and did a three-minute decompression hang somewhere between 15 and 20 feet. I was immediately nauseous again. I managed to stay the whole three minutes, thinking about keeping the second-stage regulator in my mouth if I got sick underwater. We surfaced into noticeably rougher seas and my son headed to the ladder. Now I became violently sick. Well, I have never been sick underwater; I guess that would be the worst thing. Being uncontrollably sick on the surface while being tossed about by choppy swells must be the second worst.

I managed to inflate my buoyancy control vest and involuntarily gulped seawater in between the violent abdominal contractions. I was scared. Since I was on the surface now and didn't want to screw up my regulator or possibly aspirate some of my vomit when I inhaled, I dropped the regulator from my mouth. I felt nauseous, helpless, and terrified. Waves threw me against the boat, which leaped up with every wave and then crashed down again, trying to crush me as you might step on a bug. My son was struggling at the ladder—the seas moved it cruelly as he tried to grab it. I looked up to see two more divers, geared up and backs facing me, on the gunwale above my head, about to do a rear-sitting entry right on top of me with their heavy double tanks. I didn't even know if they were aware I was under them. I moved towards the ladder. I have no idea how I managed to get up onto the boat as sick as I was, but I did.

I collapsed on the deck, winded and still sick. There would be no more dives for me today. Perhaps never. Definitely never from a boat again. In fact, I didn't think I could ever look at a glass of water again.

Some other divers did a second dive. Another diver was also sick, and he cancelled his second dive. My son, who had taken a Bonine after initial nausea but before he got sick, was okay, but he opted to stay out of the water with me. I lay curled up on the deck of the boat, still in my dry suit, unable to even lift my head. I was way way beyond all those thoughtful suggestions—the "stare at the horizon" statements and other such well-meant advice from my companions.

One of the divers had speared a large monkfish. Also called a goosefish, these horrors of the deep can be aggressive underwater and have mouths sometimes a foot across, with long, sharp teeth jutting out at crazy angles. The slimy creatures are covered with wart-like protuberances and have a little fleshy thing hanging in front of their gaping, snaggle-toothed mouths, to lure dinner to them. They are frightening creatures. The beast—bleeding in the stern of the boat—lay still alive, gasping and opening its toothy maw at anything

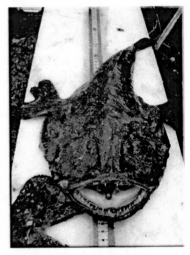

Goosefish, Courtesy of NOAA Fisheries, Northeast Fisheries Science Center

that came close. I lay also on the deck in my diving suit, unable to move an inch. Upon each roll and pitch of the boat, the horrible creature would slide towards me along a trail of bloody slime. Then the boat would roll the other way, sliding the monstrosity back away from me where it would smack against the gunwale with a sickening thud. It lived for hours, its gnarled teeth snapping at the air, teasing me from across the deck and adding to my misery in its last act of defiance.

Finally, relief! Well I didn't really feel any better—I was still getting sick periodically over the side of the boat. But now with these increasing seas and all divers out of the water, the captain announced, "It's going to get rough out here—we are leaving NOW!" But my relief at our leaving was short-lived, for after traveling about a half mile, our one remaining engine quit. Now we were totally without power, miles from home, and a storm was approaching fast. Let me add that no matter how seasick you are while the boat is underway, it is worse if you are bobbing like a cork, powerless, at the mercy of the seas. At least being under power gives consistency to the motion and eases your discomfort somewhat.

I lay on the deck moaning, my son put all my gear away for me, and we all waited. The captain called Sea Tow and consulted with them over the radio. He described recent repairs to the engine and complained about his poor luck. Sea Tow took over an hour to find us, and the Sea Tow guy's first idea was to hand us a five-gallon can of fuel, saying, "Try this." Two cans of fuel later and we were back underway. Both engines worked great! We had been out of fuel.

Right outside Shinnecock Inlet, the Sea Tow captain insisted that he tow us through the inlet. He didn't have more fuel on board and he really did not have to explain how our boat would be dashed against the two inlet rock jetties if we ran out of fuel again while traversing the inlet.

Well, we made it back. I still owe a second dive to complete my nitrox dive certification. More important than that, I learned some valuable lessons. From now on, I think I'll always take anti-seasickness medication before any boat trips. Any time I had taken it previously, I'd always gotten a wee bit drowsy—

like I do when I take a Dristan—but I never got seasick. I will forever look at other seasick divers with great compassion and try to help when I can. Also, I learned how my son, a 15-year old, can be when he sees his dad totally incapacitated. He was great! The best diving buddy I could have. And I now know that when you get on someone else's boat, you are subject to their judgment calls, and there is not much you can do other than mutiny if they do something that you feel shows poor judgment—such as not maintaining their gauges and not knowing when they are out of fuel. Or perhaps in this case the captain should have stuck to the original plan and stayed around Shinnecock Reef when we encountered heavy fog. Or maybe he should have turned back when we lost an engine early in the day. This is a good argument in favor of diving on professional dive vessels.

It is now 24 hours later, and while I have eaten and rested, I still have low energy and I feel like I'm recovering from a bout with strong opponent. I will dive again. I hope to go out to dive the USS *San Diego* again in two weeks.

Diving a Wrecked Schooner - The "Wolcott": A Lump of Coal (July 2001)

She lies, back broken, in 85 feet of water, almost wholly claimed by the drifting sands off of Fire Island some five miles out in the Atlantic Ocean. No one knows her real name. An old wooden sailing schooner, say some. On this clear and beautiful summer day, the sea is like glass, the sheen upon its surface giving no hint of the seas that might have raged on the day she sank. Divers making the descent to the wreck first get a glimpse of her from about 30 feet above. Much of the wreck is partially buried, leaving only ribs and other wooden pieces curving oddly along the sea bottom. There are three major sections of debris, with only the occasional remnant of ship's equipment—its purpose long forgotten—jutting up from the floor. Seen from above, the effect is not unlike that of an old dinosaur fossil embedded in rock, its protruding backbone

An American Clipper Ship. Off Sandy Hook Light in a Snowstorm

tracing a lazy "S" shape to beckon those who wonder about such things.

I have brought some tools with me: a gardener's three pronged claw and a little shovel in a canvas bag, which is attached to one of my three air tanks and now hangs at my side. No one knows who she is, when she sank, or why. It is a mystery. My mystery, because I am here now at 85 feet deep contemplating a sea anemone that has taken up residence upon her. I am a total romantic at heart, and I'm encouraged by the fish who gaze at me curiously. "What is he doing?" they ask with their little fish eyes, their little fish mouths making little soundless fish sounds. I open my canvas bag and pull out the gardener's claw, using it to dig against the side of the dinosaur's spine. It is puny and ineffective; the reward for my efforts is being enveloped in a cloud of silt. Digging along the old wooden timber, I feel like the wreck goes forever into the sands, as if the ocean is reclaiming it even as I work hard to uncover it. The fish continue gazing at me, occasionally looking at each other with knowing glances, not offering the least in the way of assistance. I stop working for a minute to let the cloud clear so I can see again.

There! On the left, what is that? I leave my tools at the patient's side and swim over a few yards. It is an anchor. A large old anchor, similar to what you might see outside an old seafood restaurant. It is big, probably six feet high, lying on its side just the way it would in front of that restaurant. The anchor is covered with years of sea life and sea things, but I can still easily make out its form. Too big to take on this trip. I easily drift back to my digging operation, like an astronaut floating in space on a space walk. I am ready to give up; my tools are too small for this job. I think I will spend some time swimming around and looking at the wreck.

My attention goes then to my little hole that I have dug with my little shovel with the little fish watching me. There, in the bottom, almost missed, is a lump of coal. My imagination fires up again. I thought that this was supposed to be an old sailing ship! Coal? Perhaps not a sailing ship? Perhaps a coal-burning ship? Have I solved some of the mystery?

I look up at one of the little fish, now replaced by a larger one; it sadly shakes its head at me and slowly turns away into the current. I then realize that no mystery is solved here. Perhaps I found a new one. Maybe the coal was the cargo on the ship— although there is not a lot of it. Perhaps the coal was used for a coal-burning stove which kept the crew warm in their cabins on some horrid, stormy night when she went down. Perhaps...

I look at my air gauge and realize that I must leave now. I have already been down too long. I take the lump of coal and head back for my slow trip to the surface, where a hot coffee awaits me.

Additional Information at the Engraving at the beginning of this story:

Currier and Ives (American, 1857-1907) An American Clipper Ship. Off Sandy Hook Light in a Snowstorm. 19th Century Lithograph with hand coloring. 20.5 x 32 cm (image); 28 x 37 cm (sheet) Fine Arts Museums of San Francisco, Gift of Joseph Martin Jr. 1994.120.9

The Thing That Lives in the Lake: A Story for Halloween – October, 2001

All I could think about was that piece I had read about the lake. You know, the part where they talk about how they paid laborers one dollar per body to recover the corpses from the church graveyards and cemeteries. You see, this was all dry land once. Then in 1926 they decided to block up a bunch of streams and flood the entire valley. A dam here, a earthen wall there—farms were bought up, homesteads were sold, and The Great Utility Company, through eminent domain, laid claim to lands that had been in the occupants' families for generations. It took from February through October of that year to flood the great valleys and create the largest lake in Connecticut—Candlewood Lake.

I had been diving enough years to know that a diver was less buoyant in fresh water than in salt water. I had been too lazy to remove some weight for this freshwater lake dive. Weighted heavily for salt water but diving in 30 feet of less buoyant freshwater, I was busy doing the up-and-down thing in the water column. I displayed my latest non-silting techniques as I slammed down again against the bottom. Visibility was now less than zero. All my attention was on my right arm, which held a new high-intensity light. On this time down against the silt I decided that instead of doing a body roll into the bottom of the lake I would let my light only briefly touch the bottom. This would allow me to regain my trim. The light gently touched the bottom and then kept going, and going. I was enveloped in total blackness. Even my glowing gauges were now invisible. As my arm and upper body (it seemed) continued to plunge into the quicksand like silt that lined the bottom.

Visions of *Night of the Living Dead* went through my mind as I could see the groping half decayed arms of the dead reaching up from the Stygian darkness, searching for me, the only life around to help feed their corrupted souls. I could feel the silt around my arm—it felt like my arm was in a thick soup or slurry made from the oozing effluvia of all the bodies still remaining in the soil under the lake. Agghhh! I brushed against something in the thick silt. I felt it not with my hand but along the length of my arm. It felt like something sliding up, using my arm as a guide, blindly grasping to force me to join them in their flooded sepulcher.

Before the dam was built, there were farms and homes here. I had been hoping to come across a farmhouse or perhaps the remains of an old stone wall. Maybe I would be one of the lucky divers to find an antique farm tool or an old bottle. But for now I was still fighting for my life with the zombies of the lake.

I wrestled against the pull of the silt. I could almost hear the suction sound as I got the light back out to where it could do me some good. Then I put a bit more air in my BC vest so that I'd be more buoyant. I was okay for now. I continued my explorations.

This was my second dive today at the lake. About eight of us had met this morning at 7:30 in front of the dive shop to make the one-and-a-half-hour drive up to Connecticut from New York City. It was a fun trip, despite getting lost and running out of gas. Thank goodness for cell phones. We finally arrived, and (of course) the lake area we had intended to dive was closed! Well, we grabbed a local resident and tortured him until we got some information about where the locals dive. Our caravan headed over there, to a location about two miles distant.

The air temperature was in the mid 40s with a brisk wind. There were a couple of wet-suited divers who did two dives back to back, getting into their cars to warm up in between dives, wet suits and all.

When I wasn't busy crashing against the bottom, visibility was generally okay, ranging from five to 10 feet. When the occasional cloud momentarily obscured the sun, I would plunge back into darkness. I was in a group of four divers for my first descent, and on that dive, vis was horrible. One of the divers had run a reel, and we were all tripping over each other, trying to keep near the line. This only made the vis worse. The slightest finning anywhere near the bottom roiled the silt, creating clouds that looked like miniature atomic bombs going off. I vowed that my second dive would have less people.

It did, and I even got some solo time. But because of the very thick silt, I decided not to deploy my metal detector or my new secret weapon, a homemade underwater vacuum powered by an 80-cubic-foot air tank carried on my side. I call it the "Mark II Electrolux Underwater Vacuum." The thing really churns up the silt on a good day, but besides annoying the other divers, it would have only served to anger and get me in trouble with The Thing that Lives in the Lake.

What is the underwater vacuum? Well, a couple of months ago I was glancing through a copy of the *Encyclopedia of Underwater Archaeology*. They had a picture of a device called an air lift. The device consisted of a PVC pipe just a few inches in diameter and a compressed-air hose that could inject air into the pipe through a hole situated a couple of inches from the bottom of the open end of the pipe. The diver positions the lower end of the pipe where he wants to dig and hits the button, letting air into the pipe. The air, of course, rushes up the pipe to get to the surface. This creates a powerful suction at the lower end of the pipe. Sand and whatever else is there is sucked through the pipe and comes out on the boat where it falls onto a screen. Any objects that were in the sand get trapped in the screen. Got it?

I wanted one. So I cut a three-foot section of two-inch PVC and attached a mesh netting "goodie bag" to the top of it. I drilled a hole at the lower end of the pipe, and to this I attached an air hose. There's also a small inflatable bladder attached to the upper end of the pipe (near the mesh bag) in order to keep the pipe vertical in the water. When a button is pushed, compressed air from a 80-cubic-foot SCUBA tank is injected into the tube. I wear the 80-cubic-foot tank on my right side to power this infernal contraption. Although I am still in the research phase, my underwater vacuum actually works! I am experimenting with the length of the tube and the placement of the hole in the pipe, but the tank currently provides about 15 minutes of suction at 15 feet deep, and I've been able to comfortably hold the metal detector in my left hand and the vacuum tube in my right as I cruise over the bottom of Shinnecock Bay, detecting metal and vacuuming at the same time. The sand is sucked up the pipe and falls through the bag, impacting visibility somewhat. But whatever else is present winds up in the bag. This gadget would be ideally operated by a blind diver, who might use the headphones to monitor the metal detector. He could then push the button on the vacuum when he hears a beep. Okay, so perhaps this is not how I am going to get rich, but it does beat watching *National Geographic* reruns!

Electrolux Mark II
Porta-Airlift

Some Problems on the USS San Diego – October, 2001

I went out on the *Wahoo* dive boat yesterday to dive the USS *San Diego*, and as usual I had a great time. I only had about 15 minutes of bottom time on this dive, but it was rather exciting. I encountered some unexpected surge down at 100 feet or so, and I lost my light and a little digging tool. I also had a small problem switching gas at 90 feet. I performed my usual post-mortem on the dive afterwards.

It is a very good idea to analyze what went wrong on a dive and why. Many times you will find that the cause of the problem actually originated two or three steps prior to what had seemed to be the source of the problem. It is amazing how little details can make such a difference in the unforgiving environment of the sea. Because of some minor details that I'd overlooked or hadn't paid enough attention to, I had some potentially serious problems on this dive. Because of other little details and rules that I *did* pay attention to, the problems didn't kill me.

I got a great new toy recently. It is a metal detector that is capable of being taken as deep as 200 feet underwater, and it also has a setting to ignore ferrous materials like iron and steel. I have been having a lot of fun with it recently off Long Island's bays and beaches in water up to about 25 feet deep. It is integral to my winter dive plans for the coming cold water season. I am going to use it on shallow dives along with a vacuum lift device I am developing that is powered by an 80-cubic-foot tank that you wear like a stage bottle.

Using Velcro, I had attached two small plastic clips to the detector so that I'd be able to clip it to my harness D-rings or to a stage bottle attached to my harness. The clips worked fine. They were the only plastic ones I could find, and I did not want to use metal clips on the metal detector.

Well, unfortunately, I have this skin problem on my hands—I sometimes get a rash from contact with rubber or something in my dive gear. I am okay with the rubber dry suit because of the fleece undergarment. For some reason the latex hood and wrist seals on the suit don't bother me either. But the neoprene gloves are a big problem. So on shallow beach dives I wear thin leather golf gloves to protect my hands, and I am fine. On deeper dives, though, I pull 7 mm neoprene gloves over the leather gloves. I have gotten used to it. I don't like the limited dexterity, but I've been able to work my equipment clips. Until now.

I was taking the metal detector along on this dive just to test it at depth and play around in the debris field of the *San Diego*—no artifact recovery was planned for this dive. When I jumped into the water, a crew member handed me my metal detector. I took one look at the little plastic clips on it and decided that I might have a problem unclipping the detector at depth with my double gloves on. I decided to carry the detector instead of clipping it to myself. The surface gave a false sense of calm yet there were eight-foot swells separated about 15 seconds apart. I could see other small boats in the near distance vanishing up to their gunwales as they dipped into troughs formed by the very long spaces between the swells.

Making my 80-foot descent along the anchor line to the top of the *San Diego*'s upside-down hull kept me busy. I managed to use one hand to move down the descent line, periodically passing the metal detector (which I was carrying) to my gripping hand so that I could momentarily use the *free* hand to equalize the pressure in my ears by holding my nose and gently exhaling through it.

At the bottom of the line, I was immediately pushed very hard by the strong surge and current powered by the seas above. Usually, I take a second at the bottom to establish my buoyancy and then take off for whatever destination I have in mind. But now I could barely manage to hold the line and still hang on to my detector. I looked at my red canvas tool bag and saw that it had opened. Inside, I had placed my two digging tools and my main light. Before going in the water, I had checked to make sure that the bag was closed and that the light was clipped to the bag from inside so that it could not get lost. I closed the bag, not even checking for the light—I knew it was there.

I found that if I let go of the line to play with the air bladder in my vest, the surge would knock me hard. So instead of adjusting my buoyancy, I lunged for the bilge keel, staying negative, hoping there would be some protection over the side of the ship. Now I was hanging over the side of the *San Diego*, my legs extending partly over an opening into the ship and the rest of me sticking out above the ship like a flag fluttering in the wind. First the powerful surge pushed me out away from the ship; now it tried to suck my legs and lower body into the ship. And back and forth again. In any event, my main concern continued to be preventing the delicate metal detector from slamming against anything. I decided to drop a bit lower to pass the opening in the ship, hoping that the solid hull would shelter me from the storm.

Of course, I was still negatively buoyant, so I slid down along the ship, cradling my toy like a baby. Landing on the sand in total blackness, now 105 feet deep, I found myself somewhat protected from the surge for now. I still felt it, just not as much. At least, that was the case until I moved to my right a little bit and realized that there was some kind of a hole in the shipwreck there. Standing in front of this hole, I again felt the ship try to suck me in and toss me out, the rhythm dictated by some storm or lunar influence far away. I moved back away from the opening and reached into my red bag for my light. The bag was empty except for my little shovel. I felt around for the light. No light. I put my computer up to my face to see how long I had been down. I couldn't see it. My left hand was occupied holding the detector. I couldn't hit the light button to illuminate the computer without letting go of the detector.

At this early stage, I still thought I had a dive left here. I was sure I would find my light, and then I could still play a bit with the metal detector since I was now protected by the hull of the ship. I felt again for the light and still didn't clip the detector to my harness to free up both hands. Now I started looking for my secondary light which I keep on my left harness strap, clipped below the chest D-ring. I felt down the whole length of the left strap. I still don't know why I couldn't find it. It may have been because I keep it securely attached and flush against the strap, and at this moment I had very limited dexterity due to the double gloves. Or there may have been another reason. My right hand was holding on to some protuberance on the ship, and perhaps when I let go to feel for the secondary light, I didn't look for it long enough because each surge would cause me to grab for the ship once more, to steady myself.

At this point, unable to see my gauges and find my lights, I decided it was time to abort the dive. I slowly swam directly up along the hull to the edge where the side meets the keel, a few feet below the bilge keel. As some of you may know if you have dive experience on this wreck, there are large spaces and holes in the *San Diego* there. Now I was back doing the getting-sucked-into-the-ship thing again. Hmm. Wasn't I just here doing this dance a few minutes ago? The only difference was that I was swimming upwards now. Still negatively buoyant and still cradling my detector, I made a grab for the bilge keel and hung on to it for a couple of surge sequences. Then I lunged for the anchor line.

I looked around for a couple of seconds for the lost light but didn't see it, and I decided that now—while I was hanging on to the anchor line—would be a good time to switch from my back gas to my decompression bottle. Normally when making such a switch, I remove the regulator but continue to hold it in my left hand while I start to breathe from the new regulator. This ensures that if there is a problem with the regulator I am in the process of switching to, I can always find the one that I just took out of my mouth. But my left hand was already busy holding the detector *and* the anchor line in this insanely powerful surge. So I spit the regulator out and put the deco regulator into my mouth. No air! It would have helped to turn the bottle on. Normally this would not be a big problem because I would still have a good regulator in my left hand ready to jab in my mouth.

Unfortunately, now I was in a heavy surge, hanging on a line and holding an expensive and delicate device, with no air in my lungs—and I had no idea where my just-removed regulator had gone. Fluttering somewhere behind my head in the current somewhere. Do you know that even at this point I was saying to myself, "Don't let go of the metal detector—you'll lose it!"

I wasn't panicked here, yet. I knew that my safety bottle—yet a third tank of gas I was carrying—was definitely turned on, and that I had a secondary regulator connected to my back gas on a piece of tubing around my neck. I went for that regulator and jammed it into my mouth. But a piece of tubing got caught in such a manner as to prevent a total seal of my lips around the mouthpiece. My first breath of air was almost all water. I choked and swallowed it, working the tubing out of the way and pressing the purge button at the same time. When I got that water in my mouth and throat instead of air, for a split second I remember thinking that I could possibly die down here. I felt total panic, an instinctive and very strong desire to bolt to the surface. I thanked God for that first good breath of sweet air when it came. There was no bolt to the surface, and I made a nice slow ascent complete with all required stops. There were some important lessons though.

The fundamental error here was not retaining the ability to have my two hands free in a potential emergency situation. I guess some folks may say the basic error was not dropping the metal detector, or failing to clip it to myself earlier in the dive. My only excuse for not clipping it during the ascent was my worry that it might break if I could not unclip it prior to climbing up the ladder to the boat. I wanted to be able to hand it to someone. Actually, at the 40-foot decompression stop I did try to clip it, but I was having trouble. Another diver clipped it for me, and I ultimately climbed the ladder onto the boat without damaging the detector.

I am reviewing my attitude during the dive as well as the placement of the secondary light, and I am thinking about adding a nice, big steel clip to the handle end of the metal detector. I've done some tests and have discovered that a clip in that location will not interfere with the detector's operation. At the "business end" of the device, I am leaving the plastic clip for now but will try to find a bigger one. The single metal clip will work to keep me from losing the damn machine on the next dive. I am also adding a metal clip to keep the handles of my canvas tool bag shut better.

The loss of a light can happen to anyone. But the difficulty in locating my secondary light, awkwardness in fighting the heavy surge, and the violation of my normal regulator-switching procedures all came down to the fact that I didn't have two free hands in an emergency. Let's not even mention how the general distraction caused me to neglect to turn on the deco bottle. In a sense, this dive's problems—including my potential drowning—were all due to the use of a clip that was too small. By the way, I no longer wear the double gloves.

It's all in the details. I am sure that there have been many dive incidents that, when analyzed, came down to a small decision or choice usually involving an inexpensive piece of equipment that proved to be a major contributing factor in the incident. Diver attitude plays a part too: just think of all those stories about divers refusing to drop their weights; and how I clung to my metal detector like it was made of gold. About the only thing I did really right here was to dive with numerous redundant gas supplies—also, I avoided panic and a bolt to the surface from 90 feet or so. Oh. And one other thing I am doing right. Taking the time to review the dive and learn something from it. This dive wasn't over until this story was written.

A More Serious Problem Diving the USS San Diego: The Bends – October, 2001

The 'Bends'. The slang term for Decompression Illness, or Caisson Disease. I have another definition. How about a spreading numbness that starts in your right foot and slowly, inexorably creeps up to your ankle, past your shin, to your knee? It's not a pins-and-needles feeling like you get when your foot falls asleep—it's rather like you have been given a Novocaine injection and just can't feel your foot. Combine that with extreme fatigue like you're battling a flu, add a healthy dose of denial, and there you go. The dictionary definition that I found glaringly overlooks this definition. That's funny. Because when it happened to me, I overlooked it too.

A diver can "get bent" by breathing pressurized air while at depth and then returning to the surface too fast. Air (or other mixed gases that a diver may breathe) contains mostly nitrogen. This gas builds up in the body tissues during a dive and must be allowed to come out slowly: the diver must ascend gradually. This allows the gas to come out of solution without

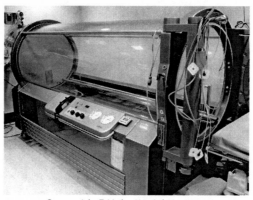

Courtesy John T. Mather Hospital, LI

forming crippling bubbles or causing a fatal embolism. First aid for a diver with decompression illness—DCI—is to provide pure oxygen. Often it requires a trip to "the chamber." The diver is placed into a chamber which is then pressurized to simulate a depth of 60 feet. The pressure is gradually reduced over the next few hours in order to allow the nitrogen to come out safely. Sometimes multiple treatments are necessary. Sometimes the diver is paralyzed anyway, if bubbles formed along nerve pathways damaging the nerves. Sometimes the diver dies. Medical science still does not fully understand DCI.

Sometimes you can get it even though you followed every rule. This is why it's important to add a measure of conservatism, as an additional safety measure, to all of your dive calculations.

On this otherwise fine October day, I did two dives. My first was to a max of 106 feet in 55-degree water. I was between 100 and 105 feet for about 19 minutes, then up around 90 feet for a while, until my total bottom time added up to about 26 minutes. This was while breathing 32% oxygen in a nitrox mix. On the way up I stopped at 40 feet for a minute and switched to 40% oxygen. I then did a decompression stop and stayed at 20 feet for about six minutes.

After a two-hour-forty-one-minute surface interval, I went back in again with 32% nitrox. I spent the first 17 minutes at about 80 feet, slowly moving down to 90 feet or so. I spent another seven minutes following the wreck down to my maximum depth of 105 feet. I stayed at that depth for four minutes, achieving a bottom time of 28 minutes. I stopped at 40 feet for two minutes, and again switched to 40% oxygen. I then stopped at 20 feet for seven minutes.

When I got out of the water I felt fine—no problem at all. I disassembled my gear and put it away, looking forward to jumping in the bunk and taking my traditional post-dive nap. Five minutes after lying down in the bunk (this would have been about 15 minutes after my dive), I noticed that my right foot was feeling funny. Like dead. I moved my leg, reached down, and massaged it. Closed my eyes and tried to go to sleep, telling myself that maybe I had "laid on it funny," or some other explanation. I started getting anxious as I noted that the area of numbness was moving up my leg at the rate of about an inch a minute. I could move it. But it was dead numb. I noted the complete absence of tingling and other familiar sensations that would have told me it had fallen asleep. I was afraid to bring it to anyone's attention because I thought I would look stupid, and that I was being a baby. The numbness continued to spread. About five minutes had passed since I first noticed the numbness, and I started to think that the numbness might just keep moving up me and that I might end up paralyzed or worse.

Finally the fear for my safety outweighed my other fears, and I hoisted myself out of the bunk with my arms. This was an upper bunk that was a bit tricky to get in and out of. My right leg gave way as I put my weight on it, and I forced myself up the ladder and through the hatch, trying to create an appearance of normalcy. I was limping and had difficulty walking, so I sat down on top of the hatch. Another diver asked me how my dive was. I said, "Great dive, but I think I might have taken a hit. My foot is feeling funny." Hearing myself say that snapped me out of my denial and I hauled myself up and found a crew member. "I think I have a problem," I started to say. He stopped me and had me lay down in the cabin. He put me on pure oxygen and had me drink a huge amount of water along with that miracle drug—an aspirin. I felt a bit foolish there in the cabin for about two hours on the oxygen, but the numbness was gone within minutes.

I could see other divers looking at me through the cabin windows and quietly making their pseudo-medical evaluations. I wondered what they were thinking. I had two hours to think and to breathe the oxygen. All sorts of stuff goes through your head: "Am I going to end up in a hyperbaric chamber? What about my big dinner tonight? I am the one who is supposed to pick up the lobsters for everyone at the fish store after the dive. Did I injure myself? Maybe it's a spinal injury…"

I actually felt fine now, but I followed the crew's advice. They were very supportive, checking on me periodically and occasionally barking at me to put the damn oxygen back in my mouth! I was very relieved that the symptoms had gone.

I could tell by speaking to the divers that they empathized with me. Some had gone through something similar or had known someone else who had. Perhaps I was going through some coming-of-age thing, or was experiencing a ritualized inauguration into the inner sanctum of northeast wreck diving. One thing I did notice was that no one told me that I had screwed up. While I was asked what my dive profiles were, no one blamed me. I felt a bit like an idiot or a hypochondriac—perhaps I had overreacted. Maybe my foot had even just fallen asleep. I told myself that I must have done something wrong. Come up too fast or something.

We pulled into the dock, and the crew asked me how I felt. I felt fine now. They then told me they thought that I had in fact "taken a hit" and they strongly recommended that I go to a local hyperbaric chamber: the hospital staff had already been notified and they were ready to man the chamber if I gave the word. My symptoms were gone except for a lingering fatigue. I thought of my upcoming dinner party and the people who were relying on me to bring the lobster. I thought of my fiancé's reaction if I told her I was on my way to the hospital. I decided not to go to the chamber. I was still shaken enough that when I loaded my car, I put my 40% oxygen deco tank in the car and turned it on in such a manner that I would be able to breathe from it while driving. If my symptoms returned, I would breathe from the deco tank while I redirected to the hospital to take up the previously declined offer of the recompression treatment. Silly, isn't it? But it made sense to me at the time.

I picked up the lobsters and made it to the dinner party (at my house). I was feeling more and more fatigued. I excused myself and went to bed at about eight p.m. I woke up about two a.m. I must have been having a dream or had slept on my arm, because my hand was numb! I shook it and felt the familiar "pins and needles." Relieved, I fell asleep again. I woke up at about nine a.m., feeling very fuzzy-headed and experiencing a strange fatigue and dullness that would not go away with my morning coffee. Suddenly, at about 11:30 a.m., like an unveiling, the strange feeling left—very abruptly. All of sudden I felt totally normal. Amazing and very weird. The next day or so was normal for me, but I had a nagging feeling that I should call the Divers Alert Network—DAN. Finally, after about three days, I made the call. I was still nervous they were going to say that I should go to a chamber. As if that were some kind of punishment or something rather than the solution. The fellow at DAN basically said that if I was symptom-free at this point there was no reason to go to a chamber now. But should I have the slightest return of symptoms, I should get to a diving doctor.

Some two months have passed since this experience. I have felt no additional effects, other than some fear that perhaps I am more susceptible to DCI than average. I have reviewed my dive profiles, and while I did not commit any outrageous violations, planned decompression diving is inherently dangerous and more prone to DCI incidents than is no-deco diving. Thus, there were still some items to ponder.

Some unusual things happened on that second dive. One is that I forgot my heavy neoprene gloves and instead dove with thin leather gloves. My hands were frozen throughout that dive. (Those damn gloves! Always causing me some problem or another.) Cold causes blood vessels throughout the entire body to constrict, thereby preserving body heat. This decreases the rate of off-gassing.

Also, I went in the water negatively buoyant. I never do that. I always go in positive, and then, once I find the line, I descend in a very controlled manner. On the day's first dive, I could see the descent line from where I jumped in the water, and I made directly for it, ignoring the "granny line" that ran from the boat's stern to the anchor line at the bow. On the second dive, I thought I would see the descent line easily again, so I jumped in negatively buoyant and did not see the line. I plummeted so fast that I could only focus on equalizing my ears, which were in excruciating pain due to the rapid increase in pressure. In seconds I was approaching the bottom. Luckily, I landed on the shipwreck after this 85-foot freefall. I will never do that negative buoyancy entry again. I could just see how someone—if his or her air were not turned on—would plummet like a rock to the bottom. They would not have time to turn on their air before their eardrums burst. I probably would not have been able to get over to the descent line even if I had seen it. There was no time to do anything except fight the pain in my ears. That second dive also had me starting shallower and then going deeper. Not a great dive profile.

Finally, because I didn't have a pee valve in my dry suit, I tended to not to drink a lot of fluids the morning of the dive. Dehydration is a big factor in DCI. The whole body chemistry changes, again significantly reducing the rate that nitrogen is off-gassed at the end of the dive.

I have had time to think. I consider myself very lucky. I love diving and am not going to stop, but there are some changes I will make. I will never again jump in negatively buoyant. Another idea is to calculate my dives for air, doing the deco time for air even when breathing a safer, higher-oxygen nitrox mix. I will avoid dive profiles that cause me to work my way deeper, like I did on my second dive.

I will also do some additional deeper decompression stops. Finally, I am considering not doing that second dive in the future. Perhaps I can extend a single dive, do a longer deco, and then call it a day. Also, maybe I need to get a pee valve—or wear a "diaper"— so that I am not discouraged from drinking a lot of water.

I am a member of DAN, the Divers Alert Network. I was a member of DAN at the time of the incident. There is no reason to not take the recompression chamber offer next time. I have read rather extensively on DCI, and science has much to learn about this mysterious illness which can only be avoided by not diving anymore. Well, maybe I wasn't actually bent. My new definition of the bends definitely includes a heavy dose of denial. Does yours?

Ice Diving at Lake Winnipesaukee New Hampshire – October, 2001

I went diving today on Long Island at the Ponquogue Bridge. There was a brisk wind, and you could just taste winter in the air. I thought back to last winter, when I had done quite a bit of cold water diving.

The *U.S. Navy Diving Manual* says that cold water diving starts at 40 degrees or lower. There can be issues with equipment freezing—even if the water temperature is above freezing—both from wind-chilling effects and from free-flowing equipment.

My interest in cold water diving all started when, at the end of last summer, I could not bear the thought of the dive season ending. So I got a dry suit with a dry-glove system, and then went out to get the appropriate training. (Okay, I know—I could have simply gone to Mexico.) I also had my breathing regulator modified for cold water. Unable to find a buddy nuts enough to join me, I settled for a pony tank as a buddy. I slipped beneath the surface at the Ponquogue Bridge one winter's day and immediately got a major brain freeze. The water temperature was somewhere around freezing there in the bay with scattered ice floes on its placid surface. I screamed into my regulator as my sinuses complained about the cold. The pain passed, and subsequent dives would find me wearing two hoods on my head. I liked ice diving! There was not much sea life in the middle of the winter, but the visibility was great.

 But on this dive I got cold and only lasted 20 minutes or so.

Don't need fish anyway. I am a digger. I must have been a walrus in a previous life. I don't mind rooting

around looking at the rocks, searching for artifacts and things. To continue with my hobby in the cold water, I had to teach myself new skills. I learned to wear my fleece smurf suit, a sweater, sweatpants, and extra socks. I also learned how to change into my gear in
the snow. I typically set up my gear while fully dressed, then quickly change into my smurf underwear and jump back into the car to warm up again. Once in my dry suit, I am usually quite toasty—at least until I get into the water.

So almost every weekend last winter I dove. I dove Rockaway, Bayville, and the Ponquogue Bridge. There was a heavy snowstorm last winter; you may recall it. Well, I was in Bayville, diving the barge. I remember leaving footprints with my DUI brand rock boots in the snow and walking through snow drifts almost up to my knee to get from the parking lot to the water. I got a bit of interest from local residents, with some of the more curious gathering to watch me on my death march to the sea.

Because I was diving alone, I thought I would be a bit conservative. I never went farther from shore than I thought was safe were my dry suit to become totally flooded with ice water. I always brought a secondary smaller air tank—a pony tank. I got very good with a reel and ran it on every dive. I restrung my reel with much heavier line so that if the current or tide kicked up unexpectedly, I could haul myself along it back to my entry point without fear of the line breaking. I stayed very warm right up until the time I went into the water. That meant that I put my gear together wearing gloves and hat and jacket, and then sat in my car for a few minutes to warm up.

The winter diving time was well-spent. One day at Rockaway, I was about 30 feet deep at the end of the small rock jetty when all of a sudden I couldn't stay down. I had just untied my reel

when I realized that one of my integrated weights had slid out of my vest-style BC. I was going up! I could not retrieve the weight. I was going UP! Very scary. Even from 30 feet. I used all of my strength to swim slightly down, doing anything and everything to slow my ascent as the laws of physics pulled me up towards the surface. I managed to go up at a safe rate, but I had to retrieve the weights on the next dive. I temporarily rigged my weights with a clip, so that if they slid out of the Velcro pocket they would hang there from my BC, but that was really unacceptable. It's a major entanglement hazard, amongst other problems. Those integrated weights are very dangerous. I believe they are going to kill some divers. I have seen quite a few divers that use clips like I did to hold the weights. That type of weight system should not be sold anymore. (Note: some later models of these vest-type BCs now have the weights also secured with a clip.)

I decided to change my entire gear configuration from a recreational BC-vest type to a Halcyon-Harness-type configuration. I moved my pony tank from my back to my left side and started calling it a "safety bottle" instead. I spent the rest of the winter working out all the kinks in my new configuration so that I would be ready to use it for wreck diving in the coming season. I got familiar with removing and putting my safety bottle on in the cold water, and with replacing my mask and switching my regulator underwater. All these things I have found to have an additional "twist" when done in very cold water.

I had heard about an ice-diving trip to New Hampshire's Lake Winnipesaukee that was sponsored by a New Jersey dive shop. I took the brief class and went off to New Hampshire. Because I was still not totally comfortable with my new harness-type setup, I used my BC-vest-type setup, complete with the integrated weights. I used clips, of course, to secure them.

Lake Winnipesaukee is New Hampshire's largest, and there is no protection from the wind. The surface of the up-to-three-foot-thick ice is interrupted here and there with these odd little outhouse-like ice fishing shacks that the locals drag onto the frozen ice with their pickup trucks to make their ice fishing a bit more comfortable.

A suitable spot was selected, and—using chain saws and brute force—we cut a triangular hole, about six feet on each side, in the ice. The block was pushed with great effort under the edge of the ice.

A safety diver in full gear sat on a milk crate at the edge of the hole for the entire day, ready to jump in if needed, and the rest of us paired up forming dive buddy teams. Each team, when its turn came to dive, would be harnessed to a line that the "line tender" on the ice would hold. Rudimentary signals would be used to give signals such as "OK" or "HELP!"

As I put on my dry suit, I watched the buddy I had been assigned as she tried to put on her rental dry suit. It was obvious she had no idea how to even put it on. I went over to the fellow who was running this operation and said to him, "I don't think she dives much. Can you pair her up with an instructor?" He looked at me and said, "You're worried? What's your certification level?" I told him it was rescue. He said, "You'll be fine!"

Hmmm…

We got in the 34 degree water. I, of course, was used to cold water and was ready to go! She could not descend and needed additional weights put in her BC pockets while we were in the water. Finally we began our descent, she gave me the OK symbol, and we were off! There was a lot more light than I thought there would be under the ice, but I was glad for the line going back to the hole. Because so much light came through the ice, the hole was impossible to see once we moved away from it. The rope came down the hole and was tied to me. Then, about 20 feet or so later, it was tied to her. For those who are interested in what the procedure is, if the line breaks and the diver gets lost, the lost diver is not supposed to search for the hole at all; valuable air would be lost, and there are no pockets of air under the three-foot-thick ice. The diver is to go up to the ice and to remain vertically upright under the ice remaining motionless conserving air. A rescue diver on a rope with twice the length of the original diver's rope goes out to the end of his rope and sweeps in a large circle. Theoretically, as the rope sweeps around it will hit the lost diver, who can grab it.

We were about 75 feet from the hole and 30 feet deep, and I watched her as she did a slow-motion roll. She looked just like one of those astronauts in the movie *Marooned*, spinning slowly in space, drifting away from the command module. Uh-oh, she was going UP! And she was definitely getting that Pillsbury Dough Boy look as her inflator uncontrollably pumped air into her rented dry suit! I swam over to her and yanked the inflator off her suit, grabbing her and putting my hand up to keep my head from hitting the thick ice above. We were now up against the bottom of the ice. She was wide eyed but giving me the OK signal. Yeah, right, she's "okay." I tilted her so that her exhaust valve could let some of the air out of the suit. She later said she had been told to not touch the inflator valve

 by the instructor. This is the valve to which a hose from the air tank attaches, allowing air to be added to the dry suit for warmth. The valve must have been defective, or else she had in fact pressed it and it froze open in the cold. I led her back to the hole in the ice, and she got out with the help of others. To get out of the ice hole, you just back up to one of the corners of the triangle cut in the ice and the others haul you out by your tank valves.

We had been in the water about 10 minutes. She was cold and did not want to continue the dive.

I surfaced in the hole, indicated that I wanted to continue alone, and had a great dive. I was the only one on the tether. I found some very sluggish fish but also spent a lot of time just looking at the beautiful undersurface of the ice. I saw fantastic ice shapes and protuberances, here and there acting as a prism on the brilliant sunlight which filtered down through the ice. I was gliding through a diamond mine, a showcase of light. My bubbles rose up through the icy water, not to surface until the spring thaw, expanding along the bottom of the ice, alive, seeking the highest points under the ice.

The next day, we explored at another spot. I was teamed up with an experienced cave diver. We dove a shipwrecked paddle-wheeler that had sunk in the 1800's. It was well-preserved in the cold lake water. Of course, one of my integrated weights slid out, but there was no real danger because it hung there on the end of the clip I had fastened to it. I slid it back in. My BC inflator valve froze shut, becoming useless, so I ended up using my dry suit to trim my buoyancy. I had a little camera with me and took some photos which accompany this story. We finished our dive to find that on today's dive, my previous buddy's suit flooded with icy water early in her dive. She had not wanted to again abort her dive so she continued, not telling her buddy she had a problem. She was now being treated for hypothermia, and it would be a couple of hours before she would be feeling warmer.

Cold water diving may not be for everyone. I find it exciting and challenging. Skills that are second nature to us have to be relearned in the extreme cold using equipment that is more likely to fail in such low temperatures. This year, I am replacing my fleece undergarment with a much heavier type—one that will retain its thermal qualities even if wet. This will give me added protection should my dry suit flood. The freshwater lake's temperature was 34 degrees but when I winter dive in the salt water ocean I have recorded temperatures as low as 28 degrees. According to the U.S. Navy, an unprotected person in water colder than 32 degrees will lose consciousness in under 15 minutes and be dead in 15 to 45 minutes. Serious stuff…

Tale of an Underwater Scooter and a Fire Truck at Rockaway – March, 2002

I always was a bit of a fire buff. I remember taking my son to a couple of fires when he was younger. I used to do a bit of news photography and had ridden along with New York Fire Department's Engine Co. 237 a couple of times, in Bushwick, Brooklyn. Well, here I was again, in a fire truck—a fire rescue truck to be exact—riding across the Atlantic Beach Bridge. Both I and my dive buddy were "well suited" for this ride, wearing our dry suits and staring at our SCUBA equipment on the floor of the truck as we headed back to Beach 6th Street in Rockaway, where our cars were parked.

The dive began as do most of my Rockaway dives: I arrived early, about 7:30 a.m., and ate my egg sandwich while looking over the railing at the water to check the vis. I hadn't dived in a couple of weeks and was looking forward to the dive. My partner showed up a few minutes later, and we joked around as we got ready. Our last two dives here had produced an antique folding-stock style admiral anchor, about three feet across. We had a great time digging it out with shovels and my scooter and lifting it to the surface. My buddy is also a digger-type diver. Visibility around us, once we get to work, is generally less than zero.

For those who are not familiar with diving at Rockaway, much of the diving is done at Beach 9th Street, where there is actually a place in the warmer weather where you can take a shower, wash your gear, and get a snack. (Author's Note: This place, *Almost Paradise*, closed its doors in October of 2003.)

Rockaway Beach 6th Street Map, artist unknown

I have never dived there, preferring to rough it three blocks east at Beach 6th street, diving the channel that to the west leads to the Atlantic Ocean through East Rockaway Inlet. East of the inlet is the Atlantic Beach Bridge, about one-quarter to one-third of a mile from the small beach where we go into the water. This is a busy boat channel; full-size tugboats, barges, and large commercial fishing vessels ply its waters year-round. The drawbridge opens and closes for these large boats throughout the day, sometimes multiple times per hour. I have looked at the sides of these boats as they've come through, and when laden, the boats can have drafts over 10 feet deep.

In the warmer weather, some divers go in from Beach 6th Street about 10 minutes before slack tide and ride the last of the incoming tide—staying on the surface and out of the main boat lanes—to the piers of the Atlantic Beach Bridge. I typically clip myself to the pilings with a line until the tide goes slack and then enjoy my dive.

The dive at the bridge is an interesting, spooky dive with lots of underwater structures, fish, and dark places that require a good dive light. After about 30 or 45 minutes you can feel the current picking up as the tide switches, now headed west and out to sea. I sometimes ride it back the quarter of a mile to 6th Street, sometimes on the surface and sometimes on the bottom, but always a bit on the north side of the channel to make sure I don't miss the beach entry point and end up in France.

In the winter, though—especially if diving alone—I don't go all the way to the bridge. To be more conservative because of the increased risk from the frigid waters I generally stay around the foot of Beach 6th Street near the underwater jetty. There is still much to do there. Sometimes I think about the sewage treatment plant directly across the channel from Beach 6th Street, with its effluent overflow pipe that empties treated water into the channel. Most of the time I try NOT to think about that. I once spoke to the fellow that runs that plant and he assured me that there is "nothing alive" in that sewage outflow and that it is tested weekly—actually twice a week in the summer—by the Department of Environmental Protection. "My own daughter grew up swimming on the beach adjacent to the sewage plant," he told me on the phone. He did not tell me if she was still alive.

Back to the story.
I wanted to test my scooter, *Apollo*, against the current, so I went in about 10 minutes before my partner. We arranged to meet at the end of the jetty in about 30 feet of water. *Apollo*

was great! I zipped this way and that, able to go against the current with ease at the medium setting. I figured that as long as I stayed east of the entry point I couldn't go wrong, because if the scooter died, the outgoing current would bring me back to the entry point the way it always did when I went to the bridge.

I found an old, intact Borden's glass milk bottle which added to the pleasure of the dive. I then headed to the rendezvous point to meet my buddy. One of the things I had planned to do was to practice towing him on the scooter. I changed the speed setting to high, in order to compensate for the extra drag, and we were off. He was comfortable hanging on to my harness, and I was fine. And we were moving at a good speed. Overconfident because of my familiarity with the dive site, I decided to tour about without really consulting my compass too often. We would stop here and there, discovering all sorts of big rocks and other things there that we had never seen before. I was now down to about one-third of my air and decided to head back.

I'd thought that we were somewhat east of the entry point, but now, when I checked my compass, everything was wrong. To the north lay deeper water, instead of shallower. And now the tide had switched, and every second it was getting stronger. I thought maybe my compass was confused because of its proximity to the scooter motor. So I shut down a couple of times, checking the compass on my wrist and turning in a circle until it showed I was facing north.

"That can't be!" I thought. That would mean that we were totally across the channel. I continued with the scooter, heading for the shallows now—to the south! The current was now strong and I could feel that the scooter had exhausted its battery and was decreasing in power. As for me, my air was down to 600 pounds per square inch (I'd started the dive with 3200 psi). I signaled to my partner that I was going to surface to see where we were. I could tell from the bottom sand and depth that we were not in the boat channel, so I tentatively surfaced. To my dismay, I saw that we were totally across the channel from our entry point, and the current was now ripping strong. I needed to tell my buddy to surface so that we could make it to the beach on this side.

To my horror, I could see from my partner's bubbles that he was heading north, trying to swim across the channel. I didn't know if he knew where we were, but he must have been feeling that current. I looked at my air, now at 500 psi. I knew he had much more air than I did, because he had come in 10 minutes after me, and I had been dragging him around the entire time. The battery-powered scooter was low on juice and I was low on air, so, remaining on the surface, I headed for the small beach near me hoping that my buddy would turn around or that I would see him surface safely across the channel. I was quite worried that the outgoing current would take him out to sea, and I wondered if I'd have to call for a rescue helicopter.

I was standing safely in the shallows on the wrong side of the channel when all of a sudden, I heard my buddy's distinctive laugh roll across the water. He'd surfaced in the middle of the boat channel. Apparently, he'd found it quite humorous when, heading north underwater, he'd seen the depth increasing rather than decreasing and had started to get hit by the current. He then must have realized that he wouldn't be able to make it back across the channel, so he'd surfaced. I was very happy to see him, but by now he had drifted about 50 yards west with the current and didn't realize he was right in the big boat lane of the channel. I screamed out his name and added the single word, "BOATS!"

He looked around and headed right to shore, then walked over to me. At least we were both okay. One of us would stay and watch the gear, and the other would walk in a dry suit across the bridge and come back with the car. I could imagine the phone calls to the police reporting me walking through a residential neighborhood, in winter, wearing a dry suit and dive mask with its built in corrective lenses.

I had never known that the Atlantic Beach Fire Rescue station was right there, across from our dive site at Rockaway. Of all places; we had actually landed on their beach, and some of the guys came running out to see what was going on. It turned out that a bunch of them had just completed a Public Safety dive course and were into diving. Trying to save face, the first words out my mouth were, "THIS isn't France! I think we made a navigational error."

They offered to drive us back to Rockaway, saving us two hours and a lot of hassle and giving me a chance to consider, in the back of their rescue truck, what I would do differently next time.

My idea of using the scooter east of the entry point as a safety measure to allow for a mechanical problem was a good idea. It's true that if I am east and the scooter dies, the outgoing tide will bring me back to my entry point. But I had not followed my own plan. I had not stayed east of the entry point. I had also not consulted my compass at the beginning of the tour, so where did I expect to end up? Finally, not being thoroughly familiar with the scooter's battery-drain rate, I should have stayed much closer to home, particularly while towing another diver. About the only really smart thing I did here was to end the dive, even though I was on the wrong side of the channel. Had I tried to make it back, especially while towing my buddy, you would be reading this story in French—if it would have been written at all!

More on that Borden's Milk Bottle I found...

I called the Borden Dairy offices in Texas, and they put me through to their resident old timer. He had a serious southern drawl and sounded very old.

"I found an old Borden's Milk bottle while SCUBA diving..."

"Awwlright, is it a brown bottle?"

"No, it's clear."

"Take a look see at her bottom. Ya see a date? Should have a date there."

"There's no date on it. It has a large 'B' on the bottom."

"Vertical lines on the bottle?"

"Yeah ! Yeah!"

"Big 'B' on the bottom?"

Borden Milk Bottle

"Yeah! That's it! How old?"

"Never heard of a bottle like that," he said.

Then: *"Jus' kiddin' boy! That bottle was produced in the Skokie, Illinois plant in the 1940s. Where'd ya find it?"*

And that's the end of the story!

The USS San Diego, One Year Later – April, 2002

My first dive on the USS *San Diego* was just one year ago. Since then I have returned to her for about 10 or 12 dives; even being stricken with decompression illness (DCI) when diving her last August. I was excited about today's dive. I looked at it like I was going back to visit a friend, one that I was still getting to know. My dives on the *San Diego* have been all from that bastion of tech sensibility—the RV *Wahoo*.

Last year, the *Wahoo* always moored at the stern end of the starboard bilge keel, and I got familiar with the shipwreck from there to the end of the stern. Although I was comfortable with a reel, my basic single-steel-tank configuration kept my gas supply too low for me to be really comfortable doing any serious penetration of the 500-foot-long wreck. I always dive with a side-slung, 30-cubic-foot safety bottle, and occasionally with an additional 80-cubic-foot bottle on my right side for even more gas, but this is usually way too cumbersome. Last year, I had an incident where I did a regulator switch at about 85 feet while holding an expensive metal detector in my hands in very strong surge. I had stupidly spit out my good regulator in order to start breathing on the one from the 80 cf bottle, only to find that it had not been turned on! Time for double tanks. Also, I wanted to be able to deco using higher percentages of oxygen, and since by this time I had a better idea of what the hell I was doing, I had recently decided it was time for advanced nitrox training. I ordered some new regulators and double tanks and booked myself for an advanced nitrox class.

Courtesy Captain Steve Bielenda

Well, I had done the reading and the class was next week, with related dives to follow. I decided to do this *San Diego* dive using my old equipment, with which I was very familiar.

The more I read about DCI and the use of more exotic gas mixtures the more frightening this whole diving thing is. So much is not known about DCI; there are factors such as dehydration, cold, and physical conditions that are critical, yet not quantifiable. For example, no one knows how much more conservative you should be if you are cold, dehydrated or overweight. So we all make a good guess and say, "Well, calculate the dive as if you are going 10 feet deeper than you actually are." My reading reveals that this is only a *guess*. No one really knows. In fact, I have gotten a shrug from many an experienced diver who is quick to add that even if you do follow the deco tables, you might get bent. Why do we do this insane sport that has an element of unpredictability, of factors outside our control, of potential death or permanent disability? Is it the taunting call of adventure and danger? The very uncertainty of whether diving a profile that has worked for us many times in the past can suddenly and inexplicably let us down like a relationship suddenly gone bad?

Well, whatever the reasons, I love diving and I intend to continue. So that means to read everything I can get my hands on. I listen to other divers' stories and advice, and I respect their experience. And I use every tool available to increase safety. Of course, I mean short of following all PADI Recreational Diver Limit restrictions, such as only diving to non-decompression depths. Hmmmm...

Typically, I would do two dives on the *San Diego*, napping in between, each dive being a few minutes longer than the recommended non-decompression limit for the gas mix I am breathing. Since my DCI incident I had toyed with the idea of just doing one longer dive with more deco time instead of two shorter dives. So for this visit back to the *San Diego*, I planned to do a single dive using 30% nitrox back gas and my trusty 30-cubic-foot tank with 40% oxygen for emergency and deco purposes. I planned a 25-minute dive at 100 feet, and I planned to do one-minute stops at 60, 40, 30, and 20 feet. Then I would do a minimum of nine minutes at 15 feet. This was based on a hypothetical deco plan for an entire dive at 110 feet for 30 minutes. The U.S. Navy tables say to do a seven-minute deco, so I added two minutes to that and then noted on my slate that I wanted to stay at 15 feet a minimum of nine minutes. But if I wasn't too cold, 14 minutes would be even better.

So, to recap, even though I'd be breathing 30% nitrox for a 25-minute dive at 100 feet and switching to 40% at about 80 feet, I would deco as if it were a 30-minute air dive to 110 feet. And then I'd basically double the deco time on top of that. Hmmm...not an exact science you say?

Because I was quite familiar with the *San Diego* stern section, I have given myself a little project. I obtained the deck plans from the Bureau of Archives in Washington DC. I laminated the stern section plans and bound them into a four-page package that can come underwater with me. It's a bit unwieldy as the original plans are seven feet long. I noted some landmarks on the plans, such as the bilge keel and elbow joints for prop shafts, etc. I then bought a standard 100-foot measuring tape (the kind that's used on a construction site), drilled drainage holes into it, added some line and a clip, and decided that I was going to survey the USS *San Diego*.

Using my newly found underwater architectural surveying skills, I would, over the coming months, record the current state of the 1918 wreck and produce a chart showing any collapses and openings into the ship. This would also serve as a future guide for planning deeper penetrations. I took an underwater slate and sketched a diagram that I could fill in underwater with some critical measurements and diagrams showing the shape of the stern collapse.

Well, today, as usual, circumstances dictated another dive plan. We hooked into the wreck at the bow end, rather than the stern. This would be my first dive ever on that section of the ship. So the laminated charts didn't come down with me. I did bring the measuring tape, thinking that I could do some work on the bow end. It turned out that the grapnel was a little off the wreck in the sand. I didn't want to go below 100 feet, so I explored a bit of the wreck uneventfully in the 95-foot range and then moved up to the keel, finally ending my dive with a chilly decompression as planned above.

That single dive was a fine introduction to a busy dive-boat season for me. I followed it with a nap and all in all had a great day. A year ago, I didn't really know too many other divers on the boat. It was all new to me. But now that I knew some of the other divers, we exchanged stories and talked. It was good seeing the RV *Wahoo* crew again too. Best of all, it was good seeing that glimpse of naval history, one of the great armored cruisers of yesteryear, the USS *San Diego*—still asleep in her watery grave.

Diving at the Strongs Neck Bridge, Setauket Long Island – April, 2002

Boy, work had me very stressed out and I needed a mental health day! I was originally going to dive at Strongs Neck, in Setauket. Due to strong northerly winds that might cause poor visibility, I decided not to. I went to two early-morning appointments for work and figured that if I got back home by 10:30 a.m, I could have my car loaded with my dive gear just in time to make the 12:49 p.m. high tide at Rockaway (a lot of times the vis is okay on the south shore when the winds are northerly).

Got to Beach 6th Street. With the high winds, vis looked to be about six inches. I could not clearly see my test rock through the water from the jetty, so I didn't go in. Oh well. I decided instead to head out to a hardware store in the Moriches to get Naval Jelly spray. I am using this stuff to prevent further deterioration of the iron admiral-style anchor recovered from Rockaway a few weeks back (more on this in a moment). I swung north to the Port Jefferson Library to return some books on the construction of clipper ships and other maritime topics. Well, Setauket is between Port Jefferson and NYC, so it was sort of on the way. I decided to go by the site of the old Strongs Neck Bridge, just to take a look. Vis looked good. I decided to dive.

The concrete Strongs Neck Bridge, with its small arch, is no more. The bridge appears on an 1886 map of the area, and once upon a time it crossed Little Bay to East Setauket. The bridge, at a bend in Dykes Road, was demolished in the 1930s. I had noticed on my last dive here about two months ago that

Site of Strongs Neck Bridge

piles of junk had collected underwater, due to the current. Today I had my trusty scooter, Apollo, to blast it all away.

I went in cautiously. Here you can easily sink into the muck while getting into the water, and I was wearing a heavy steel tank and carrying the 40-pound scooter. I did not want to sink down onto some sharp broken bottle in the mud and puncture my foot through my rubber-soled rock boots. I'd be oink-ing and squealing like a stuck pig until some good Samaritan rescued me. Hopefully they'd take care to leave the glass sticking out of me until I got to the Emergency Room so I don't bleed to death. Nope. Didn't want all that to happen! So I walked in quite slowly, feeling around carefully.

Once in the water, I realized that I had forgotten my scooter BC jacket, which allows me to add air to make the scooter neutrally buoyant so I can clip it to a D-ring on my BC and it floats alongside me as I work. No big deal: the 40-pound scooter only feels about two pounds when in the water. I would just try to keep it out of the mud. The Strongs Neck Bridge area can get pretty busy with boats and skiers in the summer, but now, on this Thursday in April, with temperatures in the 40s, it was empty. Nevertheless, I used a short polypropylene line to attach a dive flag to myself. It must have been a hell of a sight from shore: me scooting around underwater, 12 feet deep, a flag following me on the surface and moving much faster than anyone can swim.

I explored, pleased with the 15-foot visibility. The water north west of where the old bridge once stood would have originally been blocked to boats larger than a dory. But the bridge would have faced a nice sunset. Perhaps couples or friends once enjoyed those sunsets from the bridge. And perhaps they had contests, maybe throwing wine bottles (now antique) in that direction. And just maybe a few engagement rings went in there too!

South of the bridge's original location, the water is deeper. Here, Little Bay opens up to Setauket Harbor, and thence to Port Jefferson Harbor. There was once a wharf there where schooners unloaded—it stood over near the old shipbuilding areas in Setauket Harbor. Perhaps that area would produce bigger artifacts. I had heard that there may even be a wreck somewhere over there. I toured around for about 50 minutes in the 45-degree water and found a broken part of a scabbard for either a bayonet or a sword, then spent some time looking for more of it. No luck. I will return, although this area may not be safe to dive in warmer weather due to boat traffic.

As for that anchor I mentioned, what a find. I recently hauled it home from Rockaway and gave it a five-week soak in a 55-gallon drum full of fresh water, out in the garage. Then I put on an old T-shirt and jeans and pulled out a couple of chisels and a geology hammer from my fossil-hunting days. Ninety minutes later, sitting on the grease-stained floor amid the debris of probably over 100 years of encrustation, I looked at my work. Not bad. Most of the anchor was down to the pitted old iron, and in places where the metal seemed thin I left the cemented encrustation alone. I rinsed it a few more times and let it dry. The next day, I gave it two liberal coats of Naval Jelly spray, a rust converter. I prefer this to painting the artifact because the exposed iron turns blackish from the spray, yet areas that still have encrustation or other metal (such as a short copper or brass chain) retain their character without taking on color.

When I was all through, I excitedly showed the anchor to my significant other. For some reason she was less than jubilant, and in spite of her easygoing nature she flatly refused to let me suspend the anchor by an old-fashioned hemp rope from the living-room ceiling.

Admiral style folding stock anchor recovered from Rockaway

Dive Report: The Lizzie D and The Eagle's Nest – July, 2002

I had a great dive on the *Lizzie D.* It's what's left of a rum-running tugboat that sank with all hands aboard about eight miles off of Atlantic Beach in 1922. It was great doing the early-morning Sunday dive; the boat was not crowded and I was back home napping by noon. Can't beat that! I AM allowed to like BOTH the *Wahoo* and the *Eagle's Nest* dive boats, right? Each boat has its own flavor. I am actually a bit nervous that I am going to get yelled at or something when I'm on board the *Eagle's Nest*. It's a bit of a reminder of how I felt growing up around my dad, who was a military disciplinarian. On my only other dive aboard the *Eagle's Nest* last season, I had heard Captain Klein sternly address another diver for leaving the cabin door open. But the *Eagle's Nest* is an excellent dive boat, is run like a tight ship, and is clean and comfortable.

Conversations on the boat this Sunday covered all topics diving-related, including stories of "strokes" and close calls. A stroke is a derogatory term used to refer to divers who are so bad that they are dangerous to others. The crew had noticed my new advanced-nitrox-certification card when I did the paperwork—and they had especially noticed the name of my instructor. Just seeing Randi Eisen's name on the card seemed to qualify me in their eyes. She is well known among northeast wreck divers. So when talk turned to safety, I mentioned that this latest certification I had received in advanced nitrox was the first one that I had really earned and worked for. All the other certifications had been more fun than anything else, and I always felt that the instructor's point was to get people through the material as fast as possible, including the skills. This certification with Randi had been different—she had been unrelenting. I have no idea what happened to the other guy who had taken the course with me. He vanished fairly early on. The course included a lot of material and mathematical formula work, which was tough. When we had taken to the water, I had this attitude (Randi probably sensed it) that—because I dove so much and was good with running a reel—my act was all together. After the dives, she would tightly focus on anything I had not done correctly, making sure that I knew what I had to work on. At Dutch Springs, I had done my "doubles manifold air valve" exercise pretty well. That's the one where you have to go through this routine simulating emergencies and turning the air tank valves off and on underwater. On our first ocean dive aboard the *Wreck Valley* dive boat, I tried to do the same thing at 115 feet, with her watching. When I got back to the point where I had to reopen the center isolation valve that joined my two tanks, I couldn't open it! I tried again. Nope! She watched and I gestured to her to try it. She also was unable to open it. I had tightened it so much that it could not be reopened. I knew I would have to abort the dive. There was no real danger—I had lots of gas in my two now-independent tanks—but I knew this meant that I had not only failed the test but would have to ascend, leaving the *Tarantula* wreck below. Randi scratched a new deco profile for me onto a slate. I saw it and decided to try opening the valve one more time. This time, driven by anger, I found the strength to open the valve. The dive continued, and my other skill tests went well—but the valve maneuvers became my Waterloo. On subsequent dives I never made that mistake of over-tightening the valves again. Since then I have done numerous shore dives with my doubles just to practice this maneuver in shallow water (in case I turn the valves ALL off and get mixed up). On deeper dives, I go through a routine of making sure I can reach all three valves when I get to the bottom, and I double check that they are all open. Anyway, Heidi, a crew member on the *Eagle's Nest*, nodded her head upon hearing me mention how Randi worked me hard, saying something like: "Of course! I taught her!" Randi Eisen is very well-respected in the dive community.

Photo courtesy Gary Gentile

Name Board from Lizzy D.

I took my time getting ready, letting the others get in the water first, and had a good 80-foot dive with a 10- to 15-foot vis. Did a 50-minute bottom time using 40% nitrox. I deco'd two minutes at 40 feet and about eight minutes extra at 20 feet as an investment in my nitrogen paranoia. For only the second time, I was wearing my experimental diaper so I could pee underwater; again it saw no action, luckily.

Some big eels were on the wreck. It was easy to climb into the ship. I dropped slowly into an open space on the deck and descended into one of the forward areas. As my fins just touched bottom inside the wreck, I looked to my right. There, not three inches from my face, was the largest conger eel I had ever seen. Had I noticed him there, I probably would not have entered the wreck so close to him. He smiled closed mouth at me, not having to show his teeth to get his point across.

These fellows, with a bit of a dour personality, always look to me like a metallic blue-purple version of the somewhat more problematic moray eel. I have never actually heard of anyone having even the slightest problem with these critters, but I *was* in a confined space with only one way out. I shone my light at him, and he lazily turned sideways as if to show off his size—at least five or six feet long—then retired farther back into his dark area.

My reel was not needed to navigate on this wreck. I decided I wanted to go out on the sand about 50-100 feet and just go around the wreck. I attached my reel to the starboard side of the sunken tugboat and went out on the sand looking for any goodies that might be lying on the bottom. Actually, I was looking for evidence of debris patches, maybe bottles, away from the wreck. About 50 feet astern of the wreck I found a red diver's mesh bag full of mussels. This bag looked like it had been here a while. Very heavy. Tried to empty it to get the bag for myself. Clouds of silt filled the water, and the mussels weren't coming out easy. Hell with it. Big mussels! Why don't we ever see them this big in restaurants? Took a clip off the bag and left the bag for the blackfish.

I could see there was still one other diver hanging around at the base of the anchor line. I didn't realize it, but it was a crew member waiting for me to finish my dive and come up so we could leave. I was quite happy with my doubles, and I was in no rush.

Towards the end of the dive I decided to go into the *Lizzie D* again, and dropped down into one of the openings in the frame from the deck. Got my legs tangled in heavy monofilament line that I hadn't seen—my shears made short work of the mono. My shears are in a holder on my harness, and there is a Velcro flap that holds them in. My biggest problem was putting them back: I couldn't find the flap. It had Velcroed to some other thing on the holder, and I couldn't find the flap to secure the shears. I spent more time putting them away then I had cutting myself out! I was about to stick them in my red goody bag instead of in their sheath, but I gave a final big yank and the flap opened up. I was able to put them back where they belonged.

Back on the boat, I put my gear away and poked my head up front to say something nice to the Captain.

"Thanks for a nice dive! It was great!" I said.

"Next time, if you are going to make such a long dive, get in the water first!" he answered.

I turned without a word, heading back to where my gear was, to get my sandwich. And you can bet that I made sure I closed the cabin door behind me...

My First Dive at the Glen Cove Jetty – November, 2002

I went with my friend Bob to the Glen Cove Jetty, near Garvies Point. It's on the Long Island Sound in the Glen Cove area. Exit 39 on the Long Island Expressway. You park at the top of a hill, get geared up as much as possible, then use a hand truck to move your tanks a quarter of a mile to the beach entry point.

We went in on the north side of the jetty (it runs east-west in this small cove) and separated once we were in the water. Of course, as soon as Bob vanished beneath the calm waters into decent 10-foot vis, I realized that my BC inflator hose was all tangled up and inaccessible. I thought for a minute that maybe I could do the dive using just my dry suit for buoyancy, but then decided not to do that for safety reasons. I was not familiar with the site, and if I had an emergency and had to stay on the surface, it would not be comfortable doing a long surface swim with an inflated dry suit. So, while out there in about seven or eight feet of water, I decided to take off my air tank and BC, straighten out my inflator hose, and put the gear back on.

I took the BC off, and it sank immediately (which I expected). I then pushed the inflator button and the BC floated back up to me. In minutes the gear was back on, and I did a nice 48-minute dive. I followed the jetty all the way out to the end. It's a very long jetty, the longest I have ever seen. At the very end of it, I tied my reel to an old tire and then continued out due west. Explored a bit. Found that my new main dive light would not turn on for some reason. Oh well—there was enough ambient light anyway. I used my secondary light a bit. Saw lots of contemporary bottles that had been thrown off the end of the jetty by drinking fishermen, as well as some interesting pieces of wood. This site is definitely worth additional visits, and I will be back. It's a lot of work, though, between the hike from the car and the long run out to the end of the jetty. Next time I will bring my scooter, *Apollo*, and I'll be able to spend greater time at the more interesting end of the jetty.

Coming back, I could not tell how far along the jetty I was, so I surfaced to see how much farther I had to go. That jetty is SO long! I was only halfway back. I looked around for Bob—he should have been surfacing too by now—but I couldn't see him or any bubbles, so I continued back, heading due east about 15 yards north of the jetty. I came across what appeared to be a small, submerged boat, complete with the davits it would have used to tie up at its dock. As I surfaced again, closer to shore, I could at last see Bob coming out of the water. He had gone around the entire jetty and was exiting on its south side. We lugged our gear back up the hill and headed to the Garvies Point Museum (which specializes in Long Island Indian culture). I had brought along a bunch of artifacts that I'd found over the past two years during shore dives in bays and inlets around Long Island. I showed my Indian axe heads and some other ancient stone tools to one of the experts there. He agreed that some of the stuff looked good. It was very interesting and gratifying to know that I wasn't just picking up junk.

Bob headed off to the land of Thanksgiving turkey leftovers after extending me a gracious invitation, but instead I headed back home for my scheduled nap.

Trip To Dutch Springs – November, 2002

I went to Dutch Springs this past Sunday. Dutch Springs is an old 100-foot-deep, lake-sized rock quarry filled with water in the beautiful Lehigh Valley area of Pennsylvania. To make it more interesting for divers, they have dropped things into the water— items like a helicopter, a small plane, various trucks, and even a fire engine and school bus. I have been there many times.

For some reason, this time I followed the directions on one of their brochures, getting off at Pennsylvania exit 71 instead of my usual New Jersey exit 3. Boy, did I get lost! All of my familiar landmarks were there, but in reverse order. It really confused me. Finally, I got there and was only 40 minutes late in meeting my friends. Luckily for me, they were not in the water yet. We all went in together and had two great 45-minute dives. I think the water temperature was about 52 degrees, maybe a bit lower. (My wrist computer is at the bottom of my stuff now in my dive storage bin, so I'm not gonna check it.) We all dove nitrox, and Barry tested his new heavy dry-suit underwear. He was happy with it. This was my second dive this winter with my dry gloves. They worked great. Some fellow asked to tag along with us on both dives—he was working on his 50 dives towards Dive Master or something like that. He dove wet and was not visibly shivering, but I think he HAD to be a bit chilled. In between dives, Bob served up some hot soups which he heated on a camping grill. They were quite good, and we sat in our cars in our dry suits with the heat on to warm up. Visibility was excellent, and I'm glad I went. Ah choo! Ah choo!

About 2:00 p.m., Bob and Barry headed back to NY, but I had other plans. You see, I was to pick up my wife at Newark Airport at 9:02 p.m., so I did not want to go home in Queens and then back to Newark. So I went on an adventure. I took Route 22 and got off a bit before Easton, Pennsylvania. I drove down all sorts of roads which only got smaller and smaller. Finally, I found myself in a wooded area outside Steel City, near Bethlehem, Pa. I saw some interesting ruins in the woods—what may have once been an old factory, or maybe an aqueduct or railroad bridge—parked my car, and walked a quarter of a mile to take a couple of pictures of it.

This was not Queens, NY. It apparently was hunting season. I do not know if these people hunt off-gassing New York divers, but when I heard the gunshots, I decided to head back to the car. For some reason, I was listening to an old Hank Williams CD in the car, and everything suddenly came together, creating a memorable moment. "Your Cheatin' Heart," the pickup trucks with American flags in the back, the wooded hills, the ruins, the barking dog, the gunshots. I made sure my doors were locked and continued my wanderings.

Around Easton again, I surfaced back into civilization and found a tasty roadside restaurant. "Best Steak Sandwiches in the World," the sign claimed. Joe's Steaks place. I studied what the locals were eating and decided on a steak with cheese and mushrooms. The natives apparently enjoyed their steaks with some reddish-brown sauce that I assumed was barbeque. Before I could tell the lass not to put that stuff on, my sandwich was smothered in it. I had thought that I would eat while I was driving, but I took one look at this monstrosity, this apparent evidence from a grisly crime scene, and changed my mind. My new plan would be to eat it standing up next to my car, leaning forward at a 45-degree angle so I would not get it all over my shirt. As I was leaving the place with my sandwich, I clearly heard some kid ordering extra catsup on his sandwich. I am not a catsup lover, more the mayonnaise type, and was not sure how this thing would taste. Not even barbeque sauce, but catsup!

So there I was, in Easton, Pennsylvania. I turned up Hank Williams (who was whining a sad song about a wooden cigar-store Indian in love with some other wooden-Indian squaw) and took a bite. Excellent! Hmm, they'd said steak, but it was actually some kind of shredded meat. Very good, though.

Steel City Gun Club

As I finished up, I heard the shooting again. Hmm. Sounded close. I wasn't even in the woods anymore! Time to go. Off I went. Took Route 619 north for many miles, a beautiful, winding, picturesque trip. Eventually I got to Newark, after changing directions many times. Only three more hours to kill! I was happy to see my wife at the airport.

A Dive at the "Bayville Barge" and a Bit of a Fanciful Tale – December, 2002

Now I'm on a roll! Got to the water again for the second time in three days. This time I went with Bob to the famous Bayville Barge, on the north shore of Long Island near Oyster Bay. As we scooted around, exploring the still-remaining portions of the deck and a couple of cannon, I thought about the real story of this understated wreck. For those who don't know the story of the Bayville Barge, here it is...

As many may know, the famous pirate Captain Kidd operated out of Oyster Bay Harbor for quite a few years around the 1750s. Other than the deep-water harbor at the rapidly growing shipbuilding town of Port Jefferson, Oyster Bay was the only North Shore harbor able to handle his fleet of three ships. It was safe from storms, and, because of the bend at the entrance, was easy to slip into without the opening to the harbor being visible from farther away. To any pursuing British frigates from Connecticut, it would look as if Kidd's three ships simply vanished, just moments after having been spotted on the horizon.

In 1756, the scattered inhabitants on the spit of land just west of Oyster Bay got a dramatic show. It was late November, and three straight days of high winds, heavy sleet, and rain had pounded the entirety of Long Island. Any captain that cared about his ship had either secured it well in a protected berth or had gone far out to sea to weather the storm. Here though, the sound of cannon thundered, waking up the sleepy oystering and farming community. Those who followed the sounds wound up standing on a bluff overlooking what is now Ferry Beach near the site of today's Wall's Wharf Restaurant in Bayville. One of Captain Kidd's ships was foundering not 200 yards offshore. The British Man O'War HMS *Falstooth* was firing at her, but the *Falstooth* itself seemed to be trapped between two shoals, or possibly it had sustained rudder damage. It maneuvered in a curious way, first heaving to, then letting the wind quickly fill the sails to turn the ship and firing again. It would be at least an hour before the incoming tide would be enough to lift Kidd's pirate ship off the shoals to allow escape, if it were possible at all.

Spectators could just make out the name on the front of the ship. It was the number two ship in Kidd's fleet, the *Mabel Sarge*. The desperate pirate ship could not be maneuvered, rendering the cannon on the side facing away from the British ship useless. The order was given to knock out the cannon ports with axes and sledgehammers on the landward side of the ship. The 12 heavy cannon were then rolled off the tilted deck into the angry waters of the sound. Most of the sails had been taken down for the storm, and the few remaining were torn and tattered—frightening snapping sounds could be heard even from shore, giving evidence to the ferocity of the winds. And one of the masts seemed to have taken a direct hit from the British cannon. Its two largest spars had been knocked parallel to the mast. A small figure could be seen high up, trying to cut loose what remained of a flapping sail.

The *Mabel Sarge* had been lightened by the discarding of the heavy cannon—but not enough. She continued to remain aground. In spite of this, the rising tide hinted optimistically that escape might soon be possible; the ship could be seen to rock a bit on the larger storm swells.

The *Sarge*'s remaining 12 cannon were of a much lower caliber than the British cannon, but they were enough to harass the Brits. HMS *Falstooth*, because of its rudder problem, could not come around neatly enough to deliver a fatal blow to the pirate ship.

Twenty minutes had passed since the order to get rid of the starboard cannon had been given. The *Mabel Sarge* was now being captained by its first mate. The Captain, a trusted member of Kidd's inner circle, lay below deck, mortally wounded. It looked as if the ship was very close to being raised off the sands and freeing itself. It was then that the first mate gave his the order that sealed the fate of the *Mabel Sarge*.

The folks high on the bluff above the beach watched as the men on the pirate ship slid nine more of their heavy cannon off the deck and into the Long Island Sound, leaving them with just three to defend their ship. With a shudder, the ship visibly lifted and floated free. Not yet controllable and at the mercy of the gale-force winds, the ship drifted closer and closer to the British warship. The *Falstooth* crew had by this point hacked into two of their own cannon ports, enlarging them. This allowed them to use manpower to turn the cannon at a greater angle so the crew could fire with more accuracy.

Now separated by less than a hundred yards, the British ship peppered the pirate ship with grapeshot, forcing all aboard to scramble for their lives and retreat below decks. The keel of the still-drifting pirate ship had been damaged by the grounding, and she started rapidly taking on water. It was now every man for himself, and the crew of the pirate ship jumped into the cold November seas, making for the shore a short distance away. The British kept firing and launched one small boat which was quickly swamped in the rough seas. The Brits decided not to pursue the crew of the pirate ship and instead focused on repairing their rudder and setting some storm sails in order to get to deeper water.

The crew of the *Mabel Sarge* found friends amongst the spectators on the beach. The entire Oyster Bay area was pirate friendly, especially when the pirates were being pursued by the British. These early American colonial folk were already developing a strong anti-British sentiment.

For a couple of years, one of the *Mabel Sarge*'s two masts could still be seen at low tide. An effort was also made to recover her abandoned cannon. Fourteen were recovered, and they went on to have glorious and distinguished records aboard other American ships against the British in the upcoming War for Independence.

The years rolled by, and the story was forgotten. In 1912, an elderly and senile resident of the Bayville area was interviewed by a local newspaper for the occasion of the centennial observation of the town's founding. The man told a story that had been long forgotten. A tale of pirates, British warships, and a dramatic battle at sea. Unfortunately, he got a couple of minor details wrong. One of them was the name of the pirate ship. Since then, instead of remembering the valor of that stormy day with the name *Mabel Sarge*, people today refer to the site by the name which has been recorded for posterity— the Bayville Barge. And that is the REST of the story...

By the way, I made up the entire pirate story above.

The Bayville Barge is a shipwreck about 100 yards offshore in the Long Island Sound, near Bayville and near the town of

Oyster Bay, Long Island. It lies in about 20 feet of water and is fairly broken up. No one really knows what it was or where it came from. Around the 1900s, at the end of the sailing-ship era, old schooner sailing ships sometimes had their masts removed and were towed as barges to carry sand and other materials. Some say this may be one of those ships. On the other hand, if you dive the wreck you will see that its bow is flat and wide like that of a barge. Like I said, nobody really knows. Personally, I like to tell folks it's a pirate ship.

Squeezing In An Early Morning Dive at Rockaway Before Work (Dec 2002)

The shaking was getting too much for me, so I had to go diving. Too long, way too long since my last dive a couple of weekends ago. I resolved to do one of my early-morning mid-week dives. I love it. Get up real early, go dive. Get back early enough to jump in the shower and go to work. I am usually afraid to tell my clients that I've gone diving on a given morning, because I don't want them to think I'm nuts—then they'll go get another computer consultant. Actually, I *have* always thought we computer types were a bit weird anyway...

I woke up at five a.m., loaded my car, and was on my way by 5:45, stopping at a diner on Rockaway Blvd. for my traditional egg, ham, and cheese on a roll. It was still pitch dark when I arrived at the empty Beach 9th Street site. Where *was* everybody? A skinny dog chased the last meat off an old bone in an empty lot, and the occasional car on its way to work passed by, a few blocks away. The vis looked decent in the dark, and I assembled my gear.

Today's plan was to reactivate my Weezle Extreme Plus thermal undergarment. I had already been wearing my dry gloves for the past couple of dives, but I planned to be in polar bear mode from now through the rest of the winter. I tend to delay going to the Weezle, because there are buoyancy issues. That underwear is very warm, but it sure does hold a lot of air.

And the Weezle gives up its air very slowly, creating ascent concerns when worn. I need to bleed the air slowly out of my dry suit to avoid popping to the surface too quickly. I thought I had added an extra three pounds of lead weight to my belt last year to combat this tendency, as well as four additional pounds in a tank pocket. Hmm. Who remembers! I decided on a four pound weight and another two pounds in the other tank pocket, and figured that was close enough.

I made sure *Apollo* was on the fastest setting. The scooter would be an option in an emergency if I found myself caught in the current, but I wasn't really planning on using it too much for cruising around on this dive.

No emergencies on this dive. I saw a small stingray. Went out due south from the end of Beach 9th Street until I was down to half of my air and still examining the abandoned summer homes of mussels, starfish, and spider crabs along the sandy bottom. It wasn't too cold. I turned the dive and headed back at a slow pace. I usually keep my dry suit exhaust valve shut at depth so that I don't lose valuable warmth. But because of the Weezle's venting problems, this time I opened the valve so that it could start exhausting earlier as I gradually ascended, following the slope up from 42 feet. On my way back, when I was closer to the north side of the channel, I used the scooter in short bursts and did some touring about.

I was wary of the Weezle's effect on my buoyancy and went shallower from 35 feet with the scooter off, moving very slowly. At about 25 feet I got that bad buoyancy feeling. You may know it. Where previously your breath was enough to control your depth in the water column, all of a sudden you feel like you must swim down to keep from going up. I hate that feeling! Oh well, I sort of expected it. I went back down to about 32 feet and was okay. Found a nice, heavy piece of brickwork and picked it up. Went back up the slope. At about 20 feet, I turned over so that my exhaust valve would vent.

And it did. Tentatively letting go of the bricks, I was okay for my three-minute safety stop, and then I surfaced.

The sun had risen, and I still had some air. I had hardly used the scooter. I noticed a fisherman at the end of Beach 8th Street, so I decided to show off a bit. I held the scooter's propeller a bit out of the water and powered up. Having gotten the man's attention, I started scooting at high speed on the surface and dipping below maybe two to three feet. Lots of fun! Felt like I was flying! The vis was good enough that I could see the tops of the underwater jetties as I flew above them. After a while, I realized that the rest of the world was waking up, and soon I would be back in reality. I headed for the beach, having had a nice 45-minute dive.

As I got out of my dry suit and into my car, at about 8:55, my cell phone rang. I answered it the way I always do—with the name of my business. It was a customer with a computer problem. I talked her through re-mapping a database drive as I headed back. It looked like it would end up being just another day at the office...

A Somewhat Less Productive Dive at the Ponquogue Bridge – December, 2002

It was a brilliant December morning, and as I drove along Dune Road from Quogue to Hampton Bays, I looked at the ice forming on parts of Shinnecock Bay and remembered seeing seals last year in the area while out on a Sunday drive. But today was to be no Sunday drive. Actually it was Saturday, and I had a 10:15 a.m. date with destiny and the slack tide at Ponquogue Bridge.

Seals have teeth right? In fact, are their mouths not similar to that of man's best friend? Perhaps they can be thought of as swimming dogs. Little cute coral loving canines that look at you with their big brown eyes – as they open their massive dog like jaws, engulfing an entire arm of an unsuspecting diver? Like a Mastiff or Pit Bull, their jaws could lock requiring the helpless diver to have to resort to using his Sea Shears or knife to behead the cross between a dog and Flipper, so he could escape before his limited air runs out!

In other words, I was a little nervous about seals on this dive.

I met Bob as scheduled, and we walked out on the old bridge to check conditions. Visibility appeared to be about 18 inches. We glumly looked at each other and made the intelligent decision not to dive. Ten minutes later, we were suiting up. I had brought my scooter, always a good idea on these low-vis adventures. What I didn't tell Bob was that *Apollo* would be my first line of defense against a rabid *Phoca vitulina*, science's name for the harbor seal. No need to tell Bob about my seal fears. I'd yell "ORCA!" or "POLAR BEAR! RUN!" to trick the seal and then let my trusty scooter carry me as far away from those menacing whiskers as possible.

I had placed my scooter on the bulkhead and walked out from shore. Bob prepared to make a graceful entry directly from the bulkhead into the swirling, angry, pre-slack waters of Shinnecock Bay. Was he even aware of the seal threat? His lowered head and quiet posture made me wonder if he was making his peace or just checking vis. I wasn't about to ask. But I remembered my loved ones at home, and I imagined myself—stuffed—in some seal's living room, a trophy.

I hooked up with Bob, he grabbed onto my harness, and we were off! Ah! A scooter makes it so easy. Effortlessly, we rode into the bulkhead. I shut the power so we didn't get hurt. "Yeah, I meant to do that," I said. "Part of my pre-flight navigation check." I pointed *Apollo* northeast to avoid hitting anything, and seconds later we were out past the bulkhead. We stopped again so that Bob could untangle some fishing line from me. We continued a bit farther and then, following our dive plan, we slipped separately beneath the waves.

The vis was a bit better in places, perhaps between two and three feet. I did not use the scooter here underwater; I just looked around. The main life was blue claw crabs. Many of them. Quite the angry little fellows. I can see where the term "crabby" comes from. Though I didn't see any seals, I thought about them. Perhaps a Nerf ball or some nice, smelly bunker or mackerel would offer a diver some protection against an unprovoked attack. Sighting a seal, a potential victim might gently lob the Nerf ball underwater and take his regulator out of his mouth long enough to say "fetch!"

The water temperature on this dive was 43 degrees. Very close to the previous week's temperature. Last week I wasn't really cold at all, and I did a 50-minute dive. Today, at 20 minutes in, I was beginning to feel it, and by 30 minutes I had to end the dive. One difference was that normally on these cold winter dives I breathe nitrox. On this dive I'd expected to only go to about 25 feet deep, and I also knew I'd need a lot of air if the scooter died and the current kicked up. Because of this I opted to take a fuller air tank rather than a less full nitrox tank. I recently dove at Candlewood Lake on air and I had felt colder than I did on a subsequent dive at the same location on nitrox. Perhaps I need to do some more research on nitrox vs. air for cold water. It probably shouldn't really matter, except with respect to nitrogen uptake. Another factor contributing to coldness may be that if visibility is low, a diver moves more slowly and more cautiously.

I wondered how seals handled the cold with just their fur coats. I bet they were a lot more comfortable than a diver was at these temperatures.

Anyway, I had gone due east for a while and knew that I was nowhere near the bridge anymore. The current kicked up, fast and furious. I was upside down and leaning back, venting my dry suit, and the current was carrying me. I couldn't see a thing, and reached out to touch the bottom to reassure myself that

I wasn't ascending as well. I fully vented the air out of my dry suit, got a bit negative, and pointed my scooter southwest, knowing that I wouldn't hit anything in that direction. Operating my scooter in little bursts, I made my way back rapidly.

By the way, at Ponquogue Bridge the current can get quite strong, but there is a depression in the seafloor slightly to the north and east of the end of the old bridge, almost out to the channel. The outgoing tide goes right over this large area, allowing a diver to dive well past the time the current switches. There are lots of fish in this area—it seems they like the calm too. I have had a few 75-minute dives at Ponquogue using this depressed area some call the "Porgy Patch." Coming back without a scooter is easy. The trick is to have a good amount of air left. When exiting due south—where the bottom slopes from about 32 feet up to about 20—all of a sudden you can feel the current. Keep swimming hard due south and you will encounter a ridge. When you get there, stop fighting. Give up. Let the current carry you. It will carry you east right along the ridge, letting go of you at the end of the ridge. From there, you are in about 12 feet of water. Head southwest and you'll find yourself east of the area protected by the bulkhead. Here there's no more current issue for you. I have been doing this for a few years at Ponquogue, and the pattern has been stable. But who knows—in coming seasons, the ridge may vanish or something else may change, so be careful! And note that if you come back under the old bridge, the upwards slope creates a sort of bottleneck, and the current is therefore at its strongest towards the foot of the old bridge. Don't let the sudden darkness of the seaweed storm—all the debris borne by the fast current—freak you out. This is a dive that does not always have to end early, but making sure that you know how much gas you have left and keeping a reserve is very important.

The dive over, I said to Bob, "Now tell me again. Why do we do this again?" It was freezing out there, and I was still cold back at the car. But most importantly, we had escaped the wrath of the seals. We got out of our gear and headed to Tully's Seafood on the Hampton Bays side of the bridge for some delicious chowder and shrimp with cocktail sauce. It was a fun dive. I'm glad I did it. But, if you hear of anyone seeing any seals nearby – please let me know!

Rockaway Dive: Air Temp 11 Degrees, Water Temp 34 Degrees – February, 2003

Last week, Bob and I went to Rockaway but called the dive off because of poor visibility. It is sort of weird: snow on the ground—enough snow to leave three-inch deep tracks in—and you are considering diving. Bob had checked it out yesterday and reported good-to-excellent vis at Beach 9th Street, so that evening we made a final decision to meet the next morning at 6:00 a.m., at the dive site.

I fueled up with a small cup of coffee, muttered some semi-nurturing obscenity at my useless, sleeping cat, and left. I have to be very quiet so I don't wake up my wife. We do not want any semi-nurturing obscenities yelled at me! Tip toe out... oops, forgot my watch. Gotta crawl back into the bedroom like a commando, on my belly, then make a grab for the watch on the dresser and crawl back out just like I came in. One of these early mornings, floodlights are going to snap on, and I'll be caught like a resident of Sing Sing State Prison trying to make for the wall. Anyway...

As I lugged my gear on the cart downstairs to load into the car, my doorman said, "You're not diving *today!*"

"How many times do I have to explain to you, I don't even get wet!" I impatiently explained the principals of "Dry Suit 101" to him. Oh, he'll never get it! I even opened up my knapsack to let him feel my heavy Weezel brand thermal undergarment. But he still gave me that damn look. The one that says "you are friggin' NUTS" without actually saying it to me. Well, maybe I was nuts, in a way. With an air temperature of 11 degrees and steady winds, it would feel like negative *something*, especially on the unsheltered end of Beach 9th Street Rockaway.

It was 5:15 a.m., and off I went: Queens Boulevard to the Van Wyck Expressway to Rockaway Boulevard, stopping at the Sherwood Diner to buy a moldy old corn muffin to hold me till after the dive.

I got there at about 5:50 a.m. Boy, was it cold! Walked over to the jetty to have a look. Wow! That's why I love this cold weather diving. I could plainly see that the vis was excellent! I could see down into the water and make out the details of the jetty rocks. (With a light of course; it was still dark out.)

Bob showed up, and I excitedly walked out with him to show him the vis. We sat in the car until 6:30 a.m. The plan was to go in about 15 minutes past high tide, because we had found that here, the current still rips for a while after high tide. High tide was at 7:01 a.m., so we were going to go in at about 7:15 or so. We set up our gear. In weather like this, you usually try to do as much as possible with your gloves on, but for certain things they have to come off. This morning my hands were hurting from the cold within a minute. Our gear set up, we got back into the car to warm up. Another few minutes and we were putting on our dry suits.

I tried to work fast in the cold. My DUI-brand dry suit has suspenders, and of course I jammed my leg in them the wrong way, and the suspender wrapped itself around my right thigh. I thought of the cold and decided that I had to fix it. I didn't want the blood flow constricted anywhere in such cold conditions. It was a big hassle trying to get my leg out and then back in, as was pulling the bootie portion of the suit over the very thick insulation on my foot. In the freezing cold, this simple task was becoming a nightmare, and I was stressing out a bit. Finally the bootie pulled over my heel, and I was in the dry suit.

We entered the water at 7:21 a.m. On really cold days, I call this the "Death March to the Sea Phase." We were both breathing nitrox. Bob was carrying a two-and-a-half-foot-long steel bar sharpened at one end, and I had my six-pound underwater steel mallet. It has a large chisel that screws into the handle of the mallet, and a ring lets you attach it to your gear easily.

Equipped thusly, we entered the 30-degree water, which actually felt warm compared to the air temps we had been in. The vis was 30 feet at least! An old fellow that I have seen fishing at Rockaway from time to time drove up as we were leaving the car to tell me that yesterday two seals had been sighted near the Atlantic Beach Bridge. I was excited— perhaps we'd see a seal? Hopefully before he'd see us! We went south to the base of the jetty and started looking for bottom conditions suitable for our experiment. It was simple: we just wanted to pound the steel bar into the channel bottom to see if it would remain there as a useful reference point for later dives. There must have been a rock at the first spot we chose—the bar wouldn't go in—so we moved a bit farther away and swung away with the mallet, driving the steel into the floor. That done, I clipped the mallet back to my harness and we explored. We did not see the stingray that we had seen on our past two January dives. Lots of crabs and incredible vis this time, though.

The current had been slack when we entered, so we probably actually went in a few minutes too late. After about 20 minutes, we felt it kicking up again as Rockaway Channel started its twice-a-day emptying to the sea with the outgoing tide. So we made our way to the heavy line that runs down to the 40-foot depression that the currents have dug out. We then continued our dive, always staying within maybe 30 feet or so of the line so that we could get to it when the current got stronger.

In the past, we have actually begun and ended dives here in full current, using that line to descend from the entry area to the deepest part of the channel and then to ascend once again.

It's a bit like mountain climbing. I remember another dive one January where I had misread the tide charts, but because of great vis we decided to go in anyway. Thank goodness for that line; it allowed us to safely make a dive that day. Those familiar with this site already know that there is an area at Rockaway Beach 9th near the underwater training cages that is protected from the current and that this area can be explored when the current is strong. But if you leave that protected area and you do not have the heavy line to hang onto—well, you may be in some trouble.

The current did kick up, and we made our way to the line. I stopped to look at rocks, and Bob stopped to look at what I was doing every two seconds or so. We went up along the line, and at about 22 feet I looked up at the surface and could see every ripple. I still was not cold at all; I was quite comfy now, about 35 minutes into the dive. We hung around at a big yellow sponge we saw at about 18 feet to do a three-minute safety stop. In this great vis, the jetty's details were quite interesting to see.

Bob led us back via compass to our entry point. We did not want to do any surface swim time because of the chance that our breathing regulators could freeze from wind exposure. As I took my fins off, one of the straps broke on my Force Fins. I caught a tiny little black plastic cylinder that tried to escape from my fin strap assembly.

Standing up in the shallow water to start the walk to the car, I found that all of my exposed parts froze instantly. Gear and exposed skin. I was still not really uncomfortable. I got the tank off and opened my car, pulled out the little thing I stand on to take my dry suit off, and found that my DUI rock boot laces were frozen into a block of ice. I had taken off my two hoods. Mistake. Now my hair was frozen solid in a parody of some Elvis hairstyle. I fiddled with the laces and could not defeat the ice that now gripped the thingy that slides up and down them. I turned on my car and blasted the heat, directing it to the floor, and stood outside the car trying to defrost one foot at a time. I did not want to get into the car wearing my frozen dry suit and melt all over my car interior. So I stood there in the brisk wind, wishing I was elsewhere. After a minute, I tried the boot again. Still frozen like a rock. My dry suit was stiff with ice. I was really not that cold, but my head was now insulated by a layer of ice rather than a hood, and I knew that there was approaching urgency in my situation. I went over to Bob, who was sitting as warm as toast in his large, three-room truck. He rolled down the window. "Yes?"

"I'm frozen into my boots and can't take off my dry suit," I complained. He directed me to his bucket of hot water, which melted the ice off my laces in seconds. A minute later, I was out of my suit. I tossed it to the ground. It was so frozen and stiff with ice that instead of crumpling into a heap as it usually did, it looked like it had a dwarf in it. It still stood about three feet high—with me out of it.

I could not disassemble any gear. It was all locked together with ice. No clips could be worked at all. So I left the whole thing in the back of my Subaru wagon to be dealt with later.

We headed off to the Sherwood Diner for a hot cup of coffee and some eggs. I went to breakfast still wearing my dive underwear. It sort of looks like a snowmobile outfit. Once I ordered breakfast, I made sure the waitress knew that we had just been SCUBA diving at Rockaway. To get that special treatment. That special treatment they give all the nutcases that wander into that diner for breakfast after swimming in sub-freezing temperatures.

Three Fun Dives in One Winter Weekend at Rockaway – March, 2003

My wife went out of town for a few days, and I had nothing to do. So I went diving. Dove Friday, Saturday, and Sunday at Beach 9th and had a great time. On Friday, I went with a friend that had been out of the water since October. Normally a capable winter diver, he started having panic attacks while on land last fall. He told me that he had had one of these intense feelings of panic while diving with me in a lake last year. I remembered the dive. He had calmly signaled to me that he wanted to turn and end the dive in a dark, murky lake when we hit 77 feet deep, and so we exited together in an orderly, safe fashion. I was surprised when he told me he'd had a panic attack and that that was why he'd turned the dive. He had seemed very calm and in control during the entire dive. Perhaps things would have gone differently if I had given him a hard time underwater for prematurely turning the dive. One rule from cave diving—and a good one—is that anyone can end any dive for any reason – no questions asked.

Most of my friend's panic attacks typically occurred out of the water—at home and at work—but he'd since gone on medication and had called DAN, the Divers Alert Network, who had suggested that he check with a doctor before diving.

Some months had passed since these interventions. Then, one day last week, I received a call from him. He was feeling much better, he said. He had not taken the meds for over a month, and was wondering if I would babysit him on an easy dive. Well, just when I was getting a bit ho-hum about diving at Rockaway! Of course I would! That would liven it up a bit!

Sure, I'd dive with him. But there would have to be some ground rules. For example, normally while diving with an experienced diver in low vis, the two of us might agree in advance to NOT bother looking for each other if we became separated and to just continue instead as solo divers. Today, though, if we got separated, we would immediately head north to get away from the boat channel. When the depth decreased to about 15 feet, we would surface to look for each other. The other rule was that if he wanted to turn or cancel the dive, he could of course do so without having to try to explain underwater. Finally—and especially because of the low vis—we would stay in relatively shallow water and WOULD NOT SURFACE IN THE BOAT CHANNEL.

I was ready first and went in the water. My friend followed a minute or so later. Having put on his fins, he'd realized that he had left his mask locked in his car. Luckily for him, a fellow diver who was bubble watching was able to run back to the car and get the mask for him. Once we were together, we descended and had a fine 15-minute dive around some cages which enclose five-foot-high metal pipe cubes. These are used in training, in order to give divers something to hold on to. We never went deeper than 20 feet.

Then it happened. We got separated. I immediately went north and surfaced near the bulkhead at the foot of Beach 8th Street. I watched as my friend's bubbles headed south, out towards the boat channel. I guess I was muttering to myself. Finally the bubbles turned north and began coming back, and then he surfaced. He was out in the channel. No boats, but he was in the wrong spot. I yelled at him, "What are you DOING? Get over here!"

He explained that he had looked for me for a couple of minutes (that was when his bubbles headed south), failed to realize that he was so far out, and then came back and began heading up a slope. He hit 18 feet, found some rocks, and then surfaced along the rocks (which were about six feet beneath the surface). I knew exactly the spot he was talking about. From the bulkhead on the east side of the Almost Paradise restaurant beach property, you can swim straight out and you encounter a ridge. If you are heading south, which is *away* from the beach, it actually gets shallower for a while, even though you'd expect it to get deeper. If you are going north, it looks like you have hit the beginning of the slope for the beach. I understood his mix-up, but still, 18 feet deep was not the 15 feet deep where we had agreed it was safe to surface. Anyway, I wanted to continue the dive so together, we again descended.

We stayed near the cages and had an uneventful 15 minutes of diving. We ended the dive when my friend indicated that he was cold. His hands and wet gloves had finally succumbed to the 34-degree water. He told me later that he'd felt great getting back in the water again, and I felt like I had helped out a friend. By the way, this guy is one of the best and safest divers I know. He had real courage gently pushing himself until he was comfortable again in the water.

That was Friday. Max depth 20 feet, total bottom time 30 minutes, and a water temperature of 34 degrees.

Saturday, it was back to Beach 9th Street for the 11:10 high tide with my other diving pal, Bob. We have experience at this location with current, so we planned to enter at the western jetty, swim due south, and look for a steel rod we had hammered into the bottom a couple of dives ago. Then we'd fin due east, possibly running a line as far as the east jetty near the foot of Beach 8th Street. We'd continue east and then ride the tide back. We each had full air tanks and a 30- or 40-cubic-foot safety bottle, and I had my scooter— fully charged as a backup—to help us to get back if needed.

We entered the water, and Bob ran a line as we headed east. We could not find the steel rod. The vis was only slightly better than Friday's one- or two-foot vis. In spite of the poor vis we decided to go back and remove the reel guide line. Bob put his reel away, and we just followed cables on the sandy channel bottom in an eastward direction. We kept going east, and later estimated that we'd gone as far as Beach 7th Street. Then, all of a sudden, the current started up.

Okay, no problem. This WAS in the dive plan. The current propelled us at a decent clip back west, and we rode it freely.

We did not strike any objects. At one point I was going to use the scooter as well, but immediately thought better of it due to the limited visibility. Somehow Bob knew we were about lined up with the entry point, and he indicated that we could now go north and there find the slope. In the current, we both had issues venting our dry suits at about 20 or 15 feet, and we had some fun there for a while until we found some cinderblocks, which helped keep us from doing the Pillsbury-Doughboy-style ascent which is so typical when venting the air from our dry suits. As usual, it was lots of fun. We did our safety stop while hanging onto these cinder blocks.

Out of the water now, we continued our discussion about the location of the rope at the end of the Beach 8th Street bulkhead. It leads down into the deepest 40-plus-foot area— but where was that area in reference to the beach? I thought that it was pretty much due south of the training cages and Almost Paradise, and I said so. Bob asserted that it was actually farther east out in the channel. Hmm. One of these days we will solve THAT question, once and for all.

That was Saturday. Max Depth 44 feet, total bottom time 40 minutes, Water temperature of 34 degrees.

Sunday, I met Bob at the diner. He wasn't up for diving, so it looked like I'd be going solo. My surface support team included another friend, our "warm water consultant" who had just returned from Florida. And while Bob wasn't up for diving, he wasn't against standing on the beach and doing some science.

Today I had some additional equipment and a plan. I'd brought a six-foot Halcyon orange inflatable sausage, a waterproof camera, a hundred-foot-long underwater measuring tape, a reel, and an extra safety air bottle. I would follow the cable down from the bulkhead to the deepest portion of the channel, to the very spot that Bob and I couldn't find on our last dive. I would find a suitable anchor location and then shoot up the bright orange inflatable device. Bob would photograph it from three pre-selected locations, noting compass headings and other information. Before going in, I measured out about 38 feet on the reel and put a knot in the line at that spot. This would be so that I could tell when to lock the reel. I would know that when I felt the knot, I could let out a few more feet; the bag would then definitely be visible on the surface. Because we were not sure exactly where it would come up, I planned to NOT ascend on this line to recover the orange sausage. I actually would instead follow the cable back along the slope I had descended, all the time holding the reel in such a manner that if a boat did hit it, it would be torn from my hand easily without snagging any of my gear. I would not be doing any tugboat or oil-barge water skiing today.

I went in the water near the bulkhead at the foot of Beach 8th Street, on the eastern side of the Almost Paradise beach. "Wow, the vis is lousy," I thought. I followed a cable. Oops! Wrong one. This was the cable which led to the cages. After wasting some time there, I went back to the bulkhead and found the correct one. It got very dark very fast, and soon it was pretty much pitch dark. Near the surface, general vis was about two feet or so, but now I could only see for two feet within the narrow cone of illumination from my handheld light. The cable I was following was partially buried here and there, so vis dropped even more when I pulled it up and shook it to get it on top of the silty, sandy slope. In one spot, the cable drops between two rocks which are impossible to fit yourself between, so you have to let go of the cable and find it again in the sand on the other side of the rocks. No problem. I descended quite slowly. I always get very spooked in these dark, low-vis conditions, and my adrenaline pumps. Some folks like roller coasters or skydiving, and water conditions like these are one reason I enjoy diving. It is sometimes scary!

Finally, down at 44 feet deep and a bit chilled because I was moving so slow, I saw the familiar spaghetti-like curls of the other cables that are down there. For a moment I tried to take in the limited layout I could see by my light, in order to minimize my chances of following the wrong cable out at the end of the dive. The water was pitch black and extremely silty, so I decided not to attach my reel to the seafloor cable itself, in case the inflatable sausage, when I released it, pulled the cable out of the sand and up to the surface, leaving me without a clear trail home to the beach. I looked for something else to tie the reel to. I saw an old tire, but it was sunk too deeply into the sand and silt, and I couldn't budge it enough to find a tie-off point. An old street-sign post sticking out of the muck over there might work, I decided. I tested it. Seemed very solid. I clipped the inflatable sausage to the end of the reel, lay the reel down on the sign post, put a dab of air in my dry suit, and disconnected my dry suit hose—I'd need that to inflate the orange sausage. I thought for a minute about using another hose—the one that inflates my buoyancy compensator—because detaching and reattaching to the dry suit introduces a bit of 34-degree water into the suit. But I went with the dry suit inflator because I can always reach its hose easily during this process, whenever I perform it. It is always possible that disconnecting the much shorter BC inflator hose it could leave it dangling behind me and hard to find if I should happen to let go of it. I double checked that none of my gear could possibly get caught in the reel or line and then proceeded to inject air into the sausage, holding it until it finally tore itself from my hands and ripped for the surface.

It stopped. The reel was stuck. I loosened the big black knob a smidgen more and then the sausage was gone. When the reel stopped un-reeling, I felt for the knot on the line and found it a couple of feet above me. I locked the reel and waited for the surface support team to complete their tasks of documentation.

Because of the low vis, I decided to hang out right there. I'd give Bob and his assistant 10 minutes to triangulate the bright, orange sausage from shore. A bit bored and cold because I was not moving around, I decided to figure out the angle from vertical that the line is making on its trip to the surface (22.5 degrees). Also, I took a compass heading on the direction the line was taking up to the surface (330 degrees). After 10 minutes—28 minutes into the dive now—I gave three big tugs on the line to alert the surface team that I was coming up, and I double checked that the reel was tightly locked. I carried the reel on my left side so that the sausage on the surface would be drifting away from my equipment and followed the heavy cable in the sand back up the slope. About every 10 feet, I reeled in some slack from the line and then continued up. At about 12 feet, I had the usual dry-suit venting issues, and then I surfaced near the bulkhead. Went over to the underwater training cages, shot the sausage up again to mark the cage locations, and then finally exited the water after a total of 43 cold minutes.

We'll see how the pictures turn out, but Bob and his assistant both agreed that the sausage was about 100 feet or so directly south of the end of Beach 8th Street, closer to where Bob had said it would be and much farther out into the channel than I had thought. I had also thought it would be in the area between Beach 9th and Beach 8th Streets. Oh well. Live and learn!

It's Getting Warmer, Winters End, Water a Balmy 39 Degrees – March, 2003

I had a great 38-minute dive this morning. I stayed around the west jetty at Beach 9th Street, and visibility was about 10 feet. I still haven't been able to find that steel rod that Bob and I hammered into the sand. We planted it near a big rock—which I also haven't been able to find. So I decided that on this dive I'd run a semi-permanent line from the base of the jetty about 50 feet due south to an object on the channel bottom and leave it there to use next Saturday as a landmark as I ride the outgoing tide, to help me find the Beach 9th exit point.

After I firmly attached this line, I tied off a reel to the line and ventured first 50 feet east and then 50 feet west looking for the steel rod. Then I returned to the line, advanced north about 20 feet, and again went east and west, searching. Oh well, I had lots of fun anyway. Kept my mind off the impending war with Iraq…

Last week, I collected some clay from the channel and stored it in a Chinese soup container. That clay is now at a local pottery shop being test-fired in a kiln. If it is suitable, they will make me a little clay fish that I can display in my living room. Probably the only clay sculpture in the world made from real 30-foot-deep East Rockaway Inlet clay.

It's getting very warm out there at Rockaway. I recorded a water temperature of 39 degrees this morning—up five degrees from the consistently cold 34-degree temperature that has held for the past couple of months.

Flounder made from Rockaway Clay

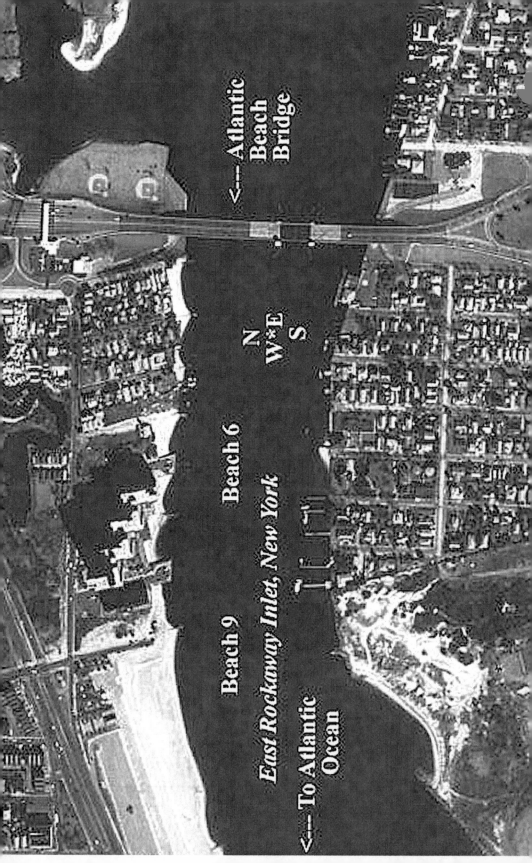

Atlantic Beach Bridge

N
W*E
S

Beach 6

Beach 9

East Rockaway Inlet, New York

To Atlantic Ocean

CHAPTER TWO

Fighting back against Seasickness, Diving Prose, Last Dives at Setauket's Strongs Neck Bridge and Rockaway's Almost Paradise.

A Trip to the Panther and Shinnecock – May 31, 2003

The weather has not been too great for offshore boat diving lately. The rain and wind seem to conspire, forcing me to wait for the next weekend. They taunt me during the week by hiding for a brief time. Then nature unleashes her full fury for the weekend, pounding the sea and sand with rain and bringing gloomy skies and hopeless weather forecasts.

This was predicted to be another weekend of just that sort. Nature's only teasing window of good weather would possibly extend from about 6:00 a.m. to 1:00 p.m. Saturday. The rest of the weekend would be all shot to hell. Bob and I decided to take our chances and play the weather. We booked onto the *Jean Marie*, a well-run dive boat out of Jackson's Marina in Shinnecock Bay, out east on Long Island.

I woke up, took my Bonine to ward off seasickness, and made the five-minute drive to the dock. This trip would take us to a late 19th century ocean going tug—the *Panther* (off Southampton Beach), and then to the *Shinnecock*, a dragger-type fishing trawler a mile out of Shinnecock Inlet. Both lie in about 60 feet of water. I was looking forward to the long bottom times and would use the dives to test my new Nitek 3 dive computer.

Bob and I had a few words about doing such shallow-water wrecks, but he did need to play with his brand new dry suit before doing his planned 170-foot *Balaena* dive next week, so he decided to come along too.

Originally, I was going to try to take off work Friday morning, dive the Ponquogue Bridge, and then get my tanks filled out east. Of course, my customers didn't know this and chose to have computer emergencies that nixed that idea. So I ended up going through my closet and finding one tank that had a 67% nitrox mix in it, as well as another empty tank. I headed to Stingray Divers dive shop in Brooklyn and dropped them off for a fill while I went off to handle my customers' computer problems. I would dive with single 104-cubic-foot tanks and would fill my 40-cubic-foot oxygen bottle with 45% O_2 to use as a safety/supplemental supply. So I had one 104 tank of 45% O_2, another with 33%, and the additional smaller bottle with 45%. I planned for 45-minute bottom times on each wreck.

While in the closet, I'd heard something rustling in the corner, took a look, and found my scooter, *Apollo*, reminding me that while heavily used, it had never come on a boat/wreck dive—could it please come on this trip? Please? Okay. I had been using *Apollo* for about two years now and felt very comfortable using it for traveling underwater, on the surface, towing other divers—even using it to recover buried artifacts in the sand. But it had never been lowered into the water from a boat, and I had never used it in an area I wasn't already very familiar with.

I looked at the scooter. Some changes would have to be made. I had attached a piece of reel line to it so that I could clip it off to me when not using it underwater. The length of the line, of course, had been carefully selected so that it was not long enough for the clip to get caught in the propeller. I had never had to lift the heavy 40-plus pound device by this line—it had only been used underwater to clip the scooter off to me. I envisioned having the scooter lowered to me from the dive boat and did not like the picture forming in my mind. First the line would break from the weight, then the scooter would hit me in the head and knock me out, and finally sharks would be attracted to my blood. I'd be pulled underwater, dinner for some starving sea critter. Nope! Did not want that! So I put a heavier line on *Apollo*. Now I was ready to go!

Once I was out of the inlet, we found the seas to be fairly calm under overcast skies with some three- or four-foot swells. We had a 30-minute ride east to the *Panther*, following the southern Long Island beaches, about two miles offshore. Usually I take my Bonine as soon as I get up, which—along with the ride to the boat from Queens—means it is in my system for about two hours before we get underway. Today— because I stayed out east—the boat was only five minutes away. This meant that the Bonine did not have time to firmly establish itself in order to quell my usual nausea. So I had a slightly queasy time initially, but my nausea soon abated, and before I knew it I was eating my ever-present Pop Tarts. I was fine. You know, I think that Pop Tarts are the perfect dive-boat food. They are sealed in little waterproof foil packets, the jam contains huge, unhealthy amounts of sugar, and they do not really require a toaster. My favorite is the cherry with frosting. They should make some with meat in them. Maybe call them "Pop Empanadas?" If these things had been around a century ago, I am sure Admiral Peary would have taken them along on his Arctic expedition. Oh—back to diving...

We tied off at our first wreck—the *Panther*. Not a whole lot was known about her. An ocean-going tug with only the engine—rising almost 20 feet off the bottom—still providing some relief. I had been here a couple of years ago with my son and we saw some of the biggest eels we had ever seen, their heads just sticking out from under the partly buried skeleton of the ship. Today, there were a number of divers with fancy underwater cameras. I looked at my scooter, which would be making the dive with me. "Behave yourself *Apollo*! Don't muck up the water too much for these guys!" The mate who had tied the *Jean Marie* to the wreck knew that I wanted to scooter and gave me a thumbs up to let me know that visibility was adequate for scootering.

I was one of the first in the water. The mate handed *Apollo* to me, and I clipped the scooter to the down line, placing my hand under the scooter clip so that as I descended the scooter would gently follow me, sliding down the line to the wreck. That worked out great. The vis was fine, maybe 25 feet or so. I spent a while circumnavigating the lady in the sand, following the drive shaft out all the way, coming back, going past the towering engine, and continuing as far as the bow area and a bit beyond, always keeping some of the wreckage in sight. Lots of fun. It is really like flying!

Hey what was that? Off on the port side, near the wreck in the sand, a flash of yellow caught my attention. I scootered over and hovered above the object like a police helicopter in some movie. I gently lowered myself down. It was a white HID light, attached by clips to a yellow diver's goodie bag. The light was encrusted—must have been here a while—but it actually turned on! I pulled on the buried goodie bag but couldn't budge it, so I took the light and its clips and put them in my red canvas work bag.

"Come on, *Apollo*! Do your thing!" I turned my scooter around so that the prop faced the buried goodie bag, then thought for a moment that if the four or five photographer-divers caught me blowing all this sand, I might meet with an unfortunate "accident" underwater. Oh, what the hell; I was off the wreck anyway! I set *Apollo* to the medium speed and kicked furiously to prevent myself from being shot backwards like a squid. I don't recommend doing this without practice in a shallower, safer area, because you really have to be ready for this, and you should do it in short bursts so that you can offset the force of the scooter. On bigger projects like anchors, I have a line in my pocket that I attach to the object and to the scooter so that the scooter remains in place without my kicking.

I found myself immediately in a fog of sand. To anyone who might have been watching me, I would have appeared to suddenly and totally vanish, replaced by formless, swirling eddies—clouds of tan and green. As the material settled, I saw that I held in my hand a rather large, high-end, spring-loaded goodie bag that could snap shut easily. Probably a lobster hunter's bag. I pulled on the bag, but it was so full of sand that I could barely lift it. No use to me: I don't bug hunt, and the bag was about twice the size of the little red canvas tool bag that had served me well for years. I decided to leave it this time. I had the HID light anyway, a nice find. I took off again on my scooter. Back on the wreck…

Oh there was Bob. What was he doing? It looked like he found a grapnel, complete with chain. He owns a boat, so that was a nice find for him. Myself, I would have just left it, perhaps not even have noticed it. I stood by, my scooter clipped off to me now, out of his way but ready to lend assistance if he requested. Looked like he had it all under control. He cut the chain from a heavy rope and pulled out his lift bag, and in a minute or two the bag darted for the surface with his reel line trailing behind it. He tied off his reel, and I realized that in addition to getting a good grapnel, he had just had a chance to practice a major wreck skill. That skill is shooting an emergency ascent line up to the surface. Good preparation for his upcoming deep dive! I thought for a minute, imagining what must have happened on the *Jean Marie* up above when that unplanned bag shot up. The first thought must have been that there was a diver in trouble, but the mate probably gaffed the bag and tied it off to the dive boat and then must have found the grapnel. So he probably knew it was an artifact being lifted and not a diver in trouble.

I motioned to Bob to hop on, and, leaving his reel behind, he grabbed my harness, and I towed him around the wreck. We went completely around, passing the photographer-divers, who seemed to have stayed at the engine for the entire dive thus far taking pictures of the fish in the open boiler. As we came back to our starting point, I went a bit off the wreck to show Bob the goodie bag in the sand. We stopped. He picked the bag right up and dumped the sand out of it, and then we were off again. I wanted to make sure he knew that I was claiming that bag. "Of course it's yours!" he mimed, like I was being paranoid or something. We headed back to the wreck. He did some compass navigating off the wreck and back again, and then it was time for me to go back to the surface.

I did a nice, slow ascent and a five-minute stop, surfaced, and then climbed up onto the *Jean Marie*. As soon as I announced that I had found an HID light, I had everyone's attention. Turned out that it had actually been lost last November on the last trip of the 2002 season by a very grateful diver who happened to be onboard today. He had come back to retrieve it. I handed it over to him, and when Bob came up with the goodie bag, the diver got that back too. Bob joked around, saying that the guy should show us some gratitude and offer us at least one of the three nice lobsters he had gotten on today's dive.

I had some dry-suit leakage on the dive in the 45-degree water. No real problem during the dive at all—I was still comfortable. But there is an annoying micro-hole in my left dry glove that I have not been able to find, so my left hand has been getting wet on recent dives. As I had hung there during my five-minute stop, I had actually been able to get a lot of air into that left glove, and I succeeded in creating a stream of bubbles that identified the leak. Also, while coming up the line, my neck seal had burped, letting some air out but also letting some water in, so my shoulders and both arms were now wet.

Captain Ken dropped down for a quick dinner hunt with his spear gun while the rest of us began our surface interval. He returned somewhat later with a nice blackfish and a sea bass.

So now the big question was: should we stay on this wreck where the visibility was good, or should we take our chances and go to the *Shinnecock* near the mouth of Shinnecock Inlet, where conditions were unknown? Fishing boats might already be in the area, making it impossible for the dive boat to approach the wreck. We took a quick vote and decided that we had done about as much as we could at the *Panther* and that it was time to move on.

We got to the *Shinnecock*—it was not hosting fishing boats— and quickly tied off. This is an interesting wreck. About 10 years ago, this bottom-dragging fishing boat pulled up a torpedo in its net. Evidently it was discovered when the net was brought on board. The Coast Guard was called and the ship was evacuated. The Navy was called. They determined that the torpedo was unstable and blew up a carefully placed explosive charge on the torpedo which of course sank the fishing boat!

I was quite cold now. I had left my suit on, and the wetness inside from the first dive had chilled me. I expected that this second dive would be short, as I would only get colder when I got into the water.

On this dive, I left the scooter behind and dove with the 104-cubic-foot 33% O_2 tank and my still-full safety bottle containing 45% O_2. The vis was maybe 15-20 feet on this wreck. I could see the fishing trawler, now resting on her side on the sandy bottom. Probably about 50 feet long? As I circumnavigated her, I could clearly see that an explosive charge had blown through her near her bottom: all the metal was bent outwards.

I was looking at a hole that was big enough to swim through. I forgot the cold and went in to explore the hold, thinking about what the boat's owner must have felt when the Navy told him they were going to sink her. I swam forward into the hold and found a ladder and stairs, both of which were now oriented sideways; these led to a small hatch through which the crew could enter the hold from the inside of the ship. I looked at the hatch, thought maybe there was room to get through, and tried to slowly climb out of the hold via this hatch. I felt my tanks scrape the side. I looked down and realized there was no room to let me move my belly closer to the side of the hatch. I resisted the urge to brute-force myself through, and, gently backing out into the hold again, I exited it through a much larger opening which led to the deck of the fishing vessel. Glad I didn't try to force things. You do not want to get stuck in a hatch underwater and then be unable to get out. A diver watched me from outside the hatch. He moved on when it was clear I was not in any trouble.

I was having a great time and wasn't feeling the cold at all. I love diving, and in a moment of joy, I did a somersault in the water like a sea otter, just playing. As I came out of the tumble, while still upside down, I saw Bob about 10 feet in back of me—he was just floating, watching me. How long he had been there behind me I have no idea, but his smile through his mask communicated that he too was having a good dive. I followed him a bit as he ran a reel and then I went off on my own again.

All of a sudden, the vis was gone. Just like that. Evidently, the outgoing tide emptying Shinnecock Bay had hit us, and what had been decent vis was now gone. I was concerned for a minute, because I had followed Bob's line back to where he had tied it off, and this spot was a bit off the main wreck. Now I could not see the main wreck. When I had reached 1000 psi of air in my main 33% mix, I had switched to the 45% mix in the 40-cubic-foot bottle. I wanted to be breathing this higher oxygen mix for the ascent and the short safety-stop deco. A minute later, I saw two divers and followed them. In seconds I saw the trawler and made my way to the up line.

A few minutes later, back on board the *Jean Marie* with my dive gear put away and back in my nice warm clothes, I felt a noticeable shift in the wind. The clouds now filled the gray sky, the last diver was back on board, and we headed for the dock.

Before we parted in gathering winds beneath an ominous sky, Bob and I stopped by Tully's in Hampton Bays. As we had our post-dive snack, we watched our dive window close. Nature's conspiracy of wind and rain began to take hold on yet another weekend.

An Ill-Fated Trip to the Wolcott Wreck – Saturday, June 21, 2003

I went out to dive the Wolcott. This beautiful wreck is almost two hours from placid Shinnecock Bay. Due to projected bad weather, we decided to do the hour-closer *Seawolf*, a 95-foot-deep wreck. When an alternate wreck is selected, the Captain must always consider that some of the divers on board may have had gas with a higher percentage of oxygen than regular air's 21% put in their tanks for the dive. The amount of oxygen in this breathing mix, called nitrox, varies based on the depth to give the diver maximum bottom time. At the same time, oxygen becomes toxic; even deadly at depth in accordance to a complex formula based on the percentage of oxygen and the depth. The depth of the alternative wreck should not be deeper than the planned original wreck to prevent an injury or death from oxygen toxicity. The *Seawolf* was about the same depth range as the *Wolcott* so that would work well.

We got to the *Seawolf*, and as the good captain got us tied in, the sea turned ugly in the fastest time and waves and rollers began breaking, sending sheets of water to be captured by the wind and driven into our faces—a real nor'easter. Then the vomiting began. The heaving, rolling seas encouraged sympathetic reactions in the stomachs of at least five of the 10 divers on board. Myself included. Even though I was heavily dosed on Bonine. The stern board of the boat was awash many times as we dropped into wave troughs. The violent pitching made it very dangerous to walk about on deck. I remembered some of Joseph Conrad's storm-at-sea tales.

I had my dry suit half on, pulled up to my waist. Waves crashed against the boat, sending water everywhere, and I felt a slap in the back as if I had been hit. It was a wave, and I was now totally drenched—my dry suit was now a wet suit both inside and out. I was sick, cold, tired, and miserable. I was so sick that I didn't want to move, except to give space at the railing for another sick diver. So I sat right where I was, huddled like a homeless person in a doorway on a stormy night, hanging on to the railing, closing my eyes, and periodically getting drenched again, wishing I were back on the dock.

The mate offered to get my yellow hooded rain slicker, which I had joked about when I'd come onboard. I was grateful for it. The boat was now underway, and I—huddled up, hand on the railing—drifted in and out of a Bonine-induced, troubled sleep. I made the error of going to the head, was overcome with engine fumes, and rushed back up the ladder to my front-row reservation at the railing again. Finally, moving as fast as a sick man can move, I got out of my wet "dry" suit and my underwear and into some dry clothes. I donned the matching yellow slicker pants, curled up on a small bench in the cabin, and fell asleep again.

I woke up to find the boat again trying to hook into a wreck, this one the *Shinnecock*, right outside Shinnecock Inlet. Through my fitful sleep, I was relieved to feel the boat underway again—this time back to the dock. No one had dived.

Rough Seas, Used Bonine Anti-Seasickness Medicine, and an Electronic Gadget – July 5, 2003

I seem to be plagued by seasickness lately, and Saturday's trip to the USS *San Diego* was no different.

I got this gadget that goes on my wrist, has five settings, and sends an electrical shock into an alleged acupressure point on the wrist every four seconds. It feels really weird, like an electrical current going up into the fingertips. For this dive, on one of my favorite wrecks, I had taken my usual one-and-one-half Bonines at 4:30 a.m., about two hours before we were to depart. I really hate that stuff. Besides putting me in a sleepy daze for about 36 hours, it seems not to work lately; it just leaves me with a lingering post-dive grumpiness. I brought my new gadget as added protection, but decided not to wear it until seasickness symptoms appeared. According to its

Calling in the Heavy Guns, Adm. Caperton and Staff aboard USS San Diego circa 1917, Image Courtesy of US Navy Historical Center

documentation, it can be used once you are sick, and it works pretty much instantly. We'll see!

There was a forecast for three- to five-foot seas, and once we were out there, we encountered four-foot short-period swells. My Bonine seemed be working, as I discovered during the two-hour ride to the wreck, most of which was due east and parallel to the swells. The boat had a rolling gait like that of a fat drunk. I was still okay, but then I started talking to someone in the cabin and after about 10 minutes got that good ol' familiar feeling again, just sort of creeping up on me. There was no need for a sudden run to the railing, but I did realize it was time to call in the heavy guns. My battery-powered Popeil's "Relief Band" by Ronco! (It was actually called a Relief Band and while now replaced by another product, was available to purchase over the Internet for about $120.00.)

I put a bit of the included conducting gel on the inside of my wrist and positioned the band so that the shocks would cause tingling in my middle two fingers. If I felt that while touching an electrical outlet I would pull my hand back REAL FAST, thinking I was being seriously electrocuted.

But it worked, in seconds! I regretted taking my Bonine, as I was okay again.

Time passed. I was able to turn the band off for a while, turning it on again as needed. Wow! This thing really worked! One problem though. Couldn't take it underwater.

After we tied in to the wreck, I left the gadget on until the last minute. It was time to put on my dry suit, and now the gadget had to come off. Within one minute I knew I would be seeing my last meal again. I was suited up in my dry suit, almost ready to go into the water—except for one minor detail. I was going to be sick. Right now! I couldn't believe it! That gadget was off my wrist less than three minutes, and already I was rushing to the stern, returning to the sea all I had eaten and drank that morning. When I was finished being sick, I went down the ladder and immersed my head in the cold ocean. Oh, I was as miserable as I had ever been. The only consolation was that on the trip out I had been okay, and I was pretty sure that once my dive was over and I put that miracle gadget back on my wrist, I would be fine.

I heard Bob saying to me through the haze of Bonine and waves of nausea, "I'll wait for you on the line at about 60 feet." He jumped over the side. I went back up the ladder and onto the boat. I knew—having just heave-hoed so much—that I probably had at most two or three minutes to finish suiting up and to get in the water before I would be sick again. Over the side and down the line I went. Bob was there, and we descended to the wreck.

We were pleasantly surprised to find that we could see about 20 to 25 feet, and we explored the bow. I have dived 13 times on the stern section; this was just my second time on the bow area. So Bob ran a line, and I let him give me a tour. He showed me the giant Navy-style anchor, the empty hawsepipe, and other features I had never seen before. As Bob explored the bow beneath me at 115 feet, I put my nose to the very bow, marveling at how this great ship of 500 feet could come to such a sharp point. My left eye looked down the port side and my right eye looked down the starboard side of the upside-down armored cruiser.

We followed the reel line back only to find that it was no longer tied off where Bob had tied it! It appeared to go up into the water along the ascent line and out of our view. I could not figure it out. Bob followed it up a bit, saw that it was tied to the ascent line now, and cut it free. We began our ascent. We had spent about 40 minutes at depth, and we would take a while to deco. We took about 30 minutes to get back onboard. I decompressed on 100% O_2 but added a bit of time and kept Bob company on the line for much of his longer deco. We chatted about the dive and about how his line had gotten attached to the ascent line; not a good idea because if the ascent line to the boat on the surface were to break, our guideline would be in trouble too. Well, maybe we didn't really chat at 20 feet that much, but we did give matters serious thought.

Once back on the boat, we mentioned the line incident, and another diver made it seem like he had saved us. He had found our line broken off from the wreck and retied it to the ascent line.

Later we discussed another hypothesis to explain how the reel line had come to be retied so high up the ascent line. We did appreciate that the other diver had retied the line, but the only reason we could come up with to explain why it was retied so high up the ascent line was that maybe the other diver had got snagged on our line and did not realize it. Making his ascent, perhaps he'd felt it tugging, keeping him from ascending, and—now partly up the ascent line—he'd cut it to free himself, immediately reattaching it right there.

In any event, it was a great dive. I got my gear off, put my gadget back on my wrist, and was totally fine—no sea sickness at all. Just the horrid side effects of the Bonine. For my next dive, I will not take the Bonine; I'll just rely on this gadget. Also, I will get my tanks and other equipment set up in advance, before I remove the wrist gadget, to minimize the time that I need to get the rest of my gear on once I've removed the watch-like Relief Band.

Failure of Experiment with Anti-Seasickness Electronic Gadget – July 13, 2003

I will continue diving and will NOT let this discourage me. Nor will I relax my eternal vigilance in my quest for that Holy Grail, that much sought Philosopher's Stone, ultimate panacea; anything that will keep me from getting seasick on dive boats. We are all searching for something in life, my quest apparently continues ad nauseaum....

To explain the origins of my seasickness problems, I must give a brief history of my gastronomic experiences at sea. Long priding myself on my classic gourmet tastes, I'm a real connoisseur of fine foods, an occasional chef to the stars, and a creator of elaborate desserts and hors d'oeuvres. I have won gold medals for my flour, "Best of the Fair" for my apple pie, and accolades from my mom for a great Romanian steak dinner. None of that mattered as I stood this Sunday bent over the side of the dive boat, humbled by the knowledge that there is no distinction between fine foods and Pop Tarts once dropped into the alimentary canal and then expelled upon the outgoing gastric tides that accompany five-foot ocean swells.

Two years ago, I took an ill-fated trip on a boat whose name shall remain anonymous. She ran out of fuel in seven-foot seas. Foolishly, I hadn't taken any seasickness medicine, and I consequently spent much of the trip lying on the deck, moaning and getting sick.

After that, I vowed never to go out again without being well-dosed on Bonine, and that approach served me well for two years. The occasional queasy feeling always vanished, and I was able to enjoy the wreck diving I love so much. But I have to say that the side effects of Bonine or Dramamine or any drugs in that family are annoying. First of all, I am sleepy for a good 30 hours or so. There is also another weird side effect, and I wonder if anyone else has experienced it: I get real crabby, just as I do from decongestants like Benadryl. A serious personality change: I'm not just tired, but in a bad mood too. When I do a boat dive, because of the medication the whole weekend gets messed up. If only there were some way to not have to take that stuff!

So I had a couple of decent years on the boats. Not just due to the medication, but also because I had set a limit: I would not go out if seas were reported to be over two to four feet. I did lots of boat diving and had lots of great dives.

Fast forward to this boat season—2003. The weather stunk. So many weekends were blown out. My weekly shore dives were wearing thin. Wasn't I just doing shore dives to kill time until the boats started running in April? The weather did not cooperate, so I decided to go out in somewhat more dicey weather than I had previously. Those dives—to the *Wolcott* and the *San Diego*—were not easy on the stomach.

So my thinking was: since I am getting sick whether or not I take the medicine, and because I was not sick until I removed the Relief Band on the last dive, it seemed logical to use the Relief Band exclusively on my next dive and to not take the medicine. I would plan for getting sick right before going in the water. The rest of the trip, though, I would be fine. It sounded good to me. An experiment, that's what I would do! And where better to do the required research but on a research vessel taking one of its regular trips to my favorite wreck—the USS *San Diego*. Everything was in place and ready to go for my experiment, including NOAA's forecasted three- to five-foot seas that would certainly induce nausea. I was set!

As I left in the early morning darkness to meet the dive boat, I must admit, it did cross my mind to take a Bonine. I reached back into my knapsack, turned on the Relief Band to make sure it worked, and made my fateful decision to not take that Bonine. I was optimistic on the boat and even left the gadget turned off until, just out of the inlet, the boat started to take on that gait now familiar to me, that drunken, rolling lurching that's so inevitable in beam-sea swells. I confidently turned the Relief Band on and was fine!

Well, maybe not fine. But I wasn't sick. I did feel, though, that the seasickness was there simmering just beneath the surface, waiting to pick its opportunity to broach the subject with me. It would do so on its terms and when it decided. I lay down on a bunk and came back up when I heard that change in the sound of the engines as the boat maneuvered over the wreck.

We came to a stop. All forward motion ceased. The boat now knew only that ancient song of the sea, the periodic, cyclical rhythm of the swells. Oh! I also knew the rhythm and felt each lurch. About every fifth wave would really roll the boat. My stomach started to pick up the rhythm: just as your hands and feet might start tapping to some musical beat in a club, my stomach was in sync with the waves.

I got horribly sick. Experiment failed. Electronic gadget useless. I decided to not take the Bonine now. It would still take a couple of hours to work, and actually, judging by my experience two years ago, it probably wouldn't work at all if I was already sick.

I had originally thought that because I would just be doing one long dive, I would take my time getting in the water. In fact, I would wait for all the other divers to go in first. Now I realized that that would be a big mistake, because these other divers, visiting from Ohio, were taking a very long time to get ready. Every additional minute they took was another minute I was on this rolling boat instead of in the water getting that immediate relief that I knew plunging in would bring me. I started to get ready, but could now barely move my head without throwing up. Finally, gear on (with the very helpful assistance of the crew, who saw the state I was in), I jumped in the water.

Uh oh, how strange. I was in the water—but still feeling sick! The bobbing of the granny line in the swells did not help as I quickly made my way to the descent line, seeking depth as my anti-nausea drug. I descended to my friend the *San Diego*, yet still a vestige of discomfort remained—enough to trigger warning signals that this might be a short dive.

At the wreck, I actually think I saw my first shark. A two- or three-foot-long brownish blur of motion chasing a school of fish across the keel and over the side. I remember thinking, "That was cool!" without any primal shark fears being triggered. Perhaps seeing a five-foot-or-longer shark will trigger them.

My stomach still felt funny. I was very surprised. In the past, my symptoms had always left when I hit the water. I headed to the stern, dropped down next to the long shaft, and then headed inside the stern section. I was still not feeling great, so I decided to play it a bit more conservatively and come back outside, maybe stay closer to the ascent line in case things turned ugly.

I had planned a 45-minute bottom time with appropriate deco. Now, at 20 minutes, the prospect of deco at 20 feet right under the swells was not attractive to me, so I headed back up after 25 minutes of bottom time. With the mix I was breathing, I was actually okay to basically get right out of the water, but I really wanted to be very conservative, so I decided that I would do some pure O_2 deco anyway, and if I really felt sick or got sick I would surface. I did some time—actually around eight minutes—and the oxygen seemed to offset some of the queasiness caused by the rough seas at that shallow depth.

As I made my final assault on the surface, the waves of nausea increased until—as I battled with the ladder in the swell and got up onto the platform—I was very sick again. I passed my stage bottle off to a crew member, sat down, let them pull my tanks off, and hung there on the corner of the platform by the crook of my arm, quite sick.

I scrambled back on deck, got out of my dry suit as fast as possible, and put the gadget back on my right wrist. I did not get sick again but felt really lousy for the rest of the trip. I did not want to go down to a bunk because I feared not making it to the side of the ship in time if the need arose. So I headed to the bow of the dive boat and lay out on the deck, my head on a Styrofoam float, and fell asleep.

I woke up with a feeling of sunburn and a stiff neck and made my way to a bunk. I lay down and focused on the electric shocks going into my wrist and hand, actually wondering if boat diving was for me at all. I was very discouraged and saddened at the prospect that this might have been my last visit to the *San Diego*. Now, some hours later, I have recovered somewhat from the failed experiment, and I've decided that I will return to my previous rule: predicted seas are not to be over two to four feet, and I will take Bonine and bring along some salty food. I will bring the electronic gadget too. I just won't rely on it alone. Bye. Gotta lay down again.

Ponquogue Bridge – Sunday, August 3, 2003

I have been getting a bit bored at the Ponquogue Bridge, running out of stuff to do under there. I guess I am not out of rocks (I am always looking for the next great Indian artifact) but I am getting a bit bored just the same.

A couple of dives ago—figuring it was good practice if pinned in a small space in a wreck—I took all my equipment off under the new bridge in about 25 feet of water. I kept my weight belt on, though, so I wouldn't pop like a cork to the surface to be made into Moo Goo Gai Pan by some boat propeller. Even with the weight belt on, I needed to hold on to my BC Harness with its six pound steel back plate to stay down. No problem. But the changing current added an element of urgency to putting the gear back on—gear which had by this time lain on the bottom for two minutes. I held on, breathing off my long hose—even my dry suit was disconnected.

Another thing I tried—not that I recommend these types of things without a buddy—is removing my mask underwater for a couple of minutes at a time, trying to create an airspace by catching my bubbles with a cupped hand tightly over an eye. I had read in a book somewhere that you may be able to read your gauges that way in an emergency if you have lost your mask. It actually worked briefly. One would definitely need to practice this in advance of needing it.

Another sport I had tired of was hanging out in the Porgy Patch after the tides switch. This 30-foot-deep area is sheltered from the outgoing tidal currents. You can continue your dive here long after the current changes. I wanted to know how long it would take me to get back to the safety of the old bridge bulkhead with a full current blasting (five minutes) and how much gas would be used with all that huffing and puffing (about 400-500 lbs). By the way, I did this experiment with about 1500 pounds of air and felt that it was not really too dangerous.

Finally, I was also sick of practicing with my airbag with two concrete cinder blocks I had brought into the water here a few dives back. I used them to fine tune my control moving the heavy objects around here to there with the airbag while underwater.

So, it was time to activate *Apollo*. Designated by some as the ancient god that drew the sun across the sky; my *Apollo* brand underwater scooter is my chariot and a very cool toy. It is powered by a battery that takes about six to eight hours to charge up and which lasts about 45 minutes on the middle of three power settings. To change the speed on the scooter, you must stick your hand into the prop and rotate a dial. Hmmm. Not my favorite thing to do underwater. But I have developed some good habits. Whenever I touch the scooter for any reason, both out of the water and in the water, I always check the safety first to confirm that it is locked. Underwater, if the scooter is turned off—even for a few seconds—that safety switch goes back on.

The battery usage rate is related to the speed and how hard the scooter has to work; for example, going against a current or dragging another diver is sure to use up the battery faster than normal. But I've only ran out of power once in three years—I do learn from my mistakes!

Now, I count on only 30 minutes of medium-power usage. Usually in the beginning of the dive I set power to low or medium and use the scooter for no more than 10 minutes. That is more than enough time to go a fair distance. Then I either use some of the remaining time with the scooter held reversed so its prop-wash digs in the sand uncovering buried treasure, or I motor about a bit more. I generally try to save at least 10 minutes of juice for the end of the dive, using the scooter at high power to get back against the full current. At the Ponquogue Bridge, I have no doubt that I could make it back (as I always do) against the current should the scooter fail. At Rockaway, though, I end the dive on the north side of the channel and east of the entry point so that if *Apollo* lets me down, I am not in a dangerous situation. I can't swim against *that* current if I wind up in the middle of the channel or across the channel. But if I finish on the north side with a dead scooter, the outgoing tide would theoretically take me back to the beach entry point.

So, I dove with *Apollo*.

I went in early, and was far north under the new bridge, at the base of the northern wooden wall, within minutes. I shut the scooter down and explored on the lee side of that wooden structure for a while, sheltered from the current. When the current slackened, I headed north, exploring areas under the new bridge that I had never been to before. I stayed put while the current switched and then told *Apollo*, "We're goin' home!"

I had a lot of battery power left, so I decided to go east against the current a bit and then due south. My arms get a bit achy from holding the scooter, but it is well worth it. I have been using the scooter for a few years now, so I don't even think about operating the machine as I am flying around. If I want to check something out to the right, I look over there and my body flies there effortlessly. There are two major hazards to watch out for, besides getting caught in the prop. One is to never go faster than sensible in whatever visibility conditions exist (on this dive, vis was about 25 feet). You can control your speed by pressing the accelerator button in short bursts independent of the scooter's current speed setting. The second really important thing is to never ascend under power with the scooter. Usually I try to ride about three feet off the bottom, using it as a reference point for depth. I periodically check my wrist dive computer while moving to confirm my depth. If you're using the bottom as a guide and you are familiar with the site, you do not really have to keep checking your computer for depth info. But when I hit an upwards slope, I immediately let go of the accelerator and come to a stop at the base of the slope. I then swim up the slope and reactivate the scooter when it levels off again.

That is, most of the time I stop. On Sunday, I took *Apollo* out again. When I encountered some large boulders and pipes, I decided not to stop but rather to exhale fully as I veered the scooter up over the obstacle and then sharply down on the far side without losing speed. I suppose I went up about three or four feet—much faster than I should have—and then back down again. I felt like a fighter pilot hugging the ground, going over some hills and then dropping back down on the other side of them. Not really recommended. But it was exhilarating.

Now that my tour was over and the current was at full force emptying bay to sea, it was time to end the dive. I switched the scooter to full power and came back in under the old bridge. A mixture of adrenaline and exhilaration as the current tried to rip my regulator out of my mouth and as it worked with

Apollo to make my arms feel like they were being pulled out of their sockets.

As you get closer in to shore under the old bridge, the narrowing effect caused by the shallower water makes the current very strong. It reaches maximum intensity at the last few bridge pilings. The water becomes a flurry of seaweed and everything that the emptying bay can throw out in its twice-daily tribute to the ocean. Even the scooter has difficulty here. But if you go at an angle to the current, enter the sheltered area near the pilings, and then go back to the current, you can pretty easily zig-zag your way through those last 50 feet or so.

I did it as I had many times before. I stopped in the shallower water once out of the current and cleaned the seaweed off the prop. I checked my air. Hmmm. Lots left. While I was not certain how much juice was left in my scooter, I was pretty sure there was some left, so I decided to go back out along the whole length of the old bridge while the post-slack current was kicking, and I ultimately went all the way back out to the Porgy Patch. I then took the same ride all the way back in again, hooting and hollering underwater the whole time. It *is* just.like flying! I love that thing!

Had it run out of power, I would have let the current take me east and would have sunk down to the bottom. There is a north-south ridge a bit off the east side of the old bridge. You can sink down to it and make your way south, partially sheltered from the force of the current. By the time you must deal with the current, you only have to swim hard for a couple of minutes at that point.

Hopefully, I'll be on a boat next Saturday.

Peconic Bay, North Sea, Near Sag Harbor, Long Island – August 9, 2003

I dove today in Peconic Bay, in the North Sea area, west of Sag Harbor. Vis was about 10 to 12 feet. There used to be a company in Sag Harbor during one of the World Wars that made torpedoes, and the general area I was diving was the company's testing area.

I did a beach entry, used my scooter, and went out about a half mile to about 20 feet deep. The water was very warm; in the mid seventies. I towed a flag which I clipped off to a D-ring on my BC. I placed a rubber O-ring in the hookup so that if the flag got caught by a boat or something it would break off and not drag me. Yet because of the overcast skies, there were no boats in the area.

The bottom was rather featureless: silt and sand with only crabs and whelks here and there. I discovered nothing of interest, but will come back one day again with the scooter. I can cover a lot of ground with it and I have heard stories about possible ship parts in this area. Perhaps I should bring a metal detector…

Back in the car, listening to the news, I heard that because of pollution runoff from recent rains you can't take shellfish from the very area I was diving in. Hmmm….

The Mysterious "Scallop" Wreck – Saturday, August 16, 2003

I had a great dive today with the help of the *Jean Marie*, a dive boat out of Jackson's Marina on Shinnecock Bay. I really needed it, as I had been very seasick on my last three boat dives. That's it. I am only going out on days just like today. Calm seas—maybe there were two-foot waves. We were off to a new wreck, the mysterious Scallop wreck somewhere out there in the vast ocean south of Long Island. Visibility was excellent, at least 60 feet, and I had a great chance to explore this mysterious wreck. Now, captured in time at 130 feet deep, sharing the sandy ocean depths with scallops, goosefish, and ling, she waited. I could only imagine her last moments.

Her bow had been kept pointing into a heavy, frothing sea. The boat met the seas with all her strength. Built short and stubby, possibly a tug, she was powered by steam. We know this from the large engine amidships. Perhaps, finally losing her battle and now caught in a beam sea, she began taking on water as the late afternoon light dwindled in the increasing storm. Waves broke over her, pounded her, sought entry through every weakness. Every space, every seam was tested by the angry seas.

Ah, to abandon ship under such conditions. To decide to leave what had been your only warmth, your island, and jump into the roiling ocean to escape with your life—not an easy decision. We don't know her name, this little ship. We also don't know how many men had to make that fateful decision to leave her and watch from a distance as she made her final gasp and slipped beneath the rollers that black night, a din of shrieking gale winds driving her to the bottom of the sea.

We do know that she landed upright, bow still pointed home, poised in her death throes such that the bow is slightly raised but canted at an angle, mimicking the act of taking on a heavy swell or bracing for a roller to crash across the decks.

Descending to meet her, I could see her new friends clearly from the line. Spaced around the wreck like checkers on a checkerboard were many large scallops, each in its own little depression in the sand, each with its thousand eyes watching in all directions. Guardians of the wreck, the scallops called out, singing their scallop songs of the mysteries of the sea. Still 30 feet above the sand, I headed out from the wreck and spent 10 minutes in a joyful scallop narcosis, reaching down to scoop them up. I was startled when the first scallop took off, powered by a little jet of water. It moved fast. I did not know that scallops swim! But alas, he was not fast enough. I grabbed him and placed him in my canvas bag and went for another one and another one. My bag was filling up, and I got anxious for a second. I had been harvesting scallops, moving farther and farther away from the wreck without giving any attention to the wreck's location. I looked up and behind me. I still saw the ship in the distance, so I made a turn and went parallel to it until my bag was full of huge scallops. About 25 very large ones. I left behind enough of them so that the wreck would continue to be adequately guarded, and I now explored the wreck proper.

Good relief off the sand, and still very recognizable I spent the rest of my total 27-minute bottom time moving over her. I thought I saw a large cleat in the distance, as well as a few wooden ribs sticking up out of the sand. It would make sense if this were in fact a tugboat to have huge cleats to fasten heavy hawsers to for towing ships.

As my bottom time and nitrogen level increased, with my scallop bag full and my underwater peregrinations nearing their end, I had observed an immense mussel amidst the wreckage of the ship. As I maneuvered closer to take it as a prize, I suddenly noticed two very large eel heads just sticking out from under a piece of wood, just inches from the large mussel. A voice screamed in my head to pull my hand back. It was a trap!

It occurred to me that the tantalizing black mussel had been placed there by the eels and was a trap to catch unsuspecting divers. Had I reached any closer, the eels would have been upon me in a second, extracting the last of my life force as the underwater pythons exacted their price for my greediness.

It was with those thoughts that I decided it was time to end my dive, pay my long deco-obligation at the door, and get my dinner shucked and cleaned on the good ship *Jean Marie* at the top of the line.

Later, on the boat, while lying in my bunk, I heard some divers talking about how they were narced at the 130-foot depth and how they had handled it. I thought to myself with some concern that the possibility had not even occurred to me. I thought of that eel laid diver trap I had narrowly escaped and drifted off to sleep.

Traditional Japanese Haiku Dive Report David Rosenthal – Dutch Springs September 14, 2003

Here is my rather traditional dive report:

I went today to Dutch Springs in Pennsylvania. It's an old quarry that's filled with water with things like an airplane, a school bus, and other "attractions" thrown in it to make it more interesting to divers. As planned, I met a couple of other divers there.

I would have preferred a boat dive, but the weather was not great.

It rained as we geared up for the first of two dives.

As usual, there was a thermocline, or major temperature change, at about 30 feet.

Even though Dutch Springs is somewhat tame, there is a surreal otherworldliness to parts, particularly the ghostly white sediment and the complete underwater trees that still have their branches.

We did two deco dives and during the hang, with the warm water, the clarity of the water, and the bubbles drifting up and exploding from divers far below, it became a Zen-like experience for all of us.

Stop reading now if all you wanted was a standard dive report.

The Japanese have an ancient poetic tradition called Haiku. A Haiku verse is generally about an animal or nature. It consists of three non-rhyming lines, the first with five syllables, the second with seven, and the last with another five syllables. Part of the

Dutch Springs experience is sitting in traffic at the Jersey side of the Holland Tunnel when returning. I took the opportunity to take a nap, direct a film, stop a world war, interrupt a bank robbery, and save two small villages with nothing more than a spoonful of water, a moth, and a paperclip. Oh, and I also composed the following Haiku that contains the same dive report as above...

> *Summers end, dive on*
> *Boats blown out, storm far at sea*
> *The quarry calls us.*
>
> *Clouds collide, Rain falls*
> *Drive on! Quarry calls again*
> *Don our suits, check air.*
>
> *Hot then warm, now cold*
> *The thermocline embraces*
> *Frost at thirty feet*
>
> *Albatross of deep*
> *Soar and circle—see the tree?*
> *Rise, bare branch—white silt*
>
> *Up up and away*
> *Not so fast, deco is due*
> *We played, we pay, OMmmmmmmmm....*

We played, we pay, OMmmmmm..

The Demise of the Almost Paradise Dive-Related Facility at Rockaway Beach 9th Street –September 2003

Almost Paradise was a restaurant with outside showers and places for SCUBA divers to gear up to go underwater to explore East Rockaway Inlet, near the Atlantic Beach Bridge, not too far from Kennedy Airport. It had been in business for about 10 years and many NYC local divers took their training at the site. I enjoyed diving the Rockaways from Almost Paradise at the foot of Beach 9th Street, and also from other nearby locations such as Beach 6th Street. These areas boast a great abundance of flora and fauna late in the season as the warm waters of the Gulf Stream come closer to land, including giant yellow sponges, sea horses, and other brightly colored tropical fish. On October 15, 2003, Almost Paradise closed its doors forever, as the land had been sold off to a developer. I sort of liked being able to clean off my gear in the warm showers at Almost Paradise instead of in my bathroom at home over the course of two days. Below is the story I wrote of what turned out to be my last dive at Beach 9th Street shortly before the closing of Almost Paradise's facilities.

Almost Paradise, Beach 9th Street, Rockaway, Queens

Yesterday I went down to Beach 9th Street, and the vis from the jetty looked great! So today I found myself there for a 2:47 p.m. high tide. I was to meet Bob at the Sherwood Diner for lunch then dive. We found Almost Paradise's gate shut. Undeterred, Bob and I suited up next to our vehicles on Beach 9th. Of course Jay, the proprietor of Almost Paradise, showed up just as we are going into the water. The plan was to go in west of Almost Paradise, entering via the public beach area, whenever we were ready without consideration as to whether it was slack tide yet. The current was still ripping, in fact did not really let up until we were done almost an hour later...Drift Dive? No...how about we were flying a glider high up riding thermal currents, like great eagles soaring over forests and mountains...

Flying! That's what I'm doing. No maybe its more like soaring above the greenish, brownish landscape. A subtle adjustment of a tip of a fin and I turn gently, now facing to the left. Sort of like a balloon wafting on the breeze. Free, floating, flying!

I look down. There a horseshoe crab rushes by, there's a starfish, two little silver-and-brown striped fish. An old bottle, a piece of glass, sea weed, sand, grey clay. I fire my reverse thrusters, slowing myself down, and heel slightly to the left. Slowly lowering down, still ever moving forward from the current, but now I am facing into the current with my face only inches above a field of rocks. I reach out to snatch one up, to more closely examine it. Is this an old Indian stone tool? I turn it over in my hands, still drifting, and look up at Bob, also drifting a couple of feet above and to the right of me. He nods NO! I know what he means...It's not an indian arrowhead, David...As an exclamation mark, to make sure I understood he makes the international "You're Nuts!" signal with his index finger describing little circles next to his right ear. That convinces me. I open my red canvas bag and drop the rock inside.

We had by now rode the current to the 46-foot-deep "trench" and could see the curling tendrils of cable, seemingly waiting to ensnare a diver like a den of snakes. But they were welcome, we grabbed onto the cables and continued letting the current push us east, using the cable to slow our ride. As all things must end, so did the cable. Bob attached his reel and we flew out still riding the current as if we were on a 200-foot-long horizontal bungee cord...

I was surprised that the current was still blowing so hard. We decided to wait a few minutes, Bob fluttering on the end of his line like a water skier frozen in time. I pulled out my dive knife and thrust it into the channel bottom at an angle, got totally negative, and lay flat on the mussel covered bottom. We waited about five minutes. The current never stopped.

We decided to head back, me crawling on the bottom and Bob a couple of feet above me, reeling himself in. We got back to the cables, out of breath, and put the reel away, using the cables to pull ourselves westward. Finally with both our gas low—I was about 500 lbs—we slowly ascended the sandy slope, doing a three-minute stop and surfacing almost exactly where we had entered the water some 55 minutes previously. What a GREAT DIVE!

We hung out at Almost Paradise for a while after putting our gear away, agreeing that its closing is a great loss to the dive community. But it is not the end of the world and certainly not the end of diving the Rockaways. Perhaps, the beginning of a process of adventure discovering new areas and challenges.

Last Dive at Strongs Neck Bridge, Setauket, Long Island – October 5, 2003

I told myself I'd be diving the Ponquogue Bridge at 5:30, but 3:00 found me in Rocky Point on the North Shore having just transported a kayak from Hampton Bays to be stored at my mom's. I really didn't want to go back out to Ponquogue and then back to Queens, so I dove "Plan B."

I drove back west along the scenic route, following the winding shore road past Miller Place and other small hamlets that lie along hilly single-lane roads enfolded in the still-lush greenery, in the trees and vines that characterize this part of the north shore of Long Island. Around Mount Sinai, I made an abrupt right turn and headed to the Long Island Sound—just exploring, seeing where the road went. Would it take me to a place where I could park the car and dive? I still had all my dive gear in the back.

I followed the serpentine road down to where it met the beach, to a valley of sorts which cuts into the sandy bluffs that guard this side of Long Island against invasion from Connecticut. The panoramic view of the Long Island Sound opened up before me. I was on the Port Jefferson Beach; about a quarter mile down the beach were the rock jetties of Mt. Sinai Harbor, and to the left was a beach that curved away into the distance as far as the eye could see. Straight out, I could easily see Connecticut across the Sound. I left my car, ignoring the signs insisting on a town permit, and walked to the water. It looked clean and seemed like it would offer good vis, but I was worried about my car getting a ticket or being towed. I took off and continued west, deciding that since I had my metal detector, I would dive at the site of the Strongs Neck Bridge in Setauket.

I had dived the bridge before, at a max depth of about 12 feet. For some reason, I'm sure that there should be bottles and maybe the occasional hurled engagement ring here. So I have often come here to dig with my scooter and shovel, and today I would use my underwater metal detector, Excalibur. I had not used it for a year or so, and I made sure it was charged up. I have rigged the detector with two clips, such that it can hang attached to the D-rings on the right side of my harness, out

Photo K. Martin

of the way. When I want to use it, I just detach the front from the upper D-ring. It then pivots on the lower D-ring, and I can move it left and right slowly as I swim forward. I also brought the dreaded dive flag. Nothing quite like having a 20-foot polypropylene line swirling around you while you are wearing all this gadgetry!

The tide was coming in as I entered the water somewhere about 4:30 p.m. Last time I was here, I sank in the mud up to my ankles, weighted down by my equipment, so this time I scouted out a firm area for the entry point. Once I had my gear on, I didn't feel like walking that far, so I took a more direct route, making my own path to the water through the reeds. Right at the water's edge, I took a step on what seemed to be solid ground and sank past my ankle. I lost my balance and fell, landing on my rear. I was inches from what I could clearly see was good sand, so I got up, and, with immense effort I pulled my right foot up out of the muck. Even with my two hoods on, I could hear the sucking sound as I pulled out my foot and stepped onto firmer ground.

As soon as the water hit a depth of three feet deep or so, I went into face-down metal-detecting mode. It took a little while to get my technique back. (Note: I have *never* found anything of much value or interest with my metal detector on a dive—my "technique" is an ongoing learning experience.) After doing nothing more than silting up my immediate area in the five-foot vis, I got the hang of not letting the ring on the detector actually touch bottom as I swung it slowly from side to side. Occasionally, after not hearing anything for a few minutes, I would reach up to the large headphones and find they had moved up my head and off of my ears. Okay, I don't know why I do this either! I suppose I was enjoying myself, here and there getting excited over some change in the odd sounds coming out of the infernal contraption and digging or using my hand to fan the silt away.

I would scoop up some muck with my shovel and place it to the left of my little excavation and then run the detector over what I had just put there to see if I had moved a metal item out of the hole. Vis was zero around me for most of my dive, affording me a good opportunity to pretend I was in a sensory deprivation tank, like in the movie *Altered States* from years ago. There was a slight current from the incoming tide, so the water would clear fairly rapidly. I would look in the hole with my light, use the detector, and shovel again. I got a very strong signal at one particular place. I do not know how long I worked it, but it must have been a while. Then all of a sudden, I couldn't find the hole I had been digging. I must have drifted off—all the work was for naught. That was it. I'd had it. I was out of here. The ambient light had been lessening as the sun kept its appointment with the horizon in the west, and I started to head back towards shore. I do not know how long my dive was, as my computer did not trigger for much of it, the depth being too shallow. I was tired from digging and now wanted to get out of this damned hellhole before it got dark.

I decided that I would exit at the place I had originally scouted out, the place that seemed to have firmer ground, and I continued lying flat on my stomach until the water was about two feet deep. Getting up was really hard with my feet sinking up to the ankles in this fine, black, organic, stinky, gooey mud. I was wearing a very heavy steel tank and my detector, and was carrying my dive flag and fins. I shakily stood up and took my first real step. My right foot began to sink to the ankle, then to the shin, then to the knee. I stopped sinking a couple of inches above my knee. I actually felt some serious fear and concern now because I was totally off balance and did not want to take my left foot off the more solid ground it was on. So I fell.

My leg didn't shift as I fell—almost in slow motion—and it occurred to me that it might break off at the shin, as it was not giving at all. My leg was locked in a vise. So now I was down on the mud, totally off balance, my right leg a prisoner. I felt a surge of adrenaline and major fear as I realized that I was at least 15 to 20 feet from solid ground, and there was no way for me to get there. I might not even be able to get my leg up out of the mud! I still had about 1500 pounds in my tank, so I figured I had some time before the incoming tide drowned me. I was quite concerned at this point.

With my butt in the mud and taking some of the weight off my leg, I was able to extricate the leg with great difficulty. I saw a couple of old branches through the three inches of water that covered the mud and tried to step on them. Did you ever see, on National Geographic, those lizards that can run across the surface of the water? I thought maybe I'd try that, using these little sticks to step on. At this point, driven by adrenaline and totally covered with smelly, black mud, I tried to make it those last 20 feet. I didn't yet want to take my heavy tank off and have it slowly sink out of sight to be discovered by someone else with their metal detector. Every step I took, I sank in the mud to my knee or thigh. I kept moving as fast as I could, huffing and puffing and practically rolling, never stopping to give the black mud a chance to tighten its hold. Finally, totally out of breath, I got to solid ground. I was a mess. My leg muscles were aching and I was covered with mud. I got back to my car and just sat there for a few minutes, catching my breath and thanking the powers that be that I made it and that there were no broken bottles with jagged glass in that mud.

I put my gear away and headed to the Long Island Expressway for home. Later that night as I hosed the mud off my gear in the garage, my aching legs served as a reminder to me that I was done with diving the site of the Strongs Neck Bridge in Setauket—probably forever.

The USS San Diego, Columbus Day, October 13, 2003

Yesterday the NOAA Islip Buoy reported 11-foot-high waves 30 miles out in the Atlantic, but a rapid decrease in wave size brought them down to about four feet for my dive today on the USS *San Diego*. I took a Bonine as part of my anti-seasickness initiative and conked out about midnight. I am sure I set my alarm for 4:00 a.m. Positive. Hmmm. I woke up at 4:07 a.m. (luckily) to find the alarm turned off. Maybe it did go off and my wife silenced it. I don't know. I groggily got out of bed and hunted down food for the cat. I try to set up my gear and put it in the car the night before, because I am a bit intellectually challenged on only four hours of sleep and the Bonine. Somehow I always make the drive to the boat without getting hit by the cops with a Bonine DWI.

I arrived at the dock, said hello to Sean from the Sea Gypsies, loaded my gear, found an empty bunk on the *Eagle's Nest*, and went right to sleep.

I had brought a few toys and gadgets with me today. I had two dive plans, one if we hooked in near the bow and the other if we ended up at the other end of the 504-foot-long sunken armored cruiser. I had just finished an interesting book: *Anchors An Illustrated History*. So if we were near the bow, I would take an underwater writing tablet and sketch one or two of the anchors and then see what I could find out about that style of anchor later. I would also bring my scooter, *Apollo*, and tour the entire wreck. If we tied in towards the stern, I would bring my laminated deck plans down with me and explore a bit, keeping myself astern of the bilge keel.

Captain Howard announced that the dive boat was tied in somewhere on the wreck's bilge keel but more towards bow than stern, so I headed for the bow once in the water. Visibility was quite good at about 30 feet considering recent local wave-and-wind action. I used the scooter to maneuver to both sides of the bow, tracing each anchor with my light, trying to see which one I should sketch. I settled on a starboard anchor that Bob had pointed out on a previous dive earlier this year. This anchor was big; perhaps as big as a Volkswagen Beetle car. You sure wouldn't want to be under this thing if it dropped. Neutrally buoyant, I hung there at 100 feet deep with my scooter clipped off to me and drew the anchor, which was pulled up tight into its hawsepipe. Then I went to sketch a side view of the same anchor.

Starboard and port refer the right and left sides of the ship if you are on the deck of the ship facing forward in the primary direction the ship is designed to move. These terms are relative to the ship, so if the ship is upside down, as is the San Diego, then—if you are facing forward toward the bow—starboard is actually the left side and port is the right side of the wreck.

I noticed that the hawsepipe for the next anchor on the same side (aft of the first anchor) was empty. There had been some speculation that this second missing anchor was released after the San Diego had hit the German U-boat mine or torpedo, in an effort to stabilize the ship. Looking at old photos of the USS San Diego, I can see that in a number of pictures there is no anchor there at all. In some of the other photos, there is a different type of anchor for that second hawsepipe. In one photo, no second anchor is drawn up into the hawsepipe, but rather a different style of anchor is "catted" or secured to the ship a bit farther aft, with its chain leading into the second hawsepipe. There is even another photo from earlier in the ship's life (as the USS *California*) which shows that anchor's chain entering the first hawsepipe.

The anchor presently in the first hawser pipe is roughly the shape of the letter "W," with three long, heavy flukes to grab into the seafloor. It is in the style of a stockless high holding power anchor, similar to the Stokes Bower Stockless Anchor but with three flukes instead of two. I can't find the exact anchor in my book. Maybe, just maybe, I've discovered a previously unknown anchor! In the true scientific tradition, I should be allowed to name it. Let's see. I'll call it the Wilbur-type anchor, because it is shaped like a "W." Or better yet, how about *Wilburorious rosenthalium*! Yep! I like that.

The second, missing, anchor looks in the old photos to be shaped generally like the letter "J." According to my reading, that would make it a mooring-type anchor. Why the letter

"J?" Well, if the ship is moored and there is a low tide or other wave action that causes her keel to hit the anchor, we would not want a pointed fluke sticking up that could give her a nice big hole in the bottom. Holes in the bottoms of ships are bad things. So some mooring anchors are designed with flukes just on one side.

Now to be honest, I am not an anchor expert, and I am looking at some poor-quality, ambiguous old photos, so my conclusions are only tentative at this point.

After drawing the anchor, I put my slate away and decided to do some sightseeing. I set my scooter to medium speed and headed aft, past the great guns still trained on some unseen enemy, past the now decayed stern, and out past the end of the ship. I then did a U-turn and headed along the other side of the ship, back toward the bow.

The vis on the starboard side of the capsized ship was much lower—the surge was stirring up sand and silt as it hit that side of the ship. I passed clouds of sediment, and whenever I wanted better visibility I would rise a few feet, almost to the level of the bilge keel. I passed all sorts of fish, some in schools and some playing hooky, and moved through some small schooling fish with my Fish-O-Matic scooter (without any injury to any fish). Some fish turned their heads (and bodies) as I passed, like they were at mid-court watching a tennis match. Most ignored me. There were more than a few beautiful moments on this dive. Sunlight filtered down in rays, illuminating features of the wreck. I could see the expanse of the wreck flying by me as I scooted along.

Finally back at the bow, I took a last look at the anchors and headed for the ascent line after a 45-minute dive. I moved slowly up the line and switched to breathing oxygen at 16 feet deep. I felt the wind-driven small chop on the surface while fluttering like a flag on the line—this deco was tough on my arms. Ready to end the dive, I reached for my bladder inflator and found it had slipped behind me somehow despite the Velcro wrap I use to keep the inflator near the strap of my harness so that it's always within reach. I gave up trying to grab it. I will have to come up with a better way to secure it. I closed my dry-suit exhaust valve as I surfaced and put a bit of air back in the suit so I would have some positive buoyancy. Then I used the scooter on the surface to bring me to the stern of the dive boat.

There was a bit of rocking on the boat today due to the wind chop on the waters. There was no second dive for anyone today. My diving done, I found my bunk and fell fast asleep again until the changing sound of the engines, as we slowed through the inlet, let me know that we were almost home.

The Push for the Bridge – Rockaway, November 8, 2003

I had a great dive this morning at Rockaway Beach 9th Street, and once again managed to find some adventure at an otherwise mundane dive site. Vis was about 10 feet, temps were in the high 50s, and my dive was about 65 minutes. Almost Paradise, scheduled to close in October is miraculously still open now in November. But its days are numbered.

I have only been diving at Beach 9th for about a year and a half. Prior to that, I used to dive at Beach 6th Street, three blocks east. Back before the tragedy of September 11, 2001, it was fairly common for divers to go in from Beach 6th about 10 minutes before slack tide with dive flags, ride the current on the surface to the bridge, grab the pilings there, hang on until the tide slackened, and then descend for a great, sometimes dark and spooky dive amongst the pilings and bridge supports. Always lots of fish there. But after 9-11 and all the reports that the security minded Coast Guard might take your gear if you were caught near a bridge, diving the Atlantic Beach Bridge became less appealing. I never quite figured out why people were still able to dive Ponquogue Bridge after 9-11 without trouble from the Coast Guard.

Anyway, at the bridge, once you feel the current and tide start going out to sea again, the dive is over. Most divers surface at the bridge and ride the now-outgoing current back to Beach 6th Street on the surface. That's what I used to do. But then I started bringing a line with a clip at the end so that I could clip myself to the pilings while awaiting slack tide. This way I could relax, fluttering on the end of the line in the current. By the way, I still carry that line on every dive in a dry-suit pocket, and over the years it has proved invaluable. It is a 12-foot-long polypropylene buddy line with a Velcro wrist loop at each end. I made a permanent loop at one end and put a brass clip on the other. I have used it in many emergencies and situations underwater as a buddy line when visibility dropped to zero. I've used it to fasten myself to underwater objects in strong current so that I could rest, to "Tarzan" myself from piling to piling in high-current situations, to extend too-short dive flag lines, and to anchor my scooter to an object while digging. I have really found this thing useful.

Recently, Bob and I had started to plan some dives that included high-current situations at Rockaway. We had gone in a few times, letting the current carry us east for some distance, and we had even descended to the deep 45-foot area in strong current using the heavy cable as if we were mountain climbing. I decided that with proper planning, I could start considering a full "push for the bridge," the bridge being about a half a mile east of Beach 9th Street. The entire ride to the bridge and back would have to be underwater, with no surface current riding—as if this were a Navy SEAL assault on some military objective. (Okay, I'm allowed to have a bit of fun with this, right? I am still a kid at heart!)

Last week, my plan was to enter the water a good 20 to 30 minutes before slack with my scooter, *Apollo*. The scooter would remain turned off and clipped to a D-ring on my harness. I had a very full steel 104-cubic-foot tank. My ever-present canvas bag and secondary light would not be coming. I needed to stay very streamlined and hydrodynamic. I rigged my primary light so that it would be easy to reach yet out of the way of the scooter propeller. I decided not to wear a safety bottle hung off the side of my harness so that I would have less drag. I would ride the current to the bridge, or until I was down to half my gas, and then head back west riding *Apollo* at full speed.

So I went in configured as described above and let the current carry me east. After some initial excitement and anxiety about being flung into a rock or piling by the current, I relaxed and enjoyed the ride. After a while, I couldn't understand why I was not yet at the bridge, so I headed north and surfaced in shallow water to get my bearings. I was a bit east of Beach 6th Street.

Okay, back into the current. I continued east towards the bridge. Again, after what seemed to be an interminably long time, I heard one of those REAL BIG BOATS. I was in fairly deep water with no sense of how far north or south in the channel I was, so I turned on the scooter and headed due north to get out of the big boat's way. In a couple of minutes, I hit the sloping sand for the north beach and decided to surface again to see where I was. Now I was still about a half block west of the target. I looked at my remaining air, found about 1800 pounds left, and decided to abort the mission. I rode *Apollo* back to Beach 9th and decided I would try for the bridge again the following week. One of my concerns had been that, coming back on the scooter, I would miss Beach 9th Street. (It does all look very similar underwater.) No problem though: the deep 45-foot area is a unique characteristic to the Beach 9th area and makes it very easy to orientate yourself when coming back. Most of the channel on the north side is about 30 feet deep.

So much for that attempt.

This morning, with a weather forecast of a blustery but sunny day, I woke up at 4:47 a.m. as usual, a few minutes before the alarm went off. I fed the cat, packed my gear, and headed off to Rockaway to get in early for the 6:58 a.m. slack. I headed down to the water at about 6:40 a.m. and was configured exactly as I had been last weekend, except I had nitrox in my tank this time. I do much of my colder diving with nitrox to offset some of the decreased nitrogen unloading by the body's tissues caused by the extreme cold. When the water temperature drops below 50 degrees, I will switch to my heavier winter underwear, too.

I entered the water and found the vis to be a bit disappointing. So I decided that I would just tootle about locally, without running the risk of a high-speed crash into some immovable object on my scooter. I moved out into the channel, negatively buoyant, and slowly did the looking-at-rocks thing. I found an old, tarnished quarter, and then all of a sudden the current got me, moving me over the bottom. Because I was negative, I was moving slowly, basically touching and dragging on the bottom. No problem—I do this all the time. But now I saw that the vis was clearing up a bit, so I checked my air and decided to resume my mission, the push for the bridge!

Last weekend, at the end of the dive, I had lots of air left. I had turned around and headed back to my beach entry point using the scooter, with 1800 pounds of air. To my surprise I found that the trip back only consumed a few hundred pounds of air. So I decided that this week I would not surface to check where I was at all; I'd just let the current carry me to the bridge. I couldn't miss it. I remembered from a few years ago that it was very dark under the bridge, and there were huge pilings every 50 feet or so. If I missed the pilings, I would certainly notice the plunge into near-total darkness. So I put a bit more air in my dry suit and relaxed, letting the current take me.

So many spider crabs! This must be spider crab season. They are like little monsters! Some are a good two feet across with their claws extended. The bottom was carpeted with them, and when my knee or legs touched down on them, they were all over me in a second. I imagine that some divers—especially new divers—could really freak out during a mass-spider-crab attack. But they really can't do anything to you. Just keep your fingers out of their claws. Bit spooky though. If you saw the remake movie of Lost In Space, there is a scene in which these little crablike metal aliens are running rampant on the spacecraft, causing all sorts of grief. The scene is similar to what it's like if you stir up one of these nests of dozens of spider crabs. If you are diving with someone that is not prone to panic and you want to give them a visual image they will not soon forget, get their attention and then gently lie down on one of these spider crab nests so the little beasts crawl all over you. Be gentle though: we wouldn't want to hurt them now...

As I glided east, I passed at least five skates or rays, and there was a big striper that started circling me, like a boxer. When I saw him, I decided that I might be approaching the bridge now—the fish love the shelter of the bridge piers—so I turned on my light and left it hanging, in case I was suddenly in a low-light situation. I really enjoy riding the current. It's not for new divers, and gas usage and other things have to be thought out and planned in advance. But it is effortless, and when you are going as far as a half mile, quite relaxing. I rode up and down over some two- to three-foot-deep depressions or washouts that are perpendicular to the current flow. I was moving east, but I really could not tell where I was on the north-south axis.

I did know that the closer to the bridge I was, the more southerly the route of the REAL BIG BOATS would be. This was so they could make the drawbridge deep-channel section. I thought I was north of that channel, but I really couldn't tell. Now that I think about it, had I heard a REAL BIG BOAT and gone north to escape it, there would have been no guarantee that I was not south of the REAL BIG BOAT, my escape route having actually moved me into its path rather than out of its path. My plan for REAL BIG BOATS, though, was to go due north when I first heard one, so that, theoretically, those very loud engines would give me ample time to get away even if I was crossing the boat's path with my scooter at full speed. Hmmm. Those boats do get me a bit nervous. I have a book on tugboats, and from it I've learned that they have huge propellers. Some as big as eight feet across. I imagine that—even if the boats' draft was 15 feet and I was at 30 feet—maybe I could get sucked up into the prop? Or maybe the prop wash hurls you around? Have any divers been churned to chum by one of these tugboats, oil barges, or large fishing boats that regularly pass through this channel? Have you noticed how they come quite close to the Almost Paradise area because that is where the channel is deepest? These are REAL BIG BOATS.

Okay, now I've got myself ALL WORKED UP about the REAL BIG BOATS. Relax (for now).

All of a sudden, I saw a darkening up ahead. My apprehension jumped up a notch until I could see that it was a bridge pier and not a monster forming in the murky 10-foot vis. And then, like magic, the current stopped, and all of a sudden I was in a different world. Fish everywhere. Big, small—schools of tiny, metallic, reflecting fish. I saw enormous pilings on the bottom disappearing at funny angles into the total blackness of the shadow under the bridge. I checked my air. 1700 pounds! Yahoo! That meant I could even stay a few minutes and sightsee before heading back. I symbolically reached out and touched one of the bridge piers, resisting the urge to surface alongside it to see where I was on a north-south line. I was careful because I have heard that recent construction work on the bridge has left many pilings recoated with a heavy, staining layer of creosote—I didn't want to get that stuff on my dry suit or equipment! I didn't really recognize anything from my last visit here a few years ago. Oops! Time to go.

I always dive with a compass and have another attached to my scooter. I consulted them now, set a course for due west, and took off. Seconds later, I was back with all the fish, in the shadow of the bridge! Momentarily disoriented, I decided that the compasses were being thrown off by some metal in the bridge. I went in the opposite direction. Now away from the bridge, my compasses worked fine, and I felt that since I did not know my position on the north-south axis, I should get to a place where I could be certain I was on the north side of the channel, in case the current reversed and my scooter failed.

I decided to go due north now that I was certain I was a good distance from the bridge. So I went north, more north, and more north. I must have been all the way on the south side of the channel. Seeing the sandy north slope, I made a turn and now headed west for Beach 9th Street. The vis had improved and I was able to ride *Apollo* at the fastest speed without fear of hitting something. The water deepened and darkened. I slowed down and realized that I was probably in the 45-foot-deep area near the end of Beach 8th Street. Another minute and I was back at the cables that lead up to the cages at Beach 9th Street. It had taken me about 30 minutes to drift to the bridge but only six to ride back on my scooter. I was exhilarated. I turned off the scooter and followed the cable slowly up to the beach, swimming around slowly at about 16 feet deep, looking at rocks at my safety stop.

In the sheltered area at Beach 9th Street I practiced moving in the mid-water column at a constant depth with the scooter. It's not that easy. Usually, I scoot a few feet off the bottom, using the bottom to control my depth so that I don't have to keep checking my depth gauge. When using the scooter at a shipwreck, I can see the wreck and use that as a reference point. But using a depth gauge to maintain a constant depth while scootering without these other visual reference points can be tricky.

I surfaced to find my friend Bob waiting. I cleaned my gear off in the Almost Paradise showers, and then we headed over to the Sherwood Diner for breakfast.

Rockaway Diving the Dredge – November 29, 2003

High-wind conditions were not the only obstacle to overcome today at Beach 9th Street. Low visibility was compounded by the presence of one of the Weeks Marine Company dredges and the supporting boats and equipment operating at the site.

I suited up in the 35- to 45-mph gusts and decided to play it safe, slinging a 30-cubic-foot safety bottle on the side of my BC. Entry was easy, and the current immediately swept me east at a good clip. Before entering I had taken a bearing on

one of the pontoons that was supporting the huge pipe now running from the dredge in the mouth of the inlet almost to the Atlantic Beach Bridge. My scooter was fully charged and I was psyched for an exciting dive.

I had gone to both the Army Corps of Engineers website and the website for the Weeks Marine Company and had analyzed the situation. I had a good idea of what kind of dredging equipment was being used and what the dangers were. Clipped off to my harness was a three-and-a-half-foot-long piece of steel rebar that would be my "buddy" should I get sucked up into the three-foot-diameter intake pipe. All I would have to do would be to turn the steel bar perpendicular to my body; I would jam at the pipe entrance and not make that long, dark ride up into the pumping system of the dredge.

The current was still ripping, so I set *Apollo* to its fastest setting and headed for mid-channel, actually at a 45-degree angle into the current. That current was faster than I had thought. Within a couple of minutes, my steel tank clanged as I struck against something hard: it was an enormous cement block. I turned off my scooter, and, in the swirling of the incoming tide, could just make out the edges of the block. It was pyramid-shaped, with a large iron ring at the apex to which was shackled a heavy steel cable that ran up towards the surface. I touched the cable near where it was attached to the ring. It shuddered with a rhythm that echoed the wind-driven waves as they struck the pontoon anchored some 35 feet above me. I was on the lee side of the concrete block now, sheltered from the strong current, and I made sure *Apollo* was clipped off to me. I slowly began going up the cable. Every three or four seconds it vibrated greatly, and I heard a dull clanging, almost like a buoy heard in the distance through a dense fog.

I was still about 20 feet deep when it occurred to me that the sound might be the huge metal pontoon banging against the large pipe it supported, due to wave action. That was a possibility, that something was loose; perhaps I might get swept into the space between the pontoon and the pipe and get crushed to death. I decided that I would just go up high enough to see the bottom of the pontoon and no farther, and I did just that. I reached up and touched its yellow-painted exterior and descended again along the steel cable.

Just then I heard a very low thrumming sound, a sound more felt than heard. A large boat, perhaps a tug approaching. In addition to the pipe and the dredge, I had noted two large tugboats and another smaller utility boat, a barge with a buoy-deployment/retrieval apparatus on it, and a large barge with a huge crane on it. There was not much time for me to analyze the sound. I figured it was one of the tugs and decided that I would be pretty safe if I stayed right with the large concrete anchor as it would shield me from the prop wash, would give me something to hold on to, and was taller than I was; no propeller could hit me if I was right next to it. I grabbed on to the iron ring and lay flush against the side of the block. The deep sound got louder and louder and became a roar.

I had expected it to pass, but it seemed to be staying right near me. Sometimes slightly louder, sometimes a bit less, but always a roar. Now I was a bit nervous. I didn't know where the tug was, so I didn't know which way to go to safely escape. I had let go of the ring and had grabbed the steel cable right above the shackle because I saw the shackle shifting around and didn't want to lose my hand or a finger in the ring. I checked my air and saw that I was okay in that department—I still had about 2000 pounds.

About three or four minutes went by like this, me hanging on the cable, shielded against the concrete block. I noticed that the current had gone slack. Right about then, the roar also stopped, and I could hear clanging sounds. There was a sudden slackening in the steel cable, and, all of a sudden, the shade of the overhead pontoon vanished and was replaced by sunlight filtering down from the surface. At the same moment that the cable slackened, I saw a dark shape hurtling down from the surface. I rolled to the side, and another heavy shackle struck with a thud against the concrete block not two

feet from where I had been. It slid down to the channel bottom along the side of the pyramid.

Now I realized that the boat I had heard had been one of the tugboats working the barge with the buoy-deployment/retrieval apparatus; it had been engaged in pulling the pontoon above me out of the water and onto the barge. And they had then inadvertently lost the line to the concrete block in the process. It now lay on the bottom, almost at my feet. I considered doing the rescue thing. I would have loved to have seen the look on their faces as I surfaced to pass them the line to their lost concrete anchor!

As fate would have it, I was not given that opportunity. In fact, I was about to be in serious trouble. I hadn't noticed another line running up to the surface from the second shackle. It all became clear as they pulled up on it. The steel line rose off the seafloor at a rapid pace, probably being rolled up on some big drum. I didn't know what to do. This concrete block had been my friend until now, but I could be crushed in seconds if I got stuck under it or between it and the tug boat or barge. So I did the only thing I could think of. I hung on for dear life. I watched as the slack was pulled out of the steel cable, and the huge block—with me on it—began to lift off of the bottom. The machinery on the barge was so powerful that there was no hesitation between the moment at which the last bit of slack was taken up and the moment at which the block began to rise. All I could think to do was to remember to keep exhaling during the forced ascent.

As I broke the water about 20 feet from the deck of the barge, workers on the barge pointed and yelled. I thought they were yelling at me but they were yelling at each other. They must have thought I was dead and tangled in the cable. I was about 15 feet above the water and about 20 feet from the deck of the barge, hanging from some kind of derrick framework off the stern of the barge. I really didn't have a great grip on the cable, and now that I was out of the water and getting buffeted by the winds my steel tank, scooter, and safety bottle were feeling really heavy. I couldn't hold on anymore, and, weighted by all of my equipment, I slid off the block back into the water. One hand went to my mask, and with the other I braced the scooter against my side so that it wouldn't kill me when we hit the water. I sank to the bottom and decided that maybe I should not hang around here any more. I had noted, when I'd momentarily surfaced, that the tugboat was at the other end of the barge, so I turned on my scooter and headed due north for Beach 9th Street.

Okay, Okay. So I made up the story. But I did go to Beach 9th Street today to dive, and I did find a huge pipe in the middle of the channel. All the equipment described in the story was likewise present. It looks like the Weeks Marine Company is re-dredging the inlet, a job which is under contract to the U.S. Army Corps of Engineers. They last dredged East Rockaway Inlet in 1995, 1997, and 1998, and they are apparently using a Cutterhead-Pipeline-type dredge. The dredging equipment I photographed at the site today, along with the huge pipe down the center of the channel on those yellow pontoons, seems to match information on the U.S. Army Corp of Engineers website. More interesting information on the Weeks Marine Company is also available on the web. Both websites can be found by Googling them.

Bayville – Sunday, January 4, 2004
A light rain was falling as I dove at the Bayville Barge off of Wall's Wharf Sunday morning 9:00 a.m. The Long Island Sound was as smooth as glass—not a ripple. A heavy pea-soup fog reduced visibility offshore to about 100 feet. Occasionally, the early-morning stillness was punctuated by muffled explosions. A local resident informed me that the sounds were from a gun club to the southeast of the dive site. The shots echoed as if they were much closer.

The vis looked great from shore—about 12 to 15 feet, with a water temperature of 41 degrees. Last week, I got annoyed at my Weezle Booties. They are so thick that it becomes a hassle pulling the dry-suit legs over them. So for this dive I left those heavy booties at home and wore heavy ski socks over my polyethylene sock liners. Big mistake. My feet got cold. Because I was also using the scooter, my hands also got cold (as they always do when I use the scooter in cold water). So I was glad to leave the water after 51 minutes. I was towing another diver for much of the time, and as we circled around we came upon a large school of fish. There were thousands of the small, silvery, two-inch-long fish. Maybe killies or something. They were schooling around the wreck, the entire group turning this way and that as if following some invisible conductor or choreographer. Behind this large mass of schooling fish was the dark, shadowy form of the wreck. It was a bit spooky, especially as we were scootering down near the silty bottom, leaving a cloud of zero-vis water behind us. Circling around the wreck, we encountered our own trail of silt clouds and suddenly went from marveling at the little fishies to battling sea monsters in zero vis. I instantly turned off the scooter, and we drifted like spacemen, unable to see any lights or gauges. A minute or so later, it had calmed down. I motioned to my buddy to grab on again, and we headed away from the wreck for clearer pastures. We roamed around a bit, and when we returned to the wreck—this time at a higher altitude off the seafloor, so as to not silt it up—the schooling fish were gone. We enjoyed some time exploring the now-familiar wreck. Whatever the name of that wooden ship, she had been quite wide. One of these days I'm gonna measure it.

Rockaway Beach, 9th Street – Sunday, January 11, 2004

I stopped by Beach 9th Street on Saturday just to check out the visibility and the dredging. I managed to speak to one of the workers on one of the utility barges. He said that the dredge had broken down and was being fixed, I think in Carolina. In any event, they are not dredging near Beach 9th, even though that's where their base of operations is. When the dredge returns, it will continue operations off Rockaway Beach, some distance to the west of Far Rockaway.

My fictional story about a dive to the concrete blocks that anchor the yellow pontoons allowed me to exercise my creativity, but it had brought me no real answers. Curious now, I asked this worker how they REALLY anchored the pontoons. He pointed to a fairly large, four-foot-wide anchor on the deck of the work barge. So while my story mentioned pyramidal concrete blocks, actually they were using standard stockless metal anchors that are shaped just like a large ship's anchor to secure these pontoons. So much for my imagination!

I went out on the jetty. It was low tide, and I could clearly see the bottom wherever I looked. Heading back to my car, I ran into Jay, the ex-proprietor of Almost Paradise, pulling up in his grey van. He visibly shivered when I told him the vis looked great and that I would be back Sunday to dive. He also said, "It's a done deal," referring to the closure of Almost Paradise and the start of new construction. To be honest, as long as I can get to the water I am happy. Although it did help to be able to clean my gear off in the hot showers there, for $19.00 per dive.

Hearing that Sunday's morning air temperature would be about six degrees, I picked up two thermos bottles—a small one for coffee, and a big one for possible de-icing operations upon leaving the water. Sunday morning, I put boiling water in the large thermos, got an egg sandwich at the Sherwood Diner, and put a coffee in the little thermos. I got to Beach 9th at about 8:45 a.m. and went out to check the vis. Even better than Saturday. I spoke to one of the barge workers, let him know that I'd be in the water east of Beach 9th, and confirmed that they would not be going east of the Beach 9th Street jetty.

I have a whole procedure for this super-cold diving. It starts at home, where I put on long polypropylene underwear and socks and make sure that I have my gloves and a hat. At the dive site, I put on my Weezle Extreme Plus dive underwear and their thick booties, on top of the polypropylenes, and I set up my gear. Then the gear goes back into the back of my station wagon, and I sit up front again with the heat blasting for about 20 minutes. Finally, the dry suit goes on, and I do a final check of my gear. Once the dry suit and my two hoods are on, I am quite well protected from wind and chill, and, actually, the issue becomes preventing overheating—even in these very low outside temps. I don't want my underwear to get sweat soaked either.

I brought my scooter down to leave on the beach at the entry point, and, as I was heading back across the sand, I saw a NYPD Emergency Services police truck pull to a halt at the end of the road. Two cops jumped out. Hmm. With my beard, scooter, and scuba gear, I was concerned that they might think I was a terrorist of some kind.

I thought of saying "Don't shoot! Please!" Maybe they'd find it funny if I ran towards them, shouting some gibberish in a Middle Eastern accent. Maybe I *wouldn't* do that. Not this time. Perhaps I could just say, in halting English, "I am looking for the Wombatsian Embassy." Or—I have it—I could look very surprised, then disappointed, and say, "Oh, THIS isn't France. Can you nice officers just point me in the right direction please?"

Well I did none of that. But I did feel that I had do some explaining. I told them I was a regular cold-water diver here. They interrupted me to say, "Oh, don't worry, we don't care if you dive here." It turned out that one of them was a diver too—more of the warm-water type. We talked a bit about the cold-weather gear I was using, and I invited him to come to the Sea Gypsies Dive Club monthly meeting as a guest. He asked for my number, so I went back to my car and, as I came back to enter the water, I handed him my card. He took it from my dry-gloved hand, told me to stay safe, and then they were off to fight crime. I sank beneath the water's surface.

The water was 39 degrees, and the air was six degrees. Vis was at least 40 feet. I know this because—lying on my back at 40 feet and staring straight up—I could see ripples on the surface. Not much life down there except for *moi*, but I had a great time. I scootered to Beach 6th Street, trying to locate the area where I and another diver once recovered that antique, Admiral-Style Folding Stock anchor I mentioned in an earlier story. I had always wanted to dive in that general area in super-good vis, to look for other objects. Maybe there is a complete boat still down there, the source of the anchor we found on that January day.

That right glove area is still leaking a bit. Didn't bother me last week in Bayville at 20 feet, but today at 40, I got a bit wet on my right hand, wrist, and arm. My dry-suit underwear still keeps me toasty when wet, so it was not a big deal. Just annoying. And every time I use the scooter for more than a minute or so, leak or no leak, my hands get really cold from the flow of water over them. I'm either going to get some heavy concrete-mixing gloves to pull over my dry gloves, or I'll make some kind of shield for my hands and attach it the scooter. I still cannot find that pesky leak. I think my dry suit will have to go to its manufacturer, Diving Unlimited International in San Diego, soon for a neck-seal change, general inspection, and repair. I have this funny picture in my mind: my dry suit, sitting in a chaise lounge chair, poolside at some fancy place in California. It's probably sipping a drink, chatting, and exchanging dive stories with the other suits that arrive there from all over the world.

I saw a skate. I wonder if this is always the same skate I see at Beach 9th Street. Not a particularly bright one, not the sharpest knife in the draw, as my father-in-law, who is from the north of England, might say. Maybe this skate got left behind when all the others went south for the winter. I also saw a couple of crabs, and that was it in the wildlife department. Scootered back to the Beach 9th Street jetty and used my three-minute stop at 15 feet to vent the suit. That's always a bit tricky with this Weezle underwear. It takes time to get the air out. Once I had surfaced, I decided to ride the scooter on the surface a bit. I was amazed that, as I scootered out past the jetty, I could see clear to the seafloor.

My dive lasted a total of 40 minutes, and I had no gear-freeze-up problems while scootering on the surface and once out of the water. Within a few minutes, I was back in my car and enjoying a chocolate chip cookie and the steaming coffee from my thermos. What a great way to start a day!

Non-Dive Report Rockaway Beach 9th Street – Sunday, February 8, 2004

It's been almost a month since my last dive. That dive at Rockaway had 40-foot-plus visibility. This has been a brutal winter. Since that dive, I have made three trips to Beach 9th Street and have not dived due to poor vis as observed from the jetty.

Today, I awoke at 6:30 a.m. (normal time for me anyway). There is a peaceful state of mind these days heading to Rockaway in what is probably the coldest windy snowiest winter I can remember. The sun is rising, low in the sky – just the right angle to be in my eyes as I turn onto the Van Wyck Expressway heading south. Early Sunday morning talk radio keeping me company. I switch stations. Sunday morning there is generally two flavors of talk radio, Religious and Political. Neither appeals to me today, I turn the radio off as I make the right onto Rockaway Blvd. I can see the wind, the few trees as I pass Kennedy Airport wave in the 35mph gusts of wind at me, their branches seeing me off on my mission. A whistle of wind enters the car through a slightly open window – its whispering voice reminding me that with a wind such as this there is not a chance in 100 that there will be any vis. I continue. It is a beautiful morning, all blue skies and sun.

I stop at the diner to fill my thermos with hot coffee and my stomach with an egg sandwich. One hand unwraps the sandwich, the other steers and soon the breakfast is gone washed down with gulps of coffee. Now, I turn onto Beach 9th. A large patch of ice in the roadway reminds me that outside my toasty warm car its still winter out there. I see the crane on the dredge utility barge in the storage position, head down, as if sleeping and think to myself –" Good, at least they're not working today". Pulling to a stop behind some dilapidated white car, with its engine running and a bearded man asleep behind the wheel.

Oh, I forgot my hat and gloves! I close up my coat as tight as possible and step out of my warm car. Now I see the swirling clouds of sand, little tornados here and there. The wind drives the sand against my exposed face. It hurts. I wince when I think what it must be doing to the finish on my car. I hear the throaty growl of a diesel marine engine and see the tugboat next to the barge with the sleeping crane hard at work doing something. In the distance, out west I see the dredge, smokestacks belching thick black clouds of oily smoke as it does whatever it does.

Well. I'm here. So I walk out onto the jetty to look at the vis. When I walk out on the jetty, I have to remind myself to take my cold hands out of my jacket pockets – so if I slip I can use my hands to catch my fall. On an excellent day you can see the sand – maybe through five or more feet of water. A mediocre day, with your eye you can pick out a rock and follow it below the surface. Does it look clear? Try to estimate how much water is between you and the edge of that rock. Look at the area where the waves are breaking. Is there a bluish/greenish cast to the breaking waves, or is it like this morning – ripples in a cup of brown coffee?

A sigh, a couple of gulls screech as they circle overhead, teasing me for coming out with any hope on this windy winters morning. There on the end of the jetty, I scrunch up my coat closer to me and hunch up my shoulders against the wind. I turn and look at Almost Paradise, now run down and even more dilapidated looking than ever. I have only been here for a minute or so, my car is still nice and warm. I am headed home...

THE "BAYVILLE BARGE"

LONG ISLAND SOUND

RUMORED SUBMARINE DEBRIS FIELD

JETTY (underwater mostly)

HIGH WATER MARK

BEACH

WALLS WHARF RESTAURANT
EXCELLENT CHOWDER
19 GREENWICH AVE
BAYVILLE, NY 11709

HOUSES

WHITE BUOY

20' DEEP

UNKNOWN 'DARK SPOT' ON SATELLITE IMAGE

TO FERRY BEACH

N E S W

© THE WHARVES PROJECT 2005

CHAPTER THREE

Bottle Hunting, Jellyfish, Recovery of 100-year-old dates, diving the Oregon, and Home Depot

First Boat Dive of 2004 (USS San Diego) – May 1, 2004

I'm going out on the *Eagle's Nest* dive boat this morning to visit my favorite local wreck, the USS *San Diego*. When I went to sleep about 10 p.m., I put a Bonine on the night stand to be taken around 12, if I woke up then. Predictably, I did wake up, but decided to climb out of bed and check the Islip Buoy wave heights before committing myself to 48 hours of sleepy, grouchy, Bonine-induced side effects. Even though at eight p.m. the waves had been increasing in height, I saw that they had been stable at three feet for the past couple of hours. So I took the anti-seasick pill and went back to sleep.

My alarm goes off. It's 4:00 a.m. I try to shut if off, desperately hitting buttons, but now the radio comes on. Half asleep, I grope, and by chance find the right button to turn the damn thing off. Too late. Lynda, my better half, is angry.

"You wake me up AND I don't even get a kiss? Please be careful, and give me a call when you get out of the water."

I recently moved, and in this garage I can lock my car at night. So now I load the car the night before, and it's all about just throwing on some clothes I'd put aside in the living room the night before. I'm out in 10 minutes. Good, the note I put on the windshield of my car warning that I'd be leaving at four a.m. worked. I'm not blocked in. I'm outta here! (After taking another half a Bonine.)

There are a few erratic drivers out here at this hour, and I have to remind myself not to be one of them. It would not be good to get pulled over for speeding and miss the boat going to the dive site. I put on cruise control, set it for two miles over the speed limit, patch in the autopilot, and decide to take a quick snooze while my car heads for Long Beach, Long Island.

I wake up as the alarm—"Pull up! Pull up!"—is going off. That's the C.A.S., or collision avoidance system. I got the system out of an old Pan Am airliner. Though it still says "pull up," what it means now is "Slow down! Your exit's coming up!" Gotta fix that someday.

Good ol' Bob is parked on the side of the road right outside the parking lot for Howard Klein's boat, the *Eagle's Nest*. "Its not five a.m. yet," he warns. "Still have 10 minutes. Better not show up on board waking everyone up."

Courtesy of Captain
Howard Klein

You know, he's right. Why start the day off getting yelled at? So we chat for a couple of minutes and then start unloading.

Oh, the boat is really full. Every good spot for equipment is already taken, and I have to put my equipment box on the dreaded upper deck. I hate when that happens. But I'm happy as a clam to be here, excited about my dive, so what the hell!

In anticipation of Howard's great barbeque, I have brought a 36-inch-long strip of what I tenderly call minky meat. Another name for it is skirt steak. I give it to Captain Howard to marinate. It'll be cooking while we're all in the water.

Both Bob and I have some interest in underwater surveying/ mapping, and I'd taken some interesting workshops last Saturday on that subject at a diving-related event in Sandy Hook, New Jersey. I picked up a new measuring tape for underwater use, and today I've also brought a slate. Last season, I sketched one of the USS San Diego's anchors, and on this dive I want to get its measurements. So the plan is for Bob and I to have some fun measuring, and to do some exploring. We are wearing double tanks with 32% oxygen and are planning for up to 45 minutes of bottom time before ascending. I'll be decompressing on pure O_2, and Bob will use 38% and do a longer decompression.

Bottom temperatures are in the high 30s, but we are fine. We DO dive in the winter, you know. But I am slightly disorientated when we get down to the wreck. We start off swimming in one direction, and then Bob has us reverse, which brings us to the bow after a hefty swim. From the dark side, we round the bow to the starboard anchor. That anchor is eight feet across, five-feet nine-inches high, and looks, well, like a big anchor. There is a porthole under (it was originally above) the upside-down anchor. Two-inch-thick glass lays there on the sand like a yellowish, dirty crescent moon, right where it had fallen out of the porthole. We head back around the bow, back to the ascent line, and find that we still have both time and gas, so we head to the stern of the 500-foot-long ship, swim around a bit under the giant prop shafts, and then head back to the base of the ascent line. We're 40 minutes into the dive, and it's time to head for the surface.

On the way up, I have time to think. The vis is excellent— probably 30 to 40 feet or more. There were lots of fish down there, and we just had a great time. The ascent is uneventful. We stop at 70, 40, 30, and 20 feet, and we're soon back on the dive boat, after a total time in the cold water of a bit over an hour.

Time to eat. In addition to the skirt steak, there's venison, hamburger, sausage, and steak. What a feast! I generally do a single long dive rather than two shorter dives if I'm going deeper than 80 feet. So I'm out of my dive gear fast. Belly full, I lie down on one of the bunks and fall asleep. Most of the rest of the divers will do a second dive. Their dives will last about 30 minutes, from the time they enter the water until the time they're back on the boat.

I'm looking forward to a great dive season.

Bottle Hunting on the "Asfalto" Wreck – May 15, 2004

It's sometime near the beginning of the summer of 1932, perhaps mid May, just like now. The place? New York City's Lower East Side, bustling and alive.

The camera is up high, taking in New York's growing skyline from the top of the Brooklyn Bridge, which is only one year away from its 50th birthday. The camera zooms in to settle on a four-story walk-up tenement building, passing markets, street stalls, the sounds of a radio coming from this apartment, bits of conversation in some foreign language from that apartment. Finally, we settle on a third-floor family. The windows are open to the fire escape, and we are positioned there, looking into the kitchen. Supper is over, and the table has been cleared.

"... And then take the garbage downstairs please, before you start on your homework."

"Momma? Can I listen to the Dr. Doolittle show on the radio? It's about to start."

"No, take the garbage downstairs first,"

replies Momma, dropping an empty cobalt-blue bottle which had once contained cough medicine into the small paper-lined garbage bin.

The young boy carries the paper bag down the stairs to the row of garbage cans in front and removes the lid of one, squishing the bag down into the almost-full can. There is so much garbage in the can that he must leave the lid ajar. Excited to listen to his radio show, he runs back upstairs, taking them two at a time. An hour later, a young man walks by, drinking a bottle of soda pop.

He finishes it, sees the lid ajar, and slides the empty bottle under the edge of it.

Late 1920's Garbage Truck

Photo: NYC Dept. of Sanitation

Now it's later, the wee hours of the morning, and local residents are treated to the sounds of the noisy garbage truck. Burly men pick up the garbage and leave the lids on the ground, tossed aside, just like they do today.

The truck ends up at a pier, and there it is offloaded onto an old steel hulled sailing schooner left over from the days of sail. Where the deck and masts used to be is now a gaping space, some reinforcement beams have been added, some huge davits added too. But now, however graceful and fast she was in life, she has been doomed for decades to be towed behind an ungainly tug hauling her load of garbage miles out into the ocean to be dumped.

Does she cry when the rustling of garbage from a breeze reminds her of her ability to fly before the wind in a previous life? No one knows it but this will be her last trip to sea. She will rest still carrying her load of refuse, the snapshot of New York City life in the early twentieth century. There is no information on her demise other than the fact that she now lies 95 feet deep on the bottom of the Atlantic Ocean some 16 miles south of Jones Inlet. Ocean dumping here by New York City ended in 1935 as the result of lawsuits brought by New Jersey.

I am awakened by the engines of the dive boat *Jeannie II* as they throttle down. We tie into the wreck. This early in the dive season, the waters are still a cold 45 degrees, and there are only three other divers on the boat. That's great! Lots of room. I wait until the first two are in the water and then start to suit up, still a bit sluggish from my Bonine-induced nap. Word from the mate who tied us in is that vis is great—some 30 to 40 feet. The other divers will be doing two dives each, and I my usual single long dive.

The shock of the cold water hitting my face wakes me fully, and I descend the long line to the wreck. Today, instead of a measuring tape and slate, I am armed with my little red canvas bag and a small gardener's shovel. The wreck unfolds beneath me, 60 feet below. I stop for a second, trying to take in all the features and landmarks on and around this broken ship, which I have never explored before. I see that someone has placed a strobe light at about 85 feet deep on the ascent line. That's good. This wreck is sitting on a silt bottom, the result of the effluence and continuation of the Hudson River, miles to the north. Any digging on the bottom will raise clouds of this silt, reducing visibility to zero. I am glad there are only a few other divers, and I warned them on the boat that I am a digger. They may not want to come near me.

The wreck curves off to the left under me, an arc of broken hull, a shape it could never have had while still a living, working ship. There to my left some 40 feet away is the bow section, and what is that to its left? Looks like a pile of New York City trash, after 75 years underwater. This actually looks nothing like garbage now. After 75 years, paper products are gone. Food-type garbage is gone, except for a number of large bones. Hmm, some of this garbage must have come from a slaughterhouse or meat packing company. It looks like it spilled out of the barge right before she hit the bottom, forming a neat little flat pile which rises about eight inches off the silty bottom. At this time, because I have not touched the bottom, visibility is great. I do note a rising cloud in the distance as some of the other divers search her remains.

I look over the pile and instantly am rewarded by the sight of a bottle neck. I pull it out of the muck. Alas, it is broken off at the neck. I drop it. These small actions are already raising silt, enough that I can't see anything in the small area I'm exploring. I look a bit more, and now I see a tiny clear bottle, still intact. I put it carefully into my red bag. The mound I am working is circular, about 15 feet across. I decide to go around its perimeter in a circle, fanning with my hands so as to remove a couple inches of silt. Of course, you can't see anything when you do that, so my plan is to work in a circle, in several phases. First, I do the fanning thing, with my hands, to brush away the top silt. Then—because I am working in a circle—I arrive back at my starting point, which is settling down. I wait patiently a few minutes as the water clears to see what I have uncovered. Now I go around the circle, following my settling silt, looking and poking a bit with my shovel. I am rewarded with another clear, small bottle, then a larger, purple, medicinal-type bottle. Water pressure has pushed a cork down into one of the little bottles. It's like a ship in a bottle. Another small bottle has a cork still sealing the top, just as it would have had in its former life.

I have been working with this single pile for about 25 minutes and now decide to explore a bit. Visibility in my general area has become lousy as a result of my digging. Earlier, I took a compass bearing from my "mound" and noted my position in relation to a large feature on the wreck so that I'd be able to find the wreck if I became totally silted in. I am carrying a reel of line, but I've opted not to use it—I did not want to get tangled in it while doing my circling stuff. No problem—I make it the few feet to the wreck and explore around the bow, poking here and there with my shovel. I rise up to the top of the bow, about 15 feet off the ocean floor. The vis is much better here. In the distance I see the strobe light advertising where the ascent line is. The overall vis is clearing up nicely;

the other divers have all gone back up to the ship long ago. I still have a little less than half my 45 minutes of total bottom time remaining. I check my gas—lots left, even with all my digging. I'm a bit surprised, but I remember that this dive, at 95 feet, is shallower than the 110-foot dive I did two weeks ago on the USS *San Diego*.

I stay at the height of the bow for a while, surveying the rapidly clearing expanse of ribs and ship pieces beneath me. There is a large, three-foot-long davit. That must have been near the bow, to tow her. Other remains of winches and equipment can also be seen near the bow. The ribs stretch out into the distance as far as I can see. Some fish dart in and out of openings, furtively watching me to see what I am going to do with their garbage.

The ship is fairly easy to navigate by simply following its broken back, so I set off gliding a couple of feet above it, always checking for the strobe light. I follow a path of strewn debris and all of a sudden realize that I have not looked for the flashing light for a while. I can't see it. Visibility is fine. I slowly rise up about 10 feet from my position down near the bottom. Oh, there it is, that way. I turn to it, checking my bottom time, which was now at about 44 minutes. My original plan was 45 minutes on the bottom with some flexibility built in, depending on gas usage and other conditions.

Now, some 10 feet from the base of the ascent line (which ends in chain tied into the wreck), I spy a beautiful bottle neck sticking out from the steel mesh of a four-foot-square crab trap that is half buried and full of all sorts of stuff. Pieces of commercial fishing gear, nets, and traps like these are commonly found on shipwrecks in our area. They get stuck on the wreck and are cut loose by the fishing boat passing above, creating a new habitat for sea life and sometimes an entanglement hazard for SCUBA divers. There is no entanglement hazard here, though, and I am only 10 feet from the ascent line, and this bottle looks like a real nice one. I jostle it. It feels intact, but only the neck is sticking out. It is too big to pull through the two-inch-wide opening in the crab trap. I'm going in. I check my gas—lots left. I also have a lot of oxygen, in addition to my back gas, so I can stay longer and still safely decompress.

I start digging inside the crab trap with my shovel carefully so that broken glass does not cut open my dry gloves. I am now about 49 minutes into the dive. I am enveloped in my very own cloud of silt. Since I am so close to the ascent line, I do not worry. I let the cloud settle and dig a bit more. As visibility goes to zero again, I gently hold onto the corner of the crab trap so that I know where I am. I don't want to let go and reach out for it again, as there is a lot of broken glass around. Don't want to grab onto a broken bottle.

This is taking longer than I thought. I decide it's time to stop. But I can't see anything—not even my gauges. So I wait. No problem, I have lots of air. I let go of the crab trap now, and in those brief two seconds I become totally disoriented. I cannot see any gauges. I think I'm neutrally buoyant, but I can't see my depth gauge to confirm that I am not rising without knowing it. I get scared for a second and resist the instinctive urge to flee. Trying to stay very still, I slowly reach out for the crab trap but find only silt. My hand sinks into it a bit, adding to the billowing clouds. Finally, there is something there, a piece of metal. I hang onto it, keeping the rest of my body motionless, waiting for the silt to clear again. Now all I want to do is get out of here. I'll already have a longer deco than I had planned, I'm a bit chilled, I got my bottles—I just want to go home.

Just stay still and wait. Don't try to find the ascent line. You have gas. Just wait. And wait. If you do go off looking now, because of the zero vis there is a good chance you'll swirl up or hit the bottom, adding to the problem. Just wait. Seems like forever.

I start to formulate a plan to ascend 20 feet—hopefully above the cloud—and then to look for the ascent line. I decide to wait—that will be the last-ditch emergency plan. I also don't want to tie my reel to something and do a circle search for the line. It'll settle. Just wait. I dive in low/zero vis a lot—it's not new to me. Been here before. Just wait. Slowly it clears, and to my right, not three feet away, I can see a fragment of the chain at the base of the ascent line. It's coming out of one cloud of silt and rising into another cloud higher up. I move for the line, checking my bottom time. I'm at 53 minutes, way over the 30-minute no-decompression limits for the 32% nitrox I'm breathing. I begin a very slow hand-over-hand ascent to my first decompression stop, which is for one minute at 70 feet.

I'm wearing a wrist slate with a deco schedule for the USS *San Diego*, which sits at 110 feet. Before the dive, I decided to follow that schedule, a schedule for a dive which is actually 15 feet deeper than I would ever get on this dive. At the 70-foot stop, I turn off my dive light and clip it closer to me, checking that I have clipped it to double lock my red canvas bag so that I don't lose my prize finds.

Whenever I do a one-minute stop, I usually wait for two minutes to pass on my dive computer. That ensures that I stop for at least one minute plus part of another. (No second hands on dive computers.) I continue up, doing my three minutes at 40 feet and my five minutes at 30 feet. Finally I'm at 20 feet. I switch to my pure-oxygen stage bottle and settle in for the 14-minute wait. If I were not using pure oxygen at this stage, I'd have to stay here about 39 additional minutes to maintain the same level of conservativeness in my decompression schedule. While it's somewhat warmer now at 20 feet, I am still a bit cool, and I close the exhaust valve of my suit and put some air back into it to get a bit warmer. I look around for the elusive shark that awaits divers on long deco hangs. He's nowhere to be found.

Before going in, I told the dive-boat crew that my dive would be about an hour long. I am sure they see my bubbles and know that I'm on the line, so they don't get worried about me. Finally, I reopen my dry-suit exhaust valve and slowly surface. I've been down 75 minutes. I still have enough back gas to complete the longer deco had there been a problem with my oxygen bottle.

Back on the boat, I am offered a hot dog. No thanks. I get out of my gear and wolf down some barbequed chicken I brought. I find a place in the cabin to curl up for a while, but soon I awaken to find the other divers getting geared up to go back in the water. I take this as my cue to go back upstairs and find a place to lie down in the sun. I am quickly fast asleep again. Later, I learn that other divers also recovered bottles from this wreck, a wreck which will produce treasures easily for at least a few more years.

On the way back to the dock, we stop so a crew member can raise a fishing boat's anchor off of Sandy Hook, using a big lift bag. The anchor was lost some time ago by one of the party boats out of Sheepshead Bay, its location marked with a float. Captain Bill Reddan will later return it to a grateful owner.

It was a great day, and I recommend the Asfalto wreck. It's a great dive. I will go back. Maybe I'll bring *Apollo* to help me dig.

Addendum
I have a couple of books on old bottles from the New York Area. The types of bottles I found are from the early twentieth century, between 1910 and 1930. This is based on the shape of the top of the bottle, where the cork would go. A lot of late nineteenth-century bottles had bulbous tops that were more rounded (our modern garbage could easily contain stuff from 30 or 40 years ago, and the same held true back then). The cobalt blue bottle in my story contained medicine. More specifically, bottles of that color contained substances you might want to think twice about drinking, the deep blue color serving as a warning to folks. Of course, our modern Milk of Magnesia comes in a bottle of that color. I guess if you drink a whole bottle of that stuff, you'd wish it had been poison!

Bayville Barge – May 22, 2004
"A spider's web!" I thought, as the thin gossamer threads caught the sunlight some five feet above me, easy to see even through the poor vis. I didn't have time to wonder why I might be seeing a spider's web here, of all places, as I began my descent to the wreck. OUCH! It felt like my upper lip was on fire! That small space, somewhat covered by my mustache right below the mask, was BURNING!

Jellyfish tentacles. And one had found its way onto the only exposed skin I had—my upper lip. I could still see the very fine, glittering tentacles all around me. I was right in the middle of them. I used my dry-gloved finger to brush the stingers off my upper lip and kept my hand there to protect myself. Seconds later, I was out of the stinging thicket, wondering how much my lip would ultimately swell. Rubbing the stinging lip hard seemed to help.

I continued my descent. I was a bit disappointed by the poor vis. Oleg and I had planned to make a rough sketch of the wreck, which was some 20 feet deep now at mid-incoming tide. The vis looked great in the shallower water, but it turned sour here right at the wreck, this wreck without a history—the Bayville Barge.

We had tied off a dive flag to the white mooring ball that by coincidence marked the southeast corner of the wreck. We then followed the ribs of the hull to the bow—or to what we thought might be the bow. Once there, we gave up trying to draw the wreck. We could see so little of it in the lousy vis. We decided to surface to see where the bow was relative to the other end of the wreck. I tied off a reel and we ascended slowly. At about 10 feet, we paused to listen again for boat engines and then continued up. Next time, I'll use that safety sausage. I knew there was a reason I carry it.

To our surprise, there was a fishing boat complete with engine not 20 feet from where we surfaced.

Yikes, I thought. "How long have you been there with your engine off?" I yelled out to the two fishermen on board. I was wondering why I hadn't heard the motor.

"Oh, we saw the dive flag so we rowed over—the engine's been off. Can you help us? One of our traps is stuck on something."

I was attached by my reel to the wreck, so Oleg went over and freed their large crab trap. They gratefully rowed off again.

We were surprised at how long this wreck was—it seemed to be about 150 feet from where we were at the bow to the white ball buoy at the end of the wreck. Oleg and I decided to stick with the bow area and to try to sketch it roughly, maybe an additional 10 to 20 feet of the wreck as well. He started back down my line, I waited a minute, and then I followed, reeling in the line as I went. At nine feet deep, I had a problem. Couldn't clear my ears. So back up I went, all the way to the surface. I couldn't even clear my ears on the surface. The fishing boat was quietly rocking in the tiny waves about 50 yards west of me. I looked southwest and saw a work boat heading east at full throttle, between me and the beach and running parallel to it.

"Doesn't he see our dive flag?" I thought. I prepared myself to descend really fast—ears clear or not—if he headed towards me.

The work boat stopped right at the white mooring ball and hooked it, pulling it up onto the boat. "My dive flag is tied on to that!" I yelled across the water. I watched as the workers pulled my flag onto the boat. Who knew what they were doing—maybe setting SCUBA-diver pot traps or something.

I decided that I'd better go down and find Oleg, because he would not know there were all these boats running around up here and snatching up dive flags. (Aren't they supposed to stay AWAY from dive flags?) I needed to warn my partner to make sure he didn't do the surfacing-from-a-dive-chop-o-matic thing. Somehow I managed to clear my ears. I got back to the wreck, put my reel away, and went back to the bow to find Oleg. There he was, very relaxed, sketching on his slate, oblivious to the BOAT up above. I could hear the boat now, evidently taking off again. I wondered what they did with my dive flag.

The northernmost section of the wreck ended at an angle, suggesting a wedge-shaped barge hull. We stumbled upon something that looked the proper shape to hold rope, but it had no rope on it now. Perhaps it once held a guy wire which supported a structure or mast. There were a lot of pole-like items down there too. Masts? Who knew. We did a lot of digging and sketched the bow, drawing the newly discovered feature relative to it so that we could find it again.

A few weeks before, I had gone to a set of workshops given by the New Jersey Historical Divers Association at Sandy Hook, NJ. I met Dan Lieb there and was impressed with his scientific approach to mapping and underwater surveying. He showed me his homemade underwater slate. It was about four times larger than what you can get in a dive store, and it erased much more easily. I listened carefully, took notes, and then spent $3.50 at a discount store for two plastic cutting boards. I drilled one hole to tie on a pencil and another hole for a double-ended clip. I ordered some sheets of inexpensive Mylar through the Internet and pulled out the good old duct tape. The Mylar has two sides, a shiny side and a matte side. I put the matte side up, fastening the Mylar on the board with duct tape. It's a bit ugly but very functional. Lots of space to write and draw. The Mylar erases easily, even underwater. I am going to make one more change: I'll add a small Velcro strap so the pencil can't get loose unless I want to use it.

Being able to communicate underwater added a whole new dimension to the dive. For example, after I finally was able to clear my ears and join Oleg again, I wrote:

"THEY TOOK THE WHITE BUOY."

He shrugged.

I then wrote: "DON'T GO UP BOATS!"

He shrugged, then wrote, "WHEN WE GO BACK, ON BOTTOM TO BEACH"

I shrugged.

He shrugged.

We were in full communication.

The dive ended. We came back up to find the boats gone and my dive flag neatly reattached to the white mooring ball.

A Land-Based Scopolomine Experiment, Beach 9th Street – Saturday, June 5, 2004

The *Wahoo* dive boat cancelled its trips for Saturday due to the weather. It turned out that the weather was not too bad Saturday morning, so I went to Plan B—Beach 9th Street. I met a dive friend at the diner for breakfast. This guy dives A LOT. Year round. I just don't know why I can't get him to join the Sea Gypsies. Loner Type. Nice guy, though. I'll keep working on him.

Anyway, we parked on Beach 9th Street and were in the 61-degree water for the 10:20 a.m. slack tide. Vis was exactly eight feet. I know this because we brought in surveying equipment to practice taking measurements with a 100-foot-long tape and recording them on slates. We actually measured the vis. It was a great dive. I had *Apollo* with me, and I towed my buddy around a bit as we explored. Had I not measured the vis, I would have guessed it was 10 or 12 feet. Eight feet vis was good enough for scootering around. We found some kind of stone slab and spent a few minutes with the scooter trying to excavate some of it. I found a fragment of what appeared to be an antique china pitcher with an old-looking design on it. Who knows what it was! But it did go in my red canvas bag. We had a 53-minute dive time, and it was raining lightly when we came out. There was a class from a local dive shop operating at the bulkhead near the cages on the 8th Street side of the property.

As an aside, I decided to try the scopolamine patch, a prescription item, for seasickness. It worked great at Beach 9th. Seriously, this stuff is expensive. About $10 per dose. I knew by Friday night that I would not be on a boat Saturday, so I decided to do the scopolamine experiment. This way, if there were any ill side effects, I could find out about them in my apartment and not at 110 feet deep.

I told my wife what I was doing and stuck the patch on behind my right ear at 9:00 p.m. Friday night. This would allow me to feel the effects for the first few hours and also to see if I would awaken in the morning. She was concerned because, as I mentioned in my previous seasickness tales, whenever I take Dramamine or Bonine I get REALLY GROUCHY for 48 hours. Benedryl decongestant also has this odd effect on me. So, having duly warned her, I put the patch on right after dinner. I thought I noticed some effects similar to drowsiness or very mild sedation within 15 minutes. This stuff works fast, but the documentation says that you need to put it on four hours before needing it, and that a patch lasts three days.

No grouchiness at all. The mental effects seemed less severe than what I experience with Bonine, and I sat in front of a Lava Lamp for two hours talking to my cat and the little people that live in the walls. Seriously, I kept the patch on and went to bed around midnight. I woke up feeling a bit restless at about two a.m., almost as if I'd had a bit too much coffee, but I had no problem falling back to sleep. I woke up again at 4:30 a.m., a bit restless, and pulled the patch off, making sure that I washed my hands and behind my ear. I was fully awake now. I did the previous night's dishes, and at first light I began cleaning the terrace. I washed down the entire terrace and scrubbed its floor and then started getting my gear together for the dive at Beach 9th.

My wife reminds me that it is extremely unusual for me to clean the terrace and do the dishes in the wee hours of the morning, and as far as she is concerned the scopolamine patch is perfect for me. I looked again at the drug information that accompanied the scop patch and found that restlessness is listed as a side effect. I will try the patch on my next boat dive. I'll probably remove it once the anchor line comes up and we start back to the dock.

To find more info on this prescription anti-seasickness patch try googling "transdermscop."

The "Immaculata" – Saturday, June 12, 2004

The shipwreck's name, ironically, is the Immaculata. The Latin root of that word means "spotlessly clean." I dove this wreck today and found that it's apparently another old garbage barge. One clue is the bones all over the place—just like on the Asfalto.

Courtesy of Captain Bill Reddan,

I like the well kept *Jeanne II* dive boat. It runs out of Sheepshead Bay in Brooklyn making it very convenient to get to. The *Jeannie II* was supposed to go to the Immaculata and then to another local barge, the "Big Wood" wreck. I took my little gardening shovel and was ready for more bottles. I have enough bones. We got to the Immaculata, but there was a fishing boat right on top of it, so off we went to Big Wood, another 15 minutes farther out.

Big Wood gets its name from the fact that it is a large wooden wreck, apparently a barge, but with a reputation for lobsters rather than artifacts. Because I would only be doing one long dive, I decided to sit this dive out. Maybe we would try the Immaculata again for our second dive.

A diver did surface with some brown pharmacy-type or chemist's bottles, but for the most part, divers reported not-so-great vis and a somewhat-mundane wreck. I was lucky. We did get back to the Immaculata, and I was one of the first in the water as the other divers suited up for their second dive.

Conditions were great. Nice, sunny day on the surface, and good vis with an interesting low-relief wreck at 95 feet. The wreck clearly had the shape of a ship. The sides of the ship gently curved out from the bow and swept back a hundred feet or so to a stern that still had some machinery associated with it. Right behind the stern, sticking up from the sand, was an object which appeared to be the vertical shank and cross piece (or stock) of a large buried anchor. If I'd had my scooter with me, I would have tried to dig down to one of the flukes to take a look. What I could presently see of the anchor included a large one-foot-diameter ring at its top which could take a chain or rope.

Still in love with the old days of sail, I liked this wreck because it appeared to be the remains of an old, wooden-hulled ship. The Immaculata is most probably a converted schooner barge. At the demise of the sailing ship era in the early twentieth century, many elegant sailing ships ended their careers as barges.

After swimming the wreck's entire length, I went back to our tie-in point and attached my reel near the ascent line, which led to the dive boat on the surface. I swam across the wreck and, spotting a lot of bones lying on the seafloor, looped my reel around a rusty pole and began digging with my shovel and fanning with my hands. I was actually looking for plates, coffee cups, and other such artifacts, and I found a coffee cup—unfortunately broken. Soon, though, I was rewarded with a nice, clear, medium-sized bottle that had lain protected in the silt for many years. This bottle looks like a hair-tonic bottle. I am not sure how I came up with that assessment, but it sounds good to me. Unlike the bottles I had picked up a few weeks ago on the Asfalto, this bottle exhibited no "sandpapering effect."

My bottom time was 50 minutes; I'd used a 28-percent-oxygen nitrox mix. I was back on the boat after a total time of 77 minutes, which included 15 minutes spent breathing pure oxygen at 20 feet deep. By the way, I wore the scopolamine patch on this trip to prevent seasickness. Seas were one or two feet, so it wasn't much of a test. But I felt fine the whole trip. I did notice that the patch was missing after my dive. It'll probably turn up in my hood when I get around to cleaning my gear. Also, I was going to cut the patch and only wear three-quarters of it. Before I did that, I checked on the Internet, and there were actually warnings about cutting these specific patches. Cutting them may, I learned, affect the delivery rate of the medication. So I used the full patch with no problems.

Back on the boat, I had one of those depressing conversations with another diver. It started out well enough.

Me (as casually as possible): Great dive. Got a nice bottle.

Other Diver (apparently impressed and interested): Oh, let me see.

Me: Here it is.

Other Diver: Oh, very nice. Hey, let me see your reel.

Me: Here.

Other Diver: Oh, that was you!

Me (somewhat confused): Huh?

Other Diver: Oh, that was your reel I followed, the one that went across the wreck.

Me: Yeah, I ran it to where I was digging.

Other Diver: Yeah, I followed your reel and found these...

At this point, the other diver pulled out a number of beautiful, perfect bottles, including a distinctively shaped one labeled "Olive Oil." A really, really nice find.

Me (depression setting in): Oh, did you have to dig a lot for them?

Other Diver: No, they were right there, lying on the bottom in plain view.

Me: Hmmmmmm...

In any event, this was a fun dive, and I would go back to the Immaculata. Maybe one day we'll dig out that anchor and I'll put it in front of my house. Second thought, I live in an apartment building. I'm not sure they'll let me do that.

I am accumulating these antique bottles, and while they do display nicely, I try to come up with other ideas. My wife puts up with my diving (amongst other things) so I had this idea to put a romantic poem in a bottle and give it to her. It still sits proudly on her desk at work, displayed for all the world to see. A less intimate message with the name of the wreck in a nice bottle also makes a thoughtful gift for a friend or a person you have told a few of your dive adventures to.

> *Message in a Bottle*
> *Dearest Lynda,*
> *Oh wind ship of time.*
> *Wind fills sails, fly, rigging speaks.*
> *Love, blonde maiden, I.*
> *- love david*

The Wreck of Iberia – Saturday, June 27, 2004

The date is a fruit of the date palm tree and is said to have originated in the Persian Gulf region in ancient times. There are over 1500 varieties, and they all require the full sun that is so abundant in the Middle East. The date palm takes about 10 years to reach full production, with a decline in productivity after about 80 years. According to Purdue University's horticultural website, dates are prized for their keeping quality:

> *Slightly underripe 'Deglet Noor' dates will keep at 32°F*
> *(0°C) up to 10 months; fully mature, for five to six months.*
> *Freezing will extend the storage life for a much longer*
> *period. In India, sun-dried dates, buried in sand, have*
> *kept well for 1 1/2 years...*

In 1886, the 225-foot-long *Iberia*, enroute from the Middle East to Arnold & Cheney, Inc. in New York City, was carrying some 28,000 crates of the fruit when she sank in 60 feet of water sometime after being struck by the ocean liner *Umbria*.

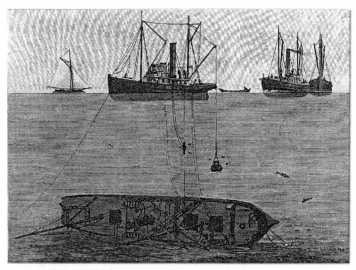

Wreckers at Work on the Iberia: Picture courtesy Herb Kaasmann, OREGON,GREYHOUND OF THE ATLANTIC

And there the steamship freighter has rested, on the sandy, silty bottom, only a few miles offshore but over a hundred years back in time.

Divers like to try to recover the crate ends, and there are still some down there. If you get a nice one, it makes a great souvenir—the printed name of the long-gone shipping company, Arnold & Cheney, makes these crates unique. I checked Mapquest.com for the company's old address—159 Water Street, in lower Manhattan. That building and address no longer exist, but you can close your eyes and picture it. The business would have been within hailing distance of the South Street Seaport. A person looking up and down the wharves near the end of Fulton Street in the late nineteenth century would have seen the masts of sailing ships through the great, black, belching clouds of smoke from the steam tugs and other ships. These steamships heralded the end of the age of sail.

I dove the *Iberia* with the Sea Gypsies on September 9, 2001, then once again with my son, and then again with Steve Edelstein of the Sea Gypsies in September of 2002. Steve's a great zero-vis diver, and together we churned up the bottom, digging for the prized crate ends. I found one, and so did he.

I thought I saw some orange dates floating around as I dug. For some reason, it seemed totally normal to see these fruits mixed in with the debris of the wreck. Back on board the dive boat, I asked if anyone else had seen dates down there. Divers responded to me as if I had been seeing things. "How could there be dates still down there? That ship went down over a hundred years ago!" I dropped the subject. Adding insult to injury, the stenciled letters on the crate end I had brought up were blurry. They had run a bit. Steve's crate, though, was as perfect as it could get. What a find he had made! I tossed my crate end over the side so that it could return to its friends at 60 feet deep.

Fast forward to this past weekend. This would be an unusual dive for a few reasons. The *Eagle's Nest* would be leaving the dock for the *Iberia* at the almost-civilized hour of 7:00 a.m. Only one dive, then back to the dock so that Captain Howard Klein could pick up another group of divers and take them to the *Iberia* to do two more dives.

I also convinced my wife, Lynda, to join me, to see what happens on a dive boat. Usually, I am trying to sneak out of the house very quietly at 3:30 a.m. or so. This time I would be banging pots and pans in an effort to wake her up. Okay, I'm not THAT stupid. No pots and pans. She came along like a little lamb, still half asleep as I led her to the car. I stuck a scopolamine patch on each of us, and we arrived at Howard's boat on time. Lynda had a great time, and Howard charmed her as we headed out past the jetties to meet the sun.

I was a bit nervous about this dive, because the last time I was on one of Captain Klein's 7:00 a.m. "one-dive trips," I did my usual thing, waiting for everyone else to get in the water first. Then I leisurely put on my gear and did a long dive with my double tanks. He was a bit annoyed with me, and rightfully so, because I had delayed him in getting back to the dock for his second trip. So, on this dive trip, I was the first in. I had brought *Apollo* to help me dig and carried a Ziploc baggie in my dry-suit pocket, along with my usual shovel and other gadgets. Very strong current on the surface forced me to cancel my scooter plans. So I declined it when the crew started to lower it to me. I descended to the wreck.

This is a great wreck that is spread out a bit. Visibility was about 15 to 20 feet, and I took a good 20 minutes orientating myself to various parts of the wreck and then finding my way back to the ascent line. There was no flashing strobe light at the end of the base of the line, and the vis would only get worse, so I wanted to make sure I could find my way back. I had a reel, but did not feel like running a line today. The long propeller shaft runs from the stern almost up to the boiler, amidships. Once you know where the ascent line is in relation to these easy-to-find objects, you'll be fine; that is, as long as you can locate one of these two major landmarks at the end of your dive.

Finally, confident that I knew where I was going, I headed forward of the boilers and found a nice spot between hull frames where it looked like there could be some wooden crates. I dug for a few minutes, fanning with my hand and using my shovel, grabbing large pieces of crate by feel alone and then pulling them out. When I was certain that I was down to virgin territory, I waited for the vis to clear and then pulled out my Ziploc bag. The black mass in the crate was clearly made up of individual dates, decayed and rotted ghosts of their former selves. Just a touch made some of them puff into nothingness like a wisp of smoke. But here and there I discovered a few which were more solid. Some were even orange-brown in color. I gave up trying to catch the good ones as they drifted away and decided to thrust my gardener's shovel into the black mass within the crate; I'd just fill the Ziploc bag and sort it all out later. It was thrilling, actually, to find these leftovers from the nineteenth century somehow preserved. It gave me a sense of the romantic history of this sunken ship, a ship in which they had lain for over a hundred years.

My Ziploc bag was now full, so I placed it in my red canvas bag. I took my reel and my light out of the bag and left them hanging outside, so that they would not bang against my delicate cargo.

I had now been down over an hour and needed to find the ascent line. Rather than going to look for it where I thought it might be, I followed my plan and went to the boiler and then to the prop shaft, following that all the way to the stern. I then came back about 20 feet and cut across the wreck. There was the ascent line. Time to go up.

I did a six-minute safety stop. No required decompression with my 57-foot-max depth and 32% nitrox. Once back on the *Eagle's Nest*, I resisted the urge to show off the dates. I knew I should leave them in their sea-water-filled baggie until I got home. Lynda and I spent the rest of the day sleeping in the sun on Lido Beach and followed that up with some mussels at the seafood place near Howard's boat. Great day.

When I got home, I cut the bag and gently dumped the contents into a large glass baking dish. I let fresh water gently run through the dish and used tweezers, pulling out the better dates and placing them in another dish where I rinsed them further. While this was going on, I looked up the *Iberia* on Dan Berg's website and read that Dan had, some years ago, collected dates off the wreck. I was doing nothing new. In spite of that, I was having fun, so I continued. I soaked them in alcohol after washing them, then let them dry. The final step was to use the tweezers to dip each of the 30 or so recovered dates into satin-finish polyurethane to help preserve them. I have taken some pictures of them and have included them with this story. I am not sure how I will display them. Perhaps in a small wooden crate from a dollhouse, or perhaps on the side of a real crate. Maybe I can glue some sand to the crate too, so that it looks like the dates are lying on the sand.

Dates, ready to serve. But don't be too quick to snack on these 115-year-old-plus polyurethane-encrusted things that look like waterbugs without legs!

Sea Gypsies Expedition, Thousand Islands – August, 2004

Forgive me for including some stories about diving in upstate NY's Thousand Islands area but the diving is great and is a popular change of scene for local divers who do not wish to endure the rigors of warm water diving.

The St. Lawrence River, called "The River That Walks" by the American Indians, has long played a crucial role in the history of Canada and in the fur trade that helped develop this part of the American continent. Explored first by de Champlain in the early seventeenth century, the river exits Lake Ontario between New York State and Ontario, draining it to the Atlantic Ocean and affording a sea route for great ships to ply their trade, an activity which continues to the present day. Man has done a lot of work to improve this route for shipping. In 1959, a joint

U.S.-Canadian project which opened the passage to larger ships was completed, allowing vessels up to 86 feet wide and with a 26-foot-and-three-inch draft to make the trip from the Great Lakes to the Atlantic using this route, the St. Lawrence Seaway. Nature too, has worked hard: immense quantities of cold, fresh, clear water from Lake Ontario have carved out an area near Clayton, New York called the Thousand Islands.

Many ships have gone down in these waters. Some, misguided, struck shoals and foundered, while others sank after fires or capsized due to sudden squalls which caused cargo to shift. The wrecks are frozen in time, preserved in the fresh water to a degree not often seen in ocean wrecks. Our expedition would include a Great Lakes freighter, an overturned drilling platform, a car ferry, a patch of sand, and a three-masted sailing ship.

My wife Lynda and I went up a day early. The rainy trip took about six or seven hours from New York City. There were little signs that we were getting into rural New York State. For example, at a certain point, the only music we could find on the dial was on Froggy 97—country songs played by a DJ

Photo Stephen Edelstein

named Cricket. Later, we turned into a gas station to use the facilities. I pulled a dollar bill out of my pocket in order to get a soda from the machine, only to realize that it was a fishing bait vending machine. We saw pickup trucks with American flags fluttering in the back (where the cargo should be) and we passed a town named Brownsville.

Harry, the Sea Gypsies Dive Club's legal counsel, was already there, sitting outside his room at the hotel, drawing slowly on his pipe as he contemplated the legal aspects of our assault on the array of sunken ships we would be diving over the coming two days. We went and had a couple of drinks at the Lost Navigator pub. In the morning, Lynda and I had a great breakfast across the street from the hotel in the Koffee Kove, and then we spent the day touring by car. Even in the intermittent rain we could see that this was a beautiful, if somewhat financially depressed, area. Lots of islands. Lots of lighthouses. Lots of river.

Now the other Sea Gypsies had arrived. It was time for a tasty dinner at the Harbor Inn. One of our club members, Eileen, a veteran diver on the Andrea Doria, wore pirate chains to dinner. It was Pirate's Week, which is sort of like Mardi Gras in these parts.

The next morning, we set out in two boats to do some diving. It's a bit different than the ocean wreck-diving I am used to; in the ocean, the dive boat has to grapple into the wreck, and a hook must be set by a mate. Here there are mooring buoys for each wreck, and the dive boat just clips on. If another dive boat arrives, it clips to the first boat. So at some of the wrecks we found a chain of three or four boats. There would be a bit of commotion if the lead boat (always ours for some reason) wanted to leave, as this would force the other boats to reconfigure their moorings. At the end of the dive, all the divers now back aboard, we unclipped, then let the current take us off the site before we started our engines.

Most northeast divers I have met are different than non-diver types; perhaps they are a bit more independent and adventurous. Dive-boat captains also are in a slightly different class than, let us say, ferry-boat captains. Captain Gary Kusilek fit right in. I spent a few minutes on the bridge listening to his stories about the eight partisans who attacked a Nazi prison in order to free his grandfather, who had not brought his cyanide capsule along on a secret mission. As we raced to the wreck site, the wind on my face, I looked out at the expanse of water in front of us, watched huge freighters navigating the shoals, felt the sun on the back of my neck, and imagined ghostly sailing ships passing in the dark depths beneath us. I turned to the Captain and said, "And then what happened?" Here in this beautiful place so deadly to ships, anything seemed possible.

Saturday
Our first dive on Saturday was the 256-foot-long coal-carrying steamer *Keystorm*, which struck a shoal and sank in dense fog in October of 1912. She lies on an incline with her bow at 20 feet and her stern at 115 feet. Visibility was very good. I took a trip to the deep end, then gradually crossed beneath the ship, about midway, through a washout beneath the hull. I then puttered about in about 60 feet of water for a while. You can still see pieces of coal here and there on the bottom of the river, although most of the original coal has been salvaged. I found a small piece that was almost a perfect cube. Then I noticed a large mast, amidships. I swam out and perched there at its end, some 75 to 100 feet away from the sunken ship. From my vantage point, I could see much of the well-preserved steel wreck, as well as the divers queuing up on the deco line which ran to the dive boat above. Very peaceful, serene, and easy. This was an easy dive and a good introduction to the St. Lawrence river.

For the past few years, I have been very conservative about dives over 80 feet deep, limiting myself to only one per day. Because we would be diving two different wrecks per day and

I did not want to sit out any dives, I decided that I would follow the deco times for my back gas (plus some additional minutes) but would actually switch from my 30% nitrox to pure oxygen at 20 feet. We had a good lunch of cold cuts and salads, and moved over to our next site, the *America*, a overturned drilling rig and barge.

The *America* is in the main shipping channel, according to the *Diver's Guide to the Upper St. Lawrence River*. We dropped down to about 30 feet and followed a line that ended in a two-way intersection of line. Which way to go? I followed the diver in front of me, who guessed right, and within seconds we were at the edge of a cliff or ridge with the wreck beneath us. The overturned rig was at 70 feet deep. Some of us tried

Photo Stephen Edelstein

to locate the boilers and firebox, which should have been near the wreck's bottom. Of course, since the wreck is overturned, the firebox is now upside-down, on top of the wreck. I peered inside and went in, careful not to silt up the cramped insides. Part of the floor had collapsed and was resting uneasily, half-supported by what had been the ceiling. In this small room, firemen had tended the boilers for the steam engines. I saw many firebricks that had lined the firebox, some with the name of the brick manufacturing company on them. The visibility was good on this dive, but it did not inspire the same kind of awe I experienced on the freighter dive.

Saturday Night

This weekend was "Pirate Weekend" in the town of Alexandria Bay. If you hadn't found treasures at depth, they were here in an atmosphere of debauchery and sin. Everyone in the town had a beer in hand and was yelling to be heard. This event attracted lots of bikers who, already in their leathers, needed just a patch over the eye or a pirate's scarf atop the head to complete the picture. One young woman bared her chest to a crowd, and I passed a few other guys who were mooning each other. Even I got into the spirit of things by cracking open a Diet Coke. Oh well! Life IS short! I decided to splurge and bought three strands of plastic jewels and a pirate hat. Avast Ye Mateys! Somehow, even with all the thousands of people milling about, Lynda and I managed to meet up with the rest of the Sea Gypsies, and we all milled about together for a while.

Sunday

Sunday morning, we headed for breakfast and then to the dock, where our two boats awaited us. The nitrox fills were late, so we had to wait a bit . When we first saw our new dive boat, there was some concern, as it was an open boat with no real toilet or "head." Saturday's dive boat had featured a traditional cabin and a small but functional deck area. As it turned out, the open boat worked fine; each diver had plenty of room to don gear, much more room than what had been available on the first boat. At the wreck sites, we lashed the boats alongside each other, effectively creating one big dive platform.

The *Wolf Islander II*, an 80-foot-long 164-car ferry, had been sunk in about 60 feet of water in 1985, as a dive attraction. I was a bit skeptical. I had been expecting a somewhat-mundane dive, but I was pleasantly surprised. This dive was a bit chillier than the dives the previous day. I kept running into Steve E. down there. We explored a bit, and I tried to photograph him sitting on the motorcycle on the car deck. For some reason, even if we don't go into the water together, we always seem to run into each other. We circled the bow just above the sand,

and there in the distance looked to be a suitcase or a piece of luggage forgotten by some passenger who was in a hurry to get off the sinking ferry. As I got closer, I could see that it was not a suitcase but rather a concrete block with a rebar loop at the top. Visibility was lower today on this dive but still decent. There was a large opening above the engine space which would allow a diver to drop down three decks into an area that was full of railing-lined catwalks and pipes. Careful! Don't stir up that silt!

I headed to the wheelhouse. Bill J. was exiting through a doorway, and I decided to go in. I had lots of gas in my doubles, so I decided to explore the inner corridors. Once inside, I headed to the forward most room, which was a semicircular space with a working and intact porthole. I dimwittedly opened and closed the porthole slowly about three times, saying to myself slowly each time, "Wow," and then exited the room. There were narrow corridors leading to the engine room, and I soon found myself on one of those catwalks I had seen earlier when I had dropped down into the engine space. Moving forward a couple of feet, then back six inches to free some equipment that was stuck on the railing, then moving forward again, I wriggled through a door and back onto the deck of the ferry. I ran into Steve again, and we headed for the ascent line. On the line a diver showed me his air gauge, it was dangerously low. He was using a single tank and had overstayed his time on the sunken ferry. I still had a good amount of air in my tanks and switched to my backup regulator so he could breathe off my long hosed main regulator to do his decompression.

Once back on board, I mentioned the porthole to Captain Gary, who explained that the original working porthole had been stolen off the wreck and the current one was installed underwater after the ship was sunk. Lunch was followed by a trip back east to do a dive that was, to say the least, out of character with the rest of the trip. We stopped off an island in about 40 feet of water. After some problems setting the hook in the sandy bottom, we were told that we being let in on a local, secret artifact area. The captain showed us a rock fall on the island that led to the bank of the river and told us there were "wooden rock cribs" in the water there. This was where rocks had been quarried in preparation for building nearby Boldt Castle in the early twentieth century. That was the same castle home that I had toured with my wife on Friday, so I found the idea a bit interesting. He added that between us and the island was an area in which possible artifacts such as bottles could be found.

I had come here to dive wrecks, but the thought of finding something got me going, and I plunged into the water. There certainly was evidence of digging here. I headed for the shallows, kicking furiously with my arms buried up to their elbows in the muck feeling for bottles. I was like a digging machine, propelled forward at the head of an increasing cloud of silt. Every time I felt something, I would hold it in front of my mask without stopping and fling it away when I saw that it was a large mussel or piece of junk. John M. said later that it had looked like I was just throwing all the silt and muck up in front of me. Most divers stayed well clear of me.

I decided to head over to the alleged rock cribs, thinking that workers on the rock fall quarry might have flung bottles and other items into the water after lunching near their work location. I found the cribs: large, wooden, underwater boxes made of heavy logs and filled with stone. Then I felt something. It was an old thermos. It appeared to be made of metal and in poor condition. I continued to dig right there and put my hand through the side of a disintegrating metal can of food. I think it was food. The can was sealed, except where my dry-gloved finger had punctured the side of it. The black, unappetizing gunk that came out the can did not look like food. Because of my mask, I was unable to smell it. Because of my regulator, I was unable to taste it. Whatever it was, let's be nice and call it food. I then stayed motionless for a few minutes, allowing everything to settle so that I could see what was going on and perhaps direct my digging efforts with a bit more purpose. I lay there, right above the bottom in eight feet of water, feeling a trickle of cold water coming in from a cut in my right dry glove soaking me to my elbow.

Normally I would have had a shovel, but that had been left in New York—I'd thought I wouldn't need it. I reevaluated my thermos and decided that since it was missing the top and was a mess, I would toss it. I then followed the shore a bit west to get opposite the dive boat. I surfaced near shore to get a bearing on the dive boat. It sure looked small from here. Rather than trying to navigate to it—possibly missing it and ending up in the channel of the BIG BOATS—or racing cigarette speed boats, I decided I would make for the boat on the surface. I inflated my big, red six-foot sausage and started out for the dive boats. The captain, who was in a large, inflatable Zodiac boat collecting lost souls, spotted my sausage and headed for me. He took the sausage on board, let me hang on to a rope, and pulled me back to the dive boat with the engine in full reverse. Lots of fun, just like water skiing in SCUBA gear. I tried to get my fins to plane so that I could stand up, but I ended up being dragged like a log on the surface behind the Zodiac as he made for the boat in reverse. I had very sore arms and shoulders that night. That evening, for some reason I repaired what I thought was a hole on my left dry glove, leaving my right glove to leak again on Monday's single dive. I still love my dry gloves, though. I used to replace them with latex wrist seals when it got warm, but for the past couple of years I have been quite happy using them year-round.

Monday
Monday was to be the day we would make the long drive back to New York City, so I opted to just do the first dive. The *A.E. Vickory*, a wooden, three-masted schooner sunk in 1889 in 120 feet of water, now lies upright on the bottom, looking like a

ghost ship. This was a great dive with excellent visibility. The wreck is well preserved, marred only by a light coating of small zebra mussels, and the light filtering down had a greenish tinge which added to the eerie feeling. Descent was tricky due to a very strong current. I had to pull myself along a line all the way to a rocky shelf which overhangs the schooner. Once on the wreck, I was sheltered from the current and could swim around.

Most divers began by entering the large, empty hull from the main deck and then swimming through the ship to the stern. I got to the end of the hold and wriggled through an opening, and all of a sudden I was out of the ship, off the stern. For a moment I hovered there looking at the ship, out of time, transported back to the night she had sunk after striking a rock. I could look down and see some of the large masts under me pointing away from the ship and down into the black depths beyond. Finally it was time to go, so I toured the main deck a bit to fulfill my deep-deco-stop obligation and then headed back to the line to make my way back.

There was a large box filled with rocks at 20 feet deep, and I was able to sit next to it, sheltered from the current. I switched to my oxygen tank to begin my deco and got a mouthful of water. Uh oh. Checking my back gas, I saw I had more than enough to do my deco, so I played a bit with the O_2 regulator. I was only able to get it to partially work. Water would fill it at the end of a breath, but I decided to carefully use it to deco anyway, my back-gas regulator hanging where I could get to it fast, if needed. I had a long drive ahead of me and really wanted to put in my deco time breathing the pure oxygen, to make me as alert as possible. Anyway, all went well, and soon we were back on the dock. The long drive was made more interesting by a very sudden hailstorm that forced drivers off the highway to wait for it to pass. I did get a photo of a tornado, which was an exciting bonus for a great trip.

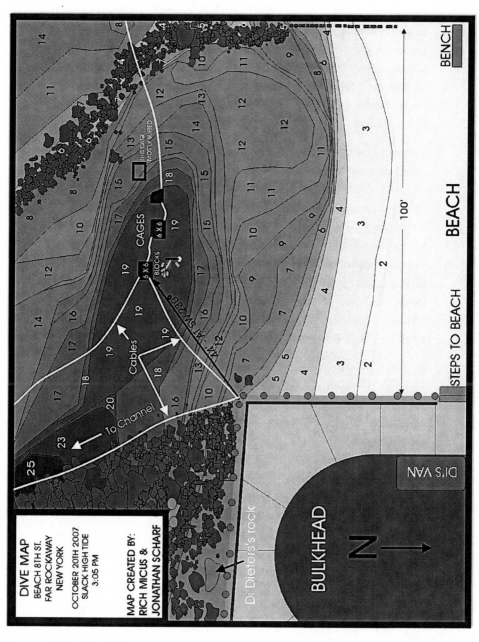

Map created by Rich Micus and Jonathan Scharf

Rockaway Beach, 9th Street – Saturday, September 5, 2004

Hurricane Frances is some 1500 miles away, but it's following close on the heels of Hurricane Charlie, and our local waters are a bit murkier than usual. I met Bob and Barry at the Sherwood Diner for breakfast, and we headed to Beach 9th Street, getting there at about 10:45 for the 12:30 p.m. high tide. We wanted to get there early so we could park—and it was a good idea, as there were a lot of fishermen and beachgoers parked there.

There was a class from Long Island's SCUBA Network parked at Beach 8th, too. We also met the NYPD patrol supervisor for that day's tour. He and his son are divers, and we invited them to come to a Sea Gypsies meeting as guests. Nice guy, and with the closing of the SCUBA haven Almost Paradise, a good contact. I do hope that people will respect property rights and will stay off of the old Almost Paradise property. That's trespassing, and it will reflect badly on divers. I did see some other divers using the benches there. It looked like they may have been the Atlantic Beach Rescue Squad—maybe they had permission. Don't know.

We could tell from the rocks at the jetty that vis was not going to be great, but we decided to go in anyway. It's a bit more challenging doing these low-visibility dives, and if you are in the mood for them, they can be fun. The simplest tasks become harder if you can't see well. It's also good practice to make sure you don't freak out if you get silted out while penetrating a wreck. The three of us descended the heavy cable down to the 40-foot-deep area which I call "the trench," even though it is nothing like a trench. The cable leads off the southwest corner of the bulkhead at Beach 8th Street, a block from where we entered the water. There are actually two cables here, positioned a few feet apart from each other where they join with the bulkhead. The western cable goes to the cages area. We used the other cable followed it into the depths of the channel.

Once we were below 25 feet, I realized that there was zero light. I mean zero. If you're the sort who likes the haunted house at the county fair, you would have LOVED this dive. Even a person who's done low-vis dives for a number of years has to confront primitive fears down here: if your leg brushes into a rock, or if you pick something up (thinking it's a rock) which tries to grab you with its spider-crab claws, you will be startled. And if your leg brushes another diver, they may move or grab your leg. Very fun. AGHHHH! I love it!. Usually after the first couple of minutes (and the ritual offering to the sea monster), the dive becomes a bit more mundane. There are still important questions to be answered, though. Such as: "I let go of the cable for a second; now where is it?" Or: "I really need a heads-up display in my mask for my compass and air pressure gauge." Anyway, I love it, and Bob and Barry seemed to enjoy it too.

We got to the bottom of the cable, at a depth of about 43 feet, and found it lying there in menacing, snakelike coils. I tied off my reel, and we continued out into the black abyss. With the light, you could see about 18 inches. We all had our lights on, but when we separated more than a few feet, I found that I could not see the lights of the other divers, even if I covered my own light.

Even if you've got years of experience, it's important to practice some skills on most dives so that in an emergency you will not be taken by surprise. I routinely take my mask off underwater, or remove my stage bottle, or test my backup regulator. Today's practice I suppose, was diving in low vis and running a reel. After we ran out about 50 feet of line, Bob indicated he was going to go off on his own; he ended up doing some of that practice stuff I just mentioned. Barry and I continued on almost to the end of my reel. We started to run his reel, felt the current starting to turn, and began heading back to base.

From the Collection of Gary Gentile "Ocean Liner Oregon"

Ascending slowly out of the inky depths is like watching the sun rise through a glass filled with coffee. Imagine slowly going from total blackness to a hint of murky, diffuse, greenish-brown light, shapeless forms now coming in and out of focus. As you ascend the slope, following the cable, there is no definite point at which you can say, "Oh I can see now, there's enough light." Because of the murky, storm-induced, pea-soup fog, all the light is diffuse, and objects are not crisp or defined. To see something clearly, you have to hold it inches in front of your mask. Of course, the route back was even worse, in terms of visibility, than on the way out, because we were retracing our own tracks and had kicked up some silt and muck in our efforts to follow the cable on our initial trip to depth.

I left Barry at about 20 feet—he wanted to go east a bit, to follow the other line to the cages. I was ready to get out of my soaked dry suit. Alas, the hole I put into my right dry glove while digging for artifacts on the recent Sea Gypsies Thousand Islands trip continued to leak. Now I know exactly where it is, and it will get fixed tonight.

My dive lasted 51 minutes in 72-degree water, and I really enjoyed it. We followed up with lunch at Bigelow's Fried Clams in Rockville Center. That place has great New England clam chowder and Ipswich-style fried clams. This is a real New-England-style fried clam restaurant, and I highly recommend it.

My First Dive on the Wreck of the Ocean Liner Oregon – Saturday, September 11, 2004

It's hard to read today's date without recalling the horror of the attacks on us some three years ago. Two days before that event, I was with other members of the Sea Gypsies aboard the dive boat *Eagle's Nest*, diving the wreck of the *Iberia*. Today found me back on Captain Howard Klein's boat, heading out to the 1881's Glasgow-built Cunard Passenger Liner *Oregon*.

Today, one gets on a large liner and tootles about the Caribbean or somewhere for a vacation. Until the mid-twentieth century, before air travel, liners were the way to get from Europe to America and elsewhere. There was fierce competition between the liner companies both for speed and accommodations. These great liners, such as the *Oregon*, had ornate rooms and every possible luxury for those willing to pay. If you close your eyes you can imagine yourself on the deck, a full moon in the sky and the breeze against your cheek, soft distant music mingling with the deep thrumping vibrations from the powerful steam engines as they drive the *Oregon* and her passengers across the Atlantic. There, a bit down the railing from you, is a couple. Her two hands rest upon the rail as she watches the moon's reflection dancing on the black seas. Her companion talks softly, one hand on her back. The smell of cigar smoke wafts through the lounge's open door.

This was the ultimate in technology for the time. It was still a bit tentative using steamship technology to cross thousands of miles of ocean, so the *Oregon* was also fitted with four masts for sailing as a backup. This approximately 500-foot-long vessel was 54 feet across and took eight hours to sink after a collision with another ship in the Atlantic Ocean some 21 miles south off the coast of Long Island.

I had 30% nitrox in my tanks left over from the Thousand Islands trip a few weeks ago, so I took them to get cranked up a bit. More air. Good thing. I think. I was also hoping that the oxygen percentage would decrease a bit so that I'd be diving a less rich mix for the wreck, which was listed as lying at 130 feet, in places. When I checked my tanks later, I found they were still a bit over 30% oxygen. Remember, too much oxygen too deep and you'll go

Oregon Steering Quadrant

into convulsions and drown. Lets see, 32% has a maximum operating depth of 130 feet at a partial pressure of oxygen (PPO) of 1.6. I called and spoke to someone familiar with the wreck just to ask if there was enough to make it worth my while at a maximum depth of 110 to 120 feet. Getting a yes from them, I then decided that I would go no deeper than 120 feet. I felt confident that if, due to some emergency, I did touch bottom at 130 feet, I would still be okay with a 1.49 PPO of oxygen. I also decided that if the visibility was not good, I would not dive. I am a bottom crawler on low-vis dives, and that would keep me at 130 feet for too long.

I had not slept well the night before and now, having loaded my car, I turned in about midnight with the alarm set for 4:00 a.m.

The boat was full and included Bill J. from the NYC Sea Gypsies and Richie Kohler of Undersea Detectives fame. I waited for the other divers to get in the water first. I could feel a strong current as I descended the yellow line. It had been tied into the wrecked steamship near the top of the large engine, amidships. I paused at 85 feet, a bit above where the line met the wreck. This is always a great time to try to orientate yourself a bit on the wreck, to note some landmarks near the line and, visibility permitting, to try to get the lay of the wreck.

I picked a direction, hoping it was towards the stern, and tied off my reel. The visibility was about 20 feet or so and I wanted to see the famed steering quadrant that had controlled the ship's rudder. Following the wreck to the stern was easy, and all of a sudden the large quadrant came into view. I swam though one of its openings, then locked and dropped my reel against the wreck. I continued out past the end of the wreck some 20 feet or so and turned around to gawk at this beautiful eight-sided, disc-shaped image from the bygone days of the great steamships. I stayed there a few minutes taking in the breathtaking scene and feeling 120-feet-deep good. All of a sudden I decided that I had been feeling good for too long. I probably had a touch of nitrogen narcosis. I picked up my reel and headed forward.

Shining my light into various crevices as I headed forward, I was not rewarded with any artifacts lying out in the open. But that was okay; my mission on this first dive was merely to reconnoiter the wreck for a more detailed assault at a later date. As it happened, I only got as far forward as the enormous boilers. They are like little cottages with alleys between them. You can go here, then make a left and then a right, swimming between them. Interesting enough for now.

Oh, many divers dive this wreck for lobsters. I am not a lobster hunter, although I am an avid fan of eating the large, armored, insect-like delicacies. There was a nice-sized one waving hello to me. I waved back. He waved an arm at me. I waved my arm. He waved his left arm. I waved my left. I was in ecstasy. I had had a breakthrough on the man-lobster communication problem. We were in lobster conversation.

Hmm...that was odd. Don't they usually try to escape divers? This good-sized fellow was trying to tell me something. I looked closer. He was stuck on monofilament. What I had taken to be a polite wave from him was actually his desperate attempt to extricate himself. Unable to find the time to do hospital volunteer work and unable to come up with the money to send to "Save The Children," I decided that an answerable call to charity was occurring right here on the wreck of the *Oregon*. I pulled out my knife and bubbled soothing sounds to the lobster as I cut him free. He dropped a few feet from the side of the boiler he had been stuck to and waved his claws at me in a threatening and most menacing manner. Was he having a lobster moment? Had he forgotten that I was his savior? Was he YELLING at me? Well, the last inclination to charity slipped out of me as I spied another diver with a lobster bag. I pointed to Mr. Ungrateful, who was promptly scooped up by the diver for dinner. Later on the boat, I must admit, I had trouble looking that lobster in the eye.

My bottom time in the 50-degree water was now 43 minutes. Time to go. I still had gas, so I decided to lazily spiral around the tall engine that we were tied into. I circled it twice, counting that as my first deep stop. Rising up the ascent line, I made additional stops at 70, 50, and 30 feet, and at 20 feet I switched to my oxygen bottle. The last time I'd used this bottle, the regulator sucked in water at the end of every breath. The problem had turned out to be that tiny zebra mussels were lodged in the regulator. A couple of weeks prior, inside some of the wrecks in the St. Lawrence River, the regulator hanging at my side on the O2 bottle had brushed against them in a couple of tight spots I had found myself in. I had cleaned the regulator out, and it seemed to breathe okay, but now—at 20 feet and with a long hang ahead of me—I found it again filling with water. Not the end of the world. I had enough back gas to do my deco. But there was also a very strong current now on the line. As I had done in Thousand Islands, I did the oxygen deco, blowing out hard after each breath to clear the regulator. I kept my back gas regulator right there, hanging over my shoulder. My utility line has been missing for two weeks; I can't find it and haven't replaced it yet. It sure would have come in handy on this ascent to attach myself to the ascent line to make my deco more comfortable. As it turned out, the same diver I had given the lobster to was ahead of me on the line and gave me her utility line when she completed her deco.

Great dive. I did about 15 minutes on the oxygen. Along with my bottom time and other deco stops, my entire dive lasted 74 minutes. I boarded the boat to Howard's famous barbeque, and as I passed, I grabbed a sausage with my dry glove before I even took my gear off. T-bone steak, venison, sausages, and chicken completed the Atkins-style menu. Gear off, stomach full, I lay down on a bunk and drifted off to sleep. In my mind's eye, recollections of what I had seen underwater intermingled with images of what the *Oregon* must have been like in her glory years.

USS San Diego – Sunday, September 29, 2004

Today we were supposed to go to the Asfalto, that great bottle wreck, but as sometimes happens, zero visibility was predicted. So instead we went to the USS *San Diego* on Dan Berg's *Wreck Valley*. Long-period swells assured us of limited vis on the bottom, but the *San Diego* is so big that we could at least hope for better conditions higher up on the wreck.

There are many different wave and current conditions that can be found in the open ocean. Some large waves are due to local winds whipping up the water. This can make for a lot of spray and whitecaps; these conditions may not produce the biggest local waves. Large waves are also produced by the long-term effect of wind and storms over a distance. It's a cumulative effect and is how a hurricane hundreds of miles away can generate 15-foot waves or greater, locally. The waves travel through the ocean combining with other waves. The distance that the wind can act over a given body of water is referred to as the "fetch." This explains why small bodies of water typically do not develop very large waves. Bodies of water like the open ocean and lakes such as the Great Lakes provide enough fetch for large waves to develop.

The seasickness comfort level aboard a small boat such as a 40-foot dive boat is related to many factors including the boat's specific handling characteristics, but the biggest factor of course is the waves. I start getting queasy once the waves go over three or four feet but I am generally okay because I take an anti-seasickness medication before all dive-boat trips regardless of predicted wave height. Sea conditions do change without much warning sometimes. The period of time between waves can also be important. For example, six-foot waves that are four seconds apart are much more uncomfortable than six-foot waves that are 20 seconds apart. As the period between the waves lengthens, the sea gets less choppier and may feel more comfortable. They are still six-foot waves, though.

I have been out diving in eight-foot waves, but there was such a long period between them that it just felt like a gentle undulating and was not horribly uncomfortable. Sitting over the wreck, another dive boat tied in at the other end of the wreck would totally disappear into the trough of the waves, gently reappearing a few seconds later. When there are these long-period waves, they form a wide wave called a swell on the surface of the ocean. From the boat it looks like large lumps are gently moving under the surface of the sea, no breaking waves; it imparts a misleading sense of serenity. These swells are actually very powerful waves moving through the water and because they are so far apart, the wavelength is so long that their effect is strong at depth. Waves with a shorter period and shorter wavelength have little or no effect at depth. Six-foot waves that are close together will make the people on the boat very uncomfortable and make it difficult for divers to exit the water to climb the ladder onto the boat, but once the diver slips beneath the surface he may find it very calm on the wreck. Six-foot waves that are farther apart make for a more comfortable boat ride but have an effect down on the wreck called surge. Surge is a powerful rhythmic current and can cause problems for shipwreck divers. It stirs up silt on the bottom, greatly reducing visibility. The surge current also powerfully moves through all the openings in the wreck, echoing the waves up above. If a diver is next to an opening in the wreck, he may be sucked into the wreck and then, a few seconds later, pushed out by the current. Combined with the poor visibility, the sharp metal edges on many wrecks can add some dangerous moments to the dive. I have had situations where my canvas bag was emptied of all my tools by the surge, times where I could barely hang on to a rope to ascend with my air regulator ripped out of my mouth, and one time where I lost my light and was positioned standing on the bottom at 105 feet, trapped in front of a two-foot-wide piece of metal that separated two ragged-edged openings into the wreck.

I waited to suit up to see if any of the earlier divers would return with news of the vis. Randi reported that there was heavy surge and current but some vis, so in I went.

I had brought *Apollo* along to help me dig, and I now checked my mental files for an alternate mission involving the scooter.

I descended to the bow. We were tied in to a spot about 40 feet down the ship from the end of the bow. *Apollo* easily battled the current on his medium speed. I remembered seeing, on a previous trip to the *San Diego*, some broken green porthole glass in the sand directly beneath a porthole, so I decided to plow the bottom, digging with *Apollo* to see if there was any glass near the first three portholes. None found, but *Apollo* and I had a great time. The surge and the current were great, clearing my dig area almost instantly when I would turn off the scooter. Getting bored, I headed aft about halfway down the ship, poking at various things and trying not to get sucked into the ship by the surge current.

Visibility was surprisingly good— about 10 feet—considering the surge action created by the wave swells 110 feet above on the surface. Anticipating a difficult deco hang, I did a shorter dive than planned and was back at the base of the ascent line after a total time of about 40 minutes.

The grey skies had changed to brilliant blue by the time I surfaced, and there was a great barbeque that included sweet and hot Italian sausage, Randi's famous ribs, and some delicious steaks.

Just another dive on the USS *San Diego*—but lots of fun.

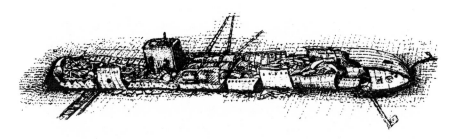

Oregon Drawing by Steve Bielenda, Picture courtesy Herb Kaasmann, OREGON, GREYHOUND OF THE ATLANTIC

Oregon – Sunday, October 10, 2004

I woke up just before the alarm went off at 4:30 a.m. (I'm not sure how I do that), pulled some steaks from the fridge, and headed down to my car. As usual, my local 7-Eleven-type store was a total disappointment, unable to produce the most rudimentary egg on a roll because "the grill is not on until 6:00 a.m." Why are they open then? The coffee is also below standard—always seems to have been sitting there for four hours or so. The bleary looking fellow behind the counter looked like I'd awakened him. "Oh, was I too noisy coming into your store, sir? So sorry to wake you up." I left there with a cup of boiling water that may as well have had a melted, brown crayon stirred in it, and an attitude. I didn't want to activate my emergency food supply (Cherry Frosted Pop-Tarts) just yet.

I was headed to Dan Berg's *Wreck Valley* dive boat to dive that sunken, speed-record-setting, ocean-crossing, nineteenth-century liner, the *Oregon*. I lucked out on the way, discovering an open diner right before I got off Sunrise Highway, and got a nice egg sandwich. It was fortuitous that I went out of my way to have a heartier-than-usual breakfast, as conditions on the boat would later delay lunch until about 3:30 p.m.

We loaded up and headed out from the dock a bit late, arriving at the wreck around 9:00 a.m. The forecast had been for three- to four-foot waves, getting worse later in the day. Hooking into the wreck proved a bit tricky with the wind coming from one direction and the currents from another. Bill J. from the Sea Gypsies was there. So was Randi Eisen and a couple from Rhode Island, as well as some other divers.

Under these overcast skies, the wreck was dark, but the vis was surprisingly good. The water temperature was 59 degrees on the bottom, and I had a nice, long dive, most of which was at the sand or right above it at 118 feet, in the area near the massive boilers. This was only my second time on the *Oregon*, and I basically was just sightseeing and trying to get the lay of her. Flattened debris on the sand is all that remains of much of the sides of this great ocean liner. You can see where others have removed portholes. In one place, I reached into the hole and grabbed the round backing of a porthole that had been previously removed. The part I held was totally free and could be moved, but since it was too large to fit through the round hole, it remains in place. I poked here and pulled there and slowly toured around. About 30 minutes into my dive, I headed towards the boilers.

Just like on my last dive here, I was struck by the size of these huge boilers. If you find the right spot, it's possible to descend between them, and you wind up in a strange space looking up at a structure of some kind above your head. Something unidentifiable forms a kind of roof (perhaps part of a deck)? In here I saw firebricks that would have lined the firebox where the coal burned. I found some loose ones, but decided to leave them for someone else, as they had no identifying marks that would make them more interesting as artifacts. After the dive I was told that they may have been from the kitchen ovens.

Forty-five minutes had passed. I reeled myself back to the ascent line and started up. The decompression schedule for my 28% oxygen mix was one minute at 80 and at 60 feet, two minutes at 50 feet, five at 40 feet, and seven at 30 feet, completed by 16 minutes on pure oxygen at 20 feet. As I moved up the ascent line, the increasing wave action on the surface became more and more pronounced as the line jerked up and down. By 20 feet, I was grateful I had a utility line (also known as a jon line) to clip to the ascent line. The jon line allowed me to maintain my proper deco depth without my shoulder being wrenched from its socket by the severely bucking ascent line.

Climbing back onto the boat's ladder at the stern was a bit tricky. The waves were making the boat and the attached ladder jump up and down some four or five feet every few seconds. This can be a dangerous moment, there is real risk of being smacked in the head by the ladder as the encumbered tired diver wearing over 100 pounds of equipment tries to climb it. I slipped a bit and went to my knees on one of the middle rungs. Captain Ed helped me out by pulling my fins off, and with a big grunt I got back to my feet and onto the boat.

Uh oh! No smell of Minkie meat on the barbeque! What's this! No food? The others on the boat recounted that while we were in the water, a passing squall had hit the boat. While it wasn't exactly a typhoon, it was enough to prevent the traditional barbeque. Time for a Cherry Pop-Tart!

I grabbed a bunk and did my third favorite thing to do on a dive boat—I napped. Reports of worse seas to come limited this trip to a single dive, which is all I usually do anyway. We headed back to the dock at a slightly reduced speed out of respect for some disobedient gauge related to the boat's engines. I awoke to the smell of meat on the barbeque drifting into the cabin.

Ah yes. Not a bad life. A great dive, some great food and conversation, and napping as needed. Now that's my idea of a fine way to spend a Sunday.

Also, as an aside, let me share this with you. There is a protocol for running a line from a reel as I did to ensure I did not get lost on the immense wreck. That protocol dictates that if you run your reel line across someone else's line, you always place your line under theirs. It's sort of like giving them the right of way, and it's a good safety practice to make it easier for them to reel back their line. I mention this here because, in spite of my training, I forgot to do this and after the dive was quietly reminded about it by the diver whose line I had violated.

The "Bald Eagle" Wreck – Saturday, October 30, 2004

My Suunto Vyper dive computer still is complaining about this last dive with a big "Er" on the face of its dial. This means that I can't upload it to my Dell computer until it calms down. So I write this report from memory without the added reminders that the dive-profile graphing software from the Suunto sometimes helps me with.

I'd gone out on the *Wreck Valley*, scopolamined against sea sickness and with a fully charged scooter battery for digging, excited about today's dive trip. We were headed back to that great source of artifacts, the Asfalto, an old garbage barge sunk in the 1920s or 30s. We were supposed to go there a couple of trips ago, but due to poor conditions we'd ended up diverting and having a fine trip to the USS *San Diego* instead.

It was a dull, overcast day. I went right below to catch some sleep in one of the bunks, nestling up into the bow. Once out of the inlet, we sped up. I woke up bouncing all over the place as we skimmed the top of waves, leaping from one to the next like a giant running across the surface of the water. The waves were not bad—about three to four feet—but we were crossing them at a perfectly perpendicular angle. It felt like the boat was jumping out of the water; then all its weight would come down onto the next wave. All the time, we were flying ahead at full speed. I pictured myself inside a giant Jet Ski or Wave Runner, leaping forward in those giant steps across the sea. I carefully rose, making sure I didn't bang my head as I climbed the ladder.

Grey fog all surrounds us; every direction looks the same. Only our wake gives evidence in the diffuse early morning light that humans are out here. I hear a faint foghorn in the distance and make a vaguely humorous remark: I feel like I'm on one of John Kerry's river swift boats as it moves up the Mekong Delta. Then I grab half a donut and head back down to my bunk. Unable to sleep—but not feeling too social this early—I make the bunk my base for the trip out, only leaving for water, the rest of the donut, a couple of trips to the head, and finally to put on my heavy dive underwear. It's freezing down here, even while I'm curled up on the narrow bunk.

As usual, I'm roused by a reduction in engine power as we approach the Asfalto. Captain Dan Berg nurses the boat gently into position over the wreck with the precision of an astronaut docking a spacecraft. "Throw in the buoy, now!" he calls out to the mate. The buoy, an old, plastic, yellow anti-freeze container, is carefully wrapped with some line that ends in a five pound weight. Dan uses the bottom sonar gadget to "see" the wreck some 100 feet below us. The buoy, thrown in to mark the spot unravels itself automatically from the lead weight. I love watching it spinning, fast at first then after the weight has hit bottom, it offers a begrudging additional turn here and there to the odd wave. But the spot is marked. Now is time to send in one of the crew to check conditions and tie the dive boat into the wreck. This morning, it'll be Ed.

Ed is known for being rather accepting of low visibility. Actually, I'm ready to dive in low vis. I'm going to be digging. There will be no vis anyway, anywhere around me today. I just need to see six to 12 inches.

Ed immediately surfaces from the wreck. This is a bad sign. Dan already knows that it can only mean zero vis. Not even a foot. Ed comes back up. The boat is quiet, hushed conversations. Where will we go now?

Oh no! Not the *Lizzie D*!

The rabble start to get a bit agitated when the name of the *Lizzie D* comes up. Apparently, when conditions are bad, the *Lizzie D* is almost always a good bet for better conditions, because it's on a sandy bottom and sticks up a good way from the bottom. With northeast diving conditions being what they are, I suppose that means a lot of trips out to the *Lizzie D* over the years.

The cry goes up from the masses: let's try something else. Dan's got an idea. Let's head three miles in that direction and do the Bald Eagle, he suggests. We're all on board for this option. Ed optimistically remains fully suited up, sitting on the gear-setup box and keeping an eye to our stern, in a position suggestive of implacable meditation and peace.

Now at the Bald Eagle, Ed is back in the water. Up comes the Styrofoam cup, the international dive-boat-crew signal that we will be diving here today. He's tying us into the wreck. While waiting, Dan mentions that they have a 3D drawing of the wreck. It's an incredibly detailed picture and a big help in visualizing this wreck, a wreck which I've never explored before.

They say that this wreck has lots of bottles and stuff, so I am not too disappointed that we won't be diving the Asfalto. This wreck is suspected of "catching bottles" from other wrecks, due to the currents. It appears also to have once carried a cargo of cobblestones. They're still here, two large piles of them sitting among the remains of the ship's schooner-like structure. Additional wreckage sits off the main wreck, adding to the mystery. Are there really two wrecks here?

I've just had a lot of dental work done and am concerned that a temporary bridge will come loose due to the stresses produced by the scuba regulator. Normally, when a diver jumps into the water from the dive boat, he or she keeps the regulator in the mouth so as to have air if something happens—if he sinks or if a wave hits him, for example. I have another plan. Not wanting to upset the crew too much, I inflate my BC bladder more than usual. I walk to the entry point, my regulator in my mouth. I jump. In midair, I take a deep breath and take the regulator out of my mouth, popping it back in once I'm in the water. I look up at the boat one final time before descending to see Dan Berg staring at me.

"What ARE you doing?" he yells. Obviously, he's seen the whole unconventional entry.

I take the regulator out of my mouth long enough to yell out. "Dental work. Bridge. Don't want to lose or break!" Through my rapidly fogging mask, I see him nod. He understands. Someone lowers me my scooter. I clip it off to me, to keep my hands free for the descent, and follow the line down to the wreck.

It's very dark. But as my eyes get accustomed, I can see that the visibility is actually fine down here today. Maybe 20 feet? I gather my senses at the base of the line, tie off my reel, and head off, holding my handheld HID light, which is really quite bright for a small light.

I am actually looking for bones. Piles of bones. I don't have a huge amount of experience in bottle hunting, but have found—on some of the old garbage-barge wrecks such as the Asfalto and Immaculata—that cut bones (probably from meat packing plants or butchers) often mark spots that prove lucky for bottle finding. If I do find these bones, I will look in the area for bottles. But will that mean that this wreck "catches" bones as well as bottles?

I've run out my reel a bit, and near a pile of cobblestones I notice a number of cut cattle bones. I'm going to dig right here. Within a minute or so, I have a beautiful round bottle, still corked. It has a chip on the lip but is otherwise intact. I really want perfect bottles, but I throw it into my canvas bag to show Ed later. He's got a good reputation as an artifact-and-bottle expert.

Now I'm hooked. There's a sole of a shoe, there's another broken bottle, here's an intact Heinz ketchup bottle. Blasting this area now with the scooter, I've dug a hole which contains all sorts of stuff. But no more bottles. I wait a few minutes for the sand to settle. Today there's a bit of a current, so it clears quickly. I'm working two areas. While one is settling, I'm power-blasting the other one with *Apollo*.

I look at my dive computer. Forty minutes already? And this is all I've got? Time to move on. I feel a pang of regret and sadness as my dive comes to its end. I always get a bit like this at the end of a dive. I take a long look around me, try to etch the experience onto my soul, and slowly start reeling back to the ascent line. I still have about 10 minutes, so I go past the ascent line and start poking around half-heartedly here and there.

Finally, time to go up.

I have been having problems with my oxygen regulator and meant to test it at 20 feet on the descent—it was just recently serviced. Forgot to do that, so I am not sure how long I will be decompressing. My dive time and air levels have been calculated so that I have more than enough back gas (32%) to do a full decompression should there be a problem with the O_2 equipment slung on my left side. After numerous stops on the way up, I switch to my oxygen at 20 feet. No problem. Great. I'll be out of here a bit sooner.

I clip off my jon line to the ascent line, get neutral, and float there. Sometimes decompression is just boring, and I can't wait to get back up on the boat. Other times I float there, excited about something I've found, something which is waiting for me there in my red canvas bag. I almost never take an object out to look at it—although I have the time, I don't want to risk dropping it and losing it. This time, I am filled with a peaceful sense of well being and I have not a care in the world. I'm just relaxing, eyes closed, feeling as if I'm floating. Oh, I am!

After I clear my oxygen computer and complete my planned stop, I wait an additional five minutes before ascending slowly the remaining 20 feet along the line to the stern of the dive boat. My second computer, the Suunto Vyper, doesn't understand about pure oxygen deco, and it is loudly accusing me of violating every law in diving. Now its display says "Er," for error, and like a petulant baby it has decided that I am done with diving today. Well I am, but by design.

Back on the boat. Everyone else has many bottles and "stuff." I show off my cute bottle with the broken top to Ed, who declares it 1920s or 1930s vintage. I move to toss it overboard, because I want a perfect bottle. He stops me.

"Are you sure you want to do that? That's a nice bottle. Finding that one would make another diver's day for sure."

I think he understands that I want a perfect one, so over it goes. Now I pull out the perfect ketchup bottle.

"Heinz Ketchup, 1930s," says Ed. I am not a Heinz fan, so over IT goes too.

Hmm. I've just thrown back everything I found. What's left?

Memories of a great dive. Had I not wasted time digging in that one spot and had instead just swam around like everyone else, I would have many bottles. Oh well. The dive was great, regardless.

Randi Eisen pulls out an intact rubber child's doll she found. It's oozing gook. Wow that's neat! I bet it was a squeak doll, and that the little hole in its back was for the squeak disk. It's dressed in late-nineteenth-century clothes and seems to be carrying a riding crop. It really reminds me that we go back into the past when we dive these wrecks. Randi sees I am interested in the doll and offers it to me. My pride surfaces. Nah, I say.

"But you seem to like it," she says.

"Yeah, but I didn't find it myself."

She understands and draws back the offered doll. Later, while loading the car up with my gear, I think about it again and ask Randi if I can still have it. The six-inch-high glimpse of the past is now soaking in fresh water until I can figure out how to display and preserve it. The rubber will certainly deteriorate very quickly if left exposed to air. Maybe I'll have it placed in a block of Lucite.

Later that night, the sobering thought that the baby who played with this toy—who loved this toy—is long grown up and probably long dead passes through my mind as I drift into a welcome sleep.

Chernobyl Inlet – Sunday, December 4, 2004
I've made it back to base. I think I'm going to be okay. Only time will tell. The incessant clicking of the Geiger counter

haunts me still as I think about this dive I did today, my first in about six weeks due to some oral surgery.

The weekend started innocently enough. I was released Thanksgiving night from the place the police took me. I don't remember much. My wife says I kept mumbling, to no one in particular, "The turkeys have left Capistrano." Maybe it was Thanksgiving that pushed me over the edge. No diving for weeks and then all this family stuff on top of no diving and I was fit to be tied. I snapped, I guess.

I was really determined to go diving today. Anywhere. Little did I know, as I tried to get water temperatures from the Islip Buoy website, that I should have been checking wind direction and melting down my lead weights to make a radiation shield. It didn't look too good. We had high winds with gusts up to 35 mph overnight, and the coastal forecast from NOAA spoke of seven- to 10-foot waves out in the ocean this morning. Only a fool or a desperate man, or maybe a desperate fool, would consider diving East Rockaway Inlet today; there would be no visibility at all.

"I'm the perfect man for the job," I thought to myself as I drove out to Rockaway Beach 9th Street around 11:00 a.m., making the obligatory stop at the Sherwood Diner for a cup of coffee.

I walked to the rock jetty and peered into the greenish-brown swirls. I thought I could see a rock. How deep was it here? There must be SOME vis. Maybe two feet?

I then walked over to the end of Beach 8th and found two other divers suiting up. I didn't know them. I checked to make sure they weren't Al Qaeda terrorists on a mission to take out the Atlantic Beach Bridge. One them was kidding around in a distinct New York accent about stabbing a diver with his dive knife. They seemed okay. I headed back to my car to suit up.

Out of the water for some six weeks now, I was extra careful suiting up. I am done with the boats until early next spring and spent some time yesterday winterizing my single-tank setup. Winterizing consists of adding 12 pounds of weight to my normal setup. I add four pounds to my belt and throw another eight pounds into some pouches in back, near my single tank. I don this extra weight so that I can add extra air to my dry suit. This keeps my Weezle underwear fluffed and dry and helps keep me toasty warm.

The vis turned out to be about three feet. Largish particulate matter floated in the water. I think this makes a difference, because finer particles cause a tougher kind of low vis. This type of vis, with the big stuff—you just leave your light off, and when your eyes adjust to the gloom, you can see three to five feet.

I swam over to the end of Beach 8th Street and found the line that descends into the 42-foot depths of the channel. Following it down, I encountered two divers coming back up the line. Hmmm, not a good sign. They had probably just entered the water, and it looked like they were heading back now, probably due to the low vis. Now I would have to deal with the mess they'd stirred up down there. I nodded an acknowledgement to them as I cursed to myself and continued down the line into total blackness. I had two lights with me, a regular one and an HID type. Both were equally ineffective in these conditions, but would be useful for reading gauges.

Vague shadows appeared out of nowhere. Things touched my legs and scampered across me, then vanished into the darkness. I kept very still, neutrally buoyant, holding the line about 20 feet deep in the inky stillness. It was relaxing, almost like being in a sensory deprivation tank. No thoughts of work, turkey, or even my family interrupted my meditative repose.

As my eyes adjusted to the darkness, I thought I saw a hint of green light in one direction. I was amazed, because that direction was down. Not up. There, in the distance. A glow, as from the core vessel of a nuclear reactor, something right out of the movies. A soft, greenish ambient glow. Pulsing with the life of nuclear reactions and beckoning me to draw closer. It reminded me also of that bluish light you've seen in a thousand science-fiction movies, the spreading glow under the mother ship. But this was green, so I thought nuclear reactor, as in the accident at the Chernobyl reactor.

I headed towards the glow, feeling as if I were descending to the alien city in the movie *The Abyss*. Slowly I pulled myself hand over hand, down the remaining 22 feet to the bottom of the line and into the reactor core. I was on a mission. I was investigating a new scientific phenomenon. I tried to take it all in. I had no slate to make notes, and I would have to remember everything, every detail, for the debriefing by the Area 51 military scientists that I knew were awaiting my return.

Once I passed into this glowing realm, the visibility opened up to over 10 feet, possibly more. Here, I could see the ambient light diffusing down from the surface. What must have happened was that the other divers had not gone all the way down the line—yet they'd stirred up so much silt near me at 20 feet that everything had been obscured at that depth. Because of some idiosyncrasy of the current as the tide finished coming in, the deeper area had cleared up first, making it appear to me that the only light was below me instead of above me.

I fastened my reel to the snarl of cable at the bottom of the channel and played it out as I moved about, in case the visibility should suddenly go. I had a great 55-minute dive. The water temperature hovered around 50 degrees. I poked at rocks and swam around like a seal, just enjoying being in the water again.

I was comfortable the entire time, except when ascending. As I passed through the low-vis area again, I felt cold water run down my arm and into my armpit. Yikes! Cold! I held up my glove and saw two tiny streams of bubbles, one from my pinky and the other from my thumb. I seem to get more leaks ever since I replaced my orange dry gloves with the heavy-duty blue ones a few months back. I'll fix them, but I should order some replacements before the water temps drop into the 30s.

I surfaced to find no immediate evidence that anyone knew of the drama unfolding 40 feet below the surface. No Area 51 scientists. But then, I thought I could hear sirens in the distance and the heavy, throbbing sounds of two black, unmarked helicopters approaching fast and low over the buildings. I headed for my car, slipped through the tightening military cordon, and made my way to Bigelow's in Rockville Center for a good bowl of clam chowder.

Bayville – Sunday, February 6, 2005
I did not feel like getting out of bed when my alarm went off at six a.m. today. But Stephen B., Oleg, and I met at 7:00 a.m. at the Bagel Deli on Route 106.

There was a flat calm, sunny skies, and what appeared to be good vis from shore. En route to the site, Oleg, driving behind me in his car, called my cell phone as we passed a totally frozen bay on our right. "It's going to be frozen," he said. I reassured him it wouldn't be, in spite of the evidence before us. I was reassuring everyone that the water temperature here in Bayville (near Oyster Bay) in the Long Island Sound was typically 10 degrees warmer than that of the Atlantic Ocean on the southern shore of Long Island. I was therefore predicting 45 degree water temperatures in Bayville, based on the 34 degrees I enjoyed last weekend at Rockaway.

I was wrong. Quite wrong.

Vis was excellent—at least 25 feet. But the water was 32 degrees. Oleg recorded 31 on his dive computer. Remember, sea water can get colder than 32 degrees before freezing. Typical seawater freezes at 28.58 degrees Fahrenheit.

Stephen had his scooter and I had mine, and I was able to tow Oleg and maintain speed with Stephen. The vis was so good that we located the wreck from the surface after we tied off a dive flag to one of the buoys about 100 yards out in the Long Island Sound. We toured the wreck of the barge for a few minutes, then headed west as per our plan, to see if we could find the deeper area which used to be the ferry channel in the early twentieth century.

There is a problem using the scooter in cold water. Even if I am otherwise okay in my dry suit and heavy thermals, my dry-gloved hands get frozen from the fast-flowing, cold water moving over them as the scooter flies through the water. After five minutes going due west (I really wanted to go 10 or 15 minutes), my hands were really cold. I guessed that Stephen was feeling the same thing, so I signaled and we headed back east.

To navigate, I used my compass on the scooter and my dive computer's timer. So I headed due west now and kept checking my computer; I knew I would be back in the area of the wreck after five minutes had elapsed. I tried shifting the position of my hands. My left hand I could take off the scooter handle—I could flex it and close my fingers, using it like a paw to hold on to the left side of the scooter. The right hand, though, needed to stay in a certain position to operate the scooter throttle, so there was no relief for that hand at all. It really began to hurt from the cold. My timer showed that we had now traveled east for five minutes, yet I could not see the wreck. I signaled to the others that we should surface to see where we were. We did, and we were not too far from the buoys near the wreck. As soon as I stopped scootering, my hands felt better, so I was ready to resume our explorations. I scootered about the wreck again for a while, searching for an intriguing piece of debris I had seen last year with Oleg—some very encrusted, rigging-related item. I couldn't find it. We went back and picked up the flag and finished the dive after about 40 minutes.

I did some meandering around near shore with the scooter and all of a sudden detected a drop in the power as its battery got ready to die. It had performed valiantly today, towing two divers around for a good period of time, but as this was the original battery that had come with the scooter when I'd bought it some three years ago, it's got to be time to replace the battery. Going to order a new one this week.

The visibility was great, and I think that while we were a bit chilly, we all enjoyed today's adventure. I really have to come with a design for some sort of shield that protects my hands on the scooter so they don't get so cold.

Rockaway (And How I Narrowly Escaped a Lynching in Home Depot) – Sunday, February 27, 2005

So, as I mentioned, when I use the scooter in frigid waters my hands get very cold. Come to think of it, this occurs in early boat-wreck-diving season too, as water temperatures on the deeper wrecks in early May are still only 40 degrees.

I called the manufacturer of my *Apollo* scooter to ask them if they knew of a hand shield that would protect my hands in the winter. No such thing. I then thought and decided that a piece of plastic—perhaps hinged—could be stuck near each handle with Velcro in the colder months. That would do the trick. I didn't want to drill into the scooter, so I called *Apollo* for advice about a suitable adhesive. Their lawyer answered with some drivel, saying, "We cannot suggest or endorse modifications." They did direct me to call one of their authorized service centers to discuss it with one of their *Apollo* experts.

Fast forward to last night. I'd been lured into Home Depot by my wife to look at some floor tiles. I slipped away into the tool corral to check out some heavy work gloves. Maybe I could pull them over my dry gloves, I thought. They just might give the protection I needed against the water flow problem. Alas, none of them were even close to big enough—they'd never fit over my dry gloves. I desperately looked around, aware that every second here in the tool corral was another second I would have to explain to "the boss" when I returned to the tile department. I guess I'm just not much a of a man. Here I was, in the manly tool corral, among other men who were each trying to outdo the others with purchases of steroidal power tools and manly construction things such as leather tool aprons and the like. That was me in the corner, cowering in the glove department near the ladies' garden gloves, sniveling around and nervously looking over my shoulder.

"Can I help you, sir?" said the Home Depot guy. He even walked, swaggering like a cowboy, right at home here in the tool corral.

How could I explain my situation? "I am looking for gloves, large gloves, like the ones you have on, but larger." I swaggered a bit, trying to hide my medium-sized hands.

He slipped to my side to peek at my hands. "What are you, a medium?"

I moved my hands farther out of his view. "No. I need large, probably EXTRA LARGE."

He nodded as if he had heard it all before, and we moved over to the large work gloves. "No, I need larger than these."

I could see, as he glanced again at my hands, that he thought I was just another manly cowboy in the tool corral, wasting his time. I had to explain.

By the time I finished explaining how I needed them for SCUBA diving—to go over my SCUBA equipment—and that I was going diving at Rockaway in 30-degree water tomorrow morning, I could

Kneepad modification to Apollo Scooter a la Home Depot

see I had his attention, as well as the attention of eight other cowboy-customers that had gathered and who were now listening in a semicircle behind me as I spoke. Was I about to get lynched? I looked up fast and whipped my head around, trying to catch the eye of just one of these would-be weekend warriors for whom leveling a door followed by a couple of beers and a belch would be the extent of their weekend activities. Not one would meet my gaze.

I could see that one or two of them had picked up the closest power tool or wooden-handled rake. This was beginning to look a lot like the mob with pitchforks in Frankenstein. I was an intruder, and strangers would not be tolerated here in the tool corral.

I slid between a display and the Home Depot guy. "Oh, what's that? Hmm...That might work!" I exclaimed. The men were caught off guard. The taunting dropped off to a muttering as I queried Mr. Home Depot. "What's that?" I said. He looked where I was pointing and then back at me, and then back where I was pointing and back at me again.

Someone behind me yelled out. "Kneepads! Says he wants gloves bigger than he's got hands and now he wants KNEEPADS? SEIZE HIM!"

Now the unruly cowboys were banging their tools against the floor in a rhythm that got faster and faster. I reached past Mr. Home Depot and grabbed the set of rubber kneepads, made a beeline for the exit, and was out of the tool corral lickety split.

Seconds later, still out of breath, I was back in the tile department where I belonged, but now I had a plan for tomorrow's dive. That freezing dive certainly would not be as demanding on me as was the visit to the manly tool corral at Home Depot.

Sunday morning at 8:30, after a brief stop at the Sherwood Diner, I was at Beach 9th Street. My scooter, *Apollo*, had a brand new battery, and I had used the Velcro on the rubber workman's kneepads, attaching one to each handle on the scooter. The kneepads really worked great. Today the water temperature was 36 degrees, and I scootered for my entire 35-minute dive at high speed. I made a push into some unexplored area west of Beach 9th Street early in the dive. I went pretty far west and decided to come up on the beach so I could see where I was. I had never been this far west before. A few weeks ago at Bayville, I'd had to stop every four or five minutes because my hands had hurt too much from the cold. Today, I was totally unaffected by the cold water on my hands. The cuplike shape of the kneepads is perfect for protection, and the hydrodynamic shape makes the water flow over the hands smoothly.

Sometimes the flow of the water would get in between the leading edge of the pad and force the leading edge of the pad to move out from the scooter, letting water flow against my hand. This only happened a couple of times. I found that flicking my elbow out forced the angle of the pad to change so that the same water flow would now push it back in place. I may make a couple of changes, but this thing is working. I can also pull my hands out of the pads instantly—good for emergencies.

I had a great dive, and the vis was about eight to 10 feet.

The Seal – Sunday, March 13, 2005
Underwater visibility along the shores and in the shallow bays of Long Island depends on a number of different factors ranging from whether the bottom is silty or sandy—to the weather. Some say that it gets bad after a rain because of the runoff from land into the sea. I tend to evaluate the vis based more on recent wind conditions.

Now, it does not really matter how bad the wind is on the day you're diving. I have gone diving in high winds. I've been sandblasted in parking lots, yet have found great visibility in the serene depths beneath the ocean's choppy surface. Prolonged wind over long fetches of ocean is what creates the swells out at sea and the corresponding deep surge. That surge scours the bottom just offshore and raises the fine silt throughout the water column.

If you think it odd that I use the term fetches, there is a nautical meaning to the word. It refers to the distance over water which a wind blows, and also to the distance traveled by waves with no obstruction. A longer fetch and a few windy days, and you have big waves. A shorter fetch, such as in a small lake, and you have smaller waves. The Great Lakes have fetches that are large—so large that their wave systems rival those of the ocean. In 1913, a famous storm generated 35-foot-plus waves in those landlocked seas.

I did not have a good source for historical wind information to help me try to predict vis, so I have been downloading daily wind data for JFK airport and data from a couple of local buoys from the National Oceanic and Atmospheric Administration (NOAA) website. When I put that data into a database program that I wrote, the program gives me average wind speed and direction for the past five days or so. I've even toyed with getting it to predict underwater visibility. It was getting to be a real pain to download this stuff. Somehow, I stumbled across *www.iwindsurf.com*. This site was designed for windsurfers, but it is giving me the information that I need. I can get specific wind data for the past week, presented graphically in an easy-to-read format.

I knew that last Tuesday was windy—but I was surprised to find that at JFK Airport there were gusts up to 55 mph and out at Shinnecock on Long Island on the same day gusts reached 70 mph. The picture of sustained winds earlier in the week made diving look pretty grim for this weekend, but I noticed that winds had dropped drastically starting Saturday around midday. The question was, would a drop to 10 mph for a period of about 24 hours after a sustained period of high winds be enough to let the vis settle down?

I needed a ride out east anyway. I was looking for a pleasant way to spend a Sunday, and perhaps I could stop by my mom's in Rocky Point on the North Shore of Long Island on the way back. I would make sure to bring my scooter and also some 18-power binoculars with image stabilization to look for seals.

Seals? Here, 90 miles from New York City? Yes. They are here. Watching us. Waiting. I have likened them to large dogs with even larger teeth. Pit bulls of the sea, I like to call them. Great white sharks may in fact be man's last defense against these chimerical beasts which resemble Charlie the Tuna crossed with a great dane.

The seals are in Shinnecock Bay in the winter. They like to hang around the commercial fishing docks a bit east of the Ponquogue Bridge. Fueled by scraps from the fishing boats and motivated by their lust for blood, they search, turning their evil heads this way and that to try to catch a glimpse of their favorite dish...SCUBA divers. Once a seal spots the unwitting diver, it slips silently beneath the surface of the bay and begins its underwater hunt. Typically, the diver never even knows what's hit him. He's stalked and then grabbed by the arm or leg and shaken like a rag doll. The seal then delivers the final blow, crushing the first stage of the diver's regulator with its massive jaws.

Okay, so I'm getting a bit carried away. Back to the story.

I arrived at the bridge about 9:30 a.m. and made the walk out to see how far down I could see into the water. Hmm. Looked like at least a couple of feet. Was that the sand all the way down there? I decided I was going in. I lugged my scooter most of the way out along the old bridge, placed it near the water's edge, and was soon in the water. The visibility was a bit disappointing—maybe three feet—and I opted to leave the scooter turned off and its buoyancy vest partially filled so that it floated in the water beside me as I slowly explored, heading north. I hadn't the foggiest idea where I was. Low vis will do that to you. Part of the fun, but not for the faint of heart.

I turned west, expecting to encounter the piers for the old bridge. Eventually I did. A ridge of rocks and sand rose up to the base of the piers. When I passed over that, I was hit with strong current and stayed low. My scooter, floating next to me, was acting like a sail in the current. I released the air from its vest so that it would instead help anchor me on the bottom. I checked my air (it was fine) and decided to continue heading north away from shore under the old bridge pier. As you move into deeper water the current weakens, though it's still always something to be respected. I reached the end of the old bridge and stood there like Samson, braced between two pilings.

I would like to say that I saw a seal and befriended him. And that we swam together, and that he taught me new, more efficient swimming techniques, and that I taught him that we divers are not just the next thing down on the food chain. This did not happen. I saw no seals underwater. But then the next best thing happened.

The vis cleared dramatically.

I switched my scooter on and sprang out from between the pilings into the current, which was rushing past me. With the scooter at top speed and the full force of the current behind me, I was going exhilaratingly fast. There was the edge of the Porgy Patch—that deeper area to the northeast of the old bridge. The current released me as I headed down the steep slope to the 33-foot-deep area. Now it was my turn to be a seal, zooming here and there. A slight twist of my body and now I was headed over that way. I feel very much like seal like when using a scooter, if I do say so myself. A few minutes of this and I decided to head back. South, that is.

As I slowly ascended out of the deeper area, the current hit again. It would only get stronger as I got closer to shore. Now I was about even with the end of the old bridge. As I went farther south, vis also started to decrease. It never got quite as bad as when I had first entered the water; perhaps my eyes had adjusted to the dim light. But the *Apollo* scooter is great. On its fastest setting, the current was no problem. I just hung on, not going really fast but going faster than I could swim, and making good progress perpendicular to the current.

About halfway back, I decided that the vis was good enough to ride the current a bit more, so I turned and went with the current for a while, then turned the scooter back on and continued south. Then I headed back to the old bridge pilings, going totally against the current. I turned off the scooter and used a piling to shelter me from the current. I held the piling.

I had kept a lot of air in my dry suit for warmth, and I thought it might be easier to do an ascent along the piling so that my suit could empty. I didn't want to suddenly scooter into a shallower area and find myself with nothing to grab onto as the expanding air in my suit launched me to the surface. I used the piling to do a very slow, controlled ascent, and, once on the surface, I could see that I was about halfway out on the old bridge. The outgoing tide formed eddies and swirls all around the pilings.

I rode the scooter back on the surface—scanning nervously for those seals I had heard about—picked up my dive flag, and went back to my car. I had been in the 36-degree water for about 40 minutes and was feeling great.

After changing back into my land clothes, I headed over to the commercial fishing docks and was rewarded by seeing a large seal. I could see his whiskers. Right after I glimpsed him, he vanished. I spent a few more minutes scanning the waters with the binoculars and again I saw him surface and look around. I caught a hint of just how big his sleek body was as he undulated along the surface. They are gorgeous creatures and true masters of this watery, icy world that we SCUBA divers invade, limited as we are by our air supply and poor tolerance for cold. I wonder how the two of us would have reacted had we met underwater in his world rather than watching each other across the air/water barrier, each of us safe and secure in our own worlds. I had been visiting in his territory not a quarter mile away. This seal had a large head and he lifted it out of the water as if trying to get a better look at me. Did he think he had seen me somewhere? I got back in my car and headed to the Quogue Market to get a hot cup of coffee.

Two Trips to Dutch Springs – March 30, 2005

I went to Dutch Springs Quarry in Pennsylvania a couple of weeks ago with Barry W. Dutch Springs used to be a quarry and there is still equipment underwater that dates back to that time. One of my favorite areas there has an 80-foot-tall steel girder tower that extends a few feet above the surface of the now water filled quarry. On my last trip to Dutch Springs I had my scooter and made two dives with my single-tank setup. Water temps were about 41 degrees, and I seemed to use up a lot of air. A while after my second dive, I noticed my BC was fully inflated and as hard a rock. I swapped some hoses around, and a couple of tests later I realized that it was the BC valve that was the problem—time for servicing! I dive over-weighted in the colder months so that I can put a lot more air in my BC and thereby stay warm. The over-weighting and the fact that I was using the scooter the whole time kept me from popping to the surface.

One of the things I wanted to practice on these dives was shooting a bag to the surface as a means of raising an emergency ascent line. I don't know if you have ever tried doing a safe, controlled, free ascent without a line, but it is not easy at all. In addition, at sea, currents will sweep the diver away from the dive boat if he ascends without a line. If that diver has to do a decompression stop—and all dives really require at least a three- to five-minute safety stop—who knows where he or she will end up. The dive boat cannot go looking for a drifting diver because the engines may mince other divers still in the water. Also, those other divers are expecting the dive boat to be where they left it. So when diving our local wrecks it is imperative that you locate the ascent line at the end of the dive so that you can come up safely. Many divers enjoying their first trip to an unfamiliar wreck will attach the line from their reel to an object near the ascent line (never attach it directly to the ascent line—you don't want to be dragged by the dive boat if the ascent line breaks free from the wreck). It is a serious emergency if a diver cannot locate the ascent line at the end of their dive. And this happens more often than you may think. A new wreck can be disorienting. Having other problems underwater can distract you and then confuse your sense of direction. Maybe another diver is digging in silt with a scooter and vis suddenly drops to zero. (That's NOT me digging, I hope!) I've neglected to run a reel on numerous dives. Somehow, I've always made it back to the ascent line, sometimes with a great sense of relief.

All wreck divers should get comfortable with a reel and use it on the wreck if needed. I carry a reel with 240 feet of strong nylon. The length of the line should be at least twice as long as your maximum depth so that even with currents blowing you sideways it can reach the surface. If I were to fail to find the ascent line, I would find a secure thing on the wreck that has no sharp edges. I'd then attach my reel and put some air in my liftbag (mine is a six-foot-long, eight-inch-across bright orange sausage) to make the bag shoot up to the surface up leaving me holding a line that goes right to the surface. I would cut the line from the reel and secure it to the wreck. Finally, I'd put my reel away and ascend, using the line as a guide. The dive boat captain sees the bright orange bag, knows that someone is surfacing away from the boat, and will keep an eye out for that diver

At the end of such a dive, you may have to cut the lift bag off the line and lose the line to the ocean—but you are vibrantly alive to dive another day. This whole process is actually very complicated, particularly if you are having other problems on your dive. And there are details to keep in mind such as making sure that the lift bag does not get caught on your equipment (thereby shooting you to the surface) and knowing how to tie a knot well enough to secure the whole thing to the wreck. Each of these sub-tasks must be practiced. You do not want to be thinking this through for the very first time during an emergency.

Fortunately for me, my idea of a fun dive is practicing stuff like this. And Dutch Springs has perfect conditions in which to do it. I was running down on my air, so I signaled Barry that I was heading back to the base of the metal girder tower to do the practicing that we had discussed before the dive. My scooter clipped off, I attached the bag to the reel, inflated it, and up it went, out of sight, presumably to the surface. I ascended along the tower, reeling the line back in as I went up very slowly. I did not want to practice cutting the line on this dive—that I would save for another day. But it's not a bad idea to take a short piece of line down on a dive and tie a knot or two after you have developed knot skills on the surface. At 40 feet I could see that my six-foot orange safety-sausage lift bag had gotten jammed into the girders of the tower structure and was not at the surface. I was surprised how much force I need to un-jam it, because the air in it had made it so buoyant. I released it, and it ran out another 40 feet to break the surface. Some lessons learned and some more practice acquired.

But I wasn't done with the quarry quite yet. I was happy to have the opportunity to squeeze in another dive at Dutch Springs before my first boat dive of the season to the USS *San Diego*. I had just got all my wreck diving equipment serviced and wanted to use it once in the relative calm of the quarry before plunging into open ocean. Good to know that the regulators will work, right?

Fast forward to today... John M. was planning to go out on a dive boat to do a wreck but poor ocean conditions caused the trip to be cancelled. So 6:30 a.m. found me driving to the rendezvous location along the Long Island Expressway where we would convoy our two cars to the Dutch Springs quarry. I was already having issues. I had bought a pre-made egg, ham, and cheese thing at a gas station market, and after a couple of bites had found a green thing in it that was unidentifiable. If I want human fingers in my food I order chili at Wendy's—this green thing was new, though. I called John excitedly on the cell to tell him I was on my way, and, "By the way, I found a green thing in my breakfast sandwich."

"Okay," he answered, not really indicating if he was actually for or against finding green things in your breakfast sandwich. Nothing ruffles this guy. Maybe that's why he's a good diver. I was already panicking about the green thing. Hell, I'd already ingested part of it. Yuck!

We got to Dutch Springs to find only a few brave souls in the light rain and went to "the pipes area," all the way on the left.

Today I would show John the pipes. He had already seen the main attractions at Dutch Springs numerous times: the helicopter, the plane, and all the rest. He had a new camera that he was looking forward to playing with. I really like the pipes area, which has structures such as the tower mentioned earlier that were used when the site was used as a quarry. All sorts of things to swim around, and roads that stretch into the surreal, white distance of the silty quarry floor. Here and there you can still find the spooky skeleton of a tree, its branches stretching up to greet a sun that will never shine brightly again down here at 80 feet.

At the end of the dive, I had one more thing I wanted to do. I had brought a "Jersey Reel," which is a large spool of heavy line that is used in a similar manner as a reel to make an emergency ascent line. The difference is that this is a much heavier/stronger and longer line and it can't be carried in a neat reel in my canvas dive bag. It's a bulky item with a whole bunch of new issues. One of the issues was where to put it so that I could reach it underwater. I tried placing it between my double tanks on my back and found that while I could reach it on land, I couldn't underwater. John actually pulled it off my tanks for me so that I could use it. I think that next time I will try placing it near the base of the doubles, going across the tanks.

It deployed well and unreeled perfectly all the way to the surface. I didn't want to tie it to the bottom and cut it so I ascended, rolling it up as I went up. Was that was a pain in the neck! Also, I had to make some creative movements to secure it at 20 feet while I switched to breathing off my deco bottle. I need some kind of line brake on it so that I can give my attention to other things without it unreeling. Though, as John reminded me after the dive, in an actual emergency I would have cut and tied the line and would not have been re-spooling it on the ascent. I am not convinced of the advantages of carrying a Jersey Reel. But I do like the fact that it can hold a stronger, longer line than a smaller reel.

As all good dives do, this one ended with food. We hit my new, secret Philly Cheese Steak place and headed home.

Just one dive in the rain today.

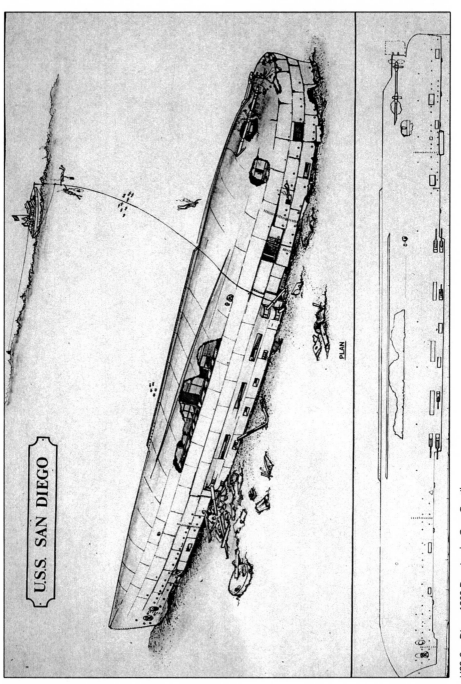

U.S.S. SAN DIEGO

PLAN

USS *San Diego* 1983 Drawing by Gary Gentile

CHAPTER FOUR

Cowboy Diving, Bumped by a Shark, Drama Diving the St Lawrence River

USS San Diego – *Saturday, April 30, 2005*
The year is 1918, the world is at war. The second battle of the River Marne, the last great German offensive of World War I, is underway. In spite of huge casualties—250,000 men will ultimately die in this battle—the allies slowly, painfully begin to turn the tide of war today, July 20, 1918, and push the German army all the way back to where it began its offensive.

When we think of the German army, we can almost hear the boots on the pavement, the men marching in perfect unison, a symbol of the German war machine. Perhaps too we can hear the scrabbling, less-coordinated sounds from the Allied side as they move to retake Europe's cobblestone lined streets from the Germans in the name of freedom. The sound of boots on pavement has always been there as a part of a land based war.

Halfway around the world one day earlier on July 19, 1918, the sound of boots could also be heard, but at sea, off of Fire Island, New York: the sounds of men scrambling for their lives on the 500-foot-long armored cruiser the USS *San Diego*.

When I think of a massive battleship, I usually picture a sort of serene bridge where the captain receives reports and gives out orders in a monotone, businesslike voice. No matter how dire the situation, the ship's command is a picture of emotionless voices and clearheadedness. Men's lives no longer specifically matter. It is the ship: she is now a single organism. Calmness and fortitude in the heat of battle.

But when a ship such as the USS *San Diego* is mortally wounded by a mine or torpedo, the rules change. Now a race begins. Get the men off the ship before she sinks. Now, its every man for himself.

I reread chapter four, "Sinking," in Gary Gentile's great book, *The USS* San Diego—*The Last Armored Cruiser* when I got back from today's dive on the *Wreck Valley* dive boat. Much of that chapter is about men running for their lives, which on a ship means the sound of sailors' shoes against metal ladders and stairs and the sound of sea boots against a wooden deck. Up on the ship's bridge, the officer of the deck—seconds after feeling the explosion in the port engine room—sends a

messenger to run to the radio room. An ensign rushes to the depth-charge racks. A lieutenant races from the bridge to the chart room to get the stricken ship's position. With the water already four feet deep in the engine spaces, two men escape, and the sound of boots against the metal ladders and stairs rings out again. The situation untenable, the captain orders his men to abandon ship. Now the sound of so many sailors moving at once...The individual footsteps combine into a low background sound of clattering sole against ship as the soul of the ship gives its last sigh..

Six men died that day on the USS *San Diego*. Twelve hundred survived.

I was excited about today's trip to the *San Diego*. It would be my first boat dive this season, and while the weather would be lousy with light rain, the forecast was for fairly calm seas. I started the day a bit on the wrong foot when I woke up at 4:30 a.m., before my alarm went off. I groped in the dark, reaching for the clock so that I could deactivate the alarm. I succeeded only in turning on the radio—very loud—and waking up my wife. The situation worsened in the dark room as I then activated the buzzer alarm. A few whispered "I'm sorries," and I was off to load my car. I would be diving with Barry W., and I met him at the boat.

I was afraid that we would divert to the *Lizzie D* wreck instead, due to the rain. We ended up going to the *San Diego* to do a single dive, planning to head back to beat the rising seas and thunderstorms that were predicted for later in the day.

I just love the sea. It's beautiful on a sunny day. It's also beautiful on a foggy, rainy, overcast day. Leaving the inlet for open ocean, I couldn't help thinking to myself—even as I tightened the hood on my slicker—that the boat ride is part of the whole lovable offshore diving experience. (You may want to check my opinion on this again if I am seasick—it might be different.)

It took about two hours to get out to the wreck, and I snoozed a bit on one of the bunks. I enjoy diving on the *Wreck Valley*. Captain Dan Berg, noted local diver, explorer, and author, runs a great boat. Someone called out, "Dolphin!" I missed it somehow, but I am sure they are out there. I had my scooter, and Barry and I planned to circumnavigate the entire 500-foot-long wreck. I'd tow him with *Apollo*.

Visibility was about 30 feet. I descended to find Barry waiting for me. He grabbed on, and after a brief time we were at the stern. I inflated the scooter's buoyancy jacket a bit so it wouldn't drag on the bottom, and we explored a few minutes around the massive twin prop shafts, finally swimming into an open area inside the stern and exiting on the "dark side" of the wreck. We were both fairly comfortable in the 41-degree water and proceeded forward along the ship, right above the sand.

About three-quarters of the way forward, we spotted what appeared to be a pile of leather military shoes, almost like work boots. These would have been what the sailors wore as they did their jobs on the ship, and what most of them must have been wearing that fatal day in July, 1918. Mixed in with them were rubber sea boots. These would have been worn in rougher seas on deck and in foul weather.

This isn't just a mass of wreckage down here. This was once alive. This is about men at war, disaster, national pride, the power of the sea. Close your eyes and hear the bosun's whistle, commands to battle stations, the boots on the deck.

One of the boots was fused with encrustation to a piece of wood—maybe its packing crate. I saw another loose boot. I picked up the loose boot and put it next to the encrusted one. A left boot and a right boot. Same size. A match. I held them together and showed Barry. He nodded. There was something about a pair of shoes from this fascinating wreck that for a second made it alive for me again.

We continued forward, scootering in a tight circle around the bow, gently rising in a safe spiral so that when we had rounded the bow we were now at the height of the anchors on the other side of the ship. I turned the scooter off and we agreed to ascend to the level of the keel. Once back on top of the upside-down warship, we scootered back to the ascent line. Barry ascended, but I still had some time left in my plan, so I decided to tour about a bit. I crossed the keel and looked back. Vis had suddenly decreased greatly, so I headed back to the ascent line—no time to get lost at the end of the dive.

I have been playing around with the placement of a Jersey-spool-type ascent reel for emergencies. On my last trip to Dutch Springs, I had placed it between my double tanks and had been unable to reach it. So I had made some changes and now just wanted to see if I could reach it. No luck. I struggled like a circus menagerie contortionist. Even though I could now reach the line and clip, I could not get the spool free of the surgical tubing I had used to fasten it to my tanks. I have an idea for next time and will try again. In the interim, of course, I have my regular reel and lift bag for emergencies, just until I figure out this Jersey spool thing.

After about 45 minutes on the bottom, I began my slow ascent back up into the rainy, overcast day, leaving the wreck to be visited another time.

I got home, and, while getting undressed for a shower and nap, I noticed my shoes. I had taken them off and had neatly lined them up near the door. They recalled to my mind the dark brown boots worn by the sailors now long dead of the USS *San Diego*.

Recommended reading:
Gentile, Gary. *USS* San Diego—*The Last Armored Cruiser.*

Berg, Daniel. Wreck Valley, *Volume II: A Record of Shipwrecks Off Long Island's South Shore and New Jersey.* (Very good section on USS *San Diego* and other local wrecks.)

A Monkfish Escapes the Monkfish Mincing Unit: A Dive on the G&D (Yankee) Wreck – Saturday, June 11, 2005

I had a great dive today on the G&D, a Great Lakes steamer with a cargo of coal that was sunk in 1919 by a collision with another ship. I was up at four a.m., loaded my gear, and could be found at 5:30 a.m. munching an egg on a roll on the deck of the *Jeannie II* out of Sheepshead Bay, Brooklyn. Whenever I'm on this boat I'm struck by the never ending, good-natured bantering of the crew. It's a fun boat with a good atmosphere.

Like the World War II shipboard meeting at Yalta between Roosevelt, Churchill, and Stalin, I found myself onboard the *Jeannie II* with Steve Burke and Janice from the Long Island Divers Association. In my capacity as President of the NYC Sea Gypsies, I initiated high-level diving talks; we then divided up the booty in advance and made some critical decisions that will affect local diving for years to come.

Last week, I was supposed to go to the wreck of the "Linda," an unidentified schooner that sits at a depth of about 135 feet, so I had a 26%-oxygen nitrox mix in my tanks. I had to cancel the Linda dive at the last minute, so the 26% mix would have to do for today's dive, which was originally scheduled to be the *Yankee*, a wreck that is farther out and about 125 feet deep. This gets confusing. There are two wrecks called *Yankee* in the same general area of the Atlantic Ocean. For more clarity you can look them up on Dan Berg's website at *www.aquaexplorers.com/shipwrecks.htm*.

So today we left Sheepshead Bay for the "Old Yankee," another wreck whose identity is unknown. Seas were a confused four feet, with an occasional six-foot breaker. It was a rough ride out, and Captain Reddan opted to go to the other, closer *Yankee*, the one also known as the G&D. No one objected. I had never been on the G&D and looked forward to it. I was pleased because it's a bit shallower, at about 110 feet. That meant I could have a longer dive.

Generally, if the depth is over 80 feet I will plan to do a single, long, decompression dive rather than two shorter dives. This is for a few reasons. Doing a single dive with a single ascent is inherently safer than doing two ascents in a day. That second dive, even with a surface interval in between the two dives, increases your risks. I also like to get out of my equipment and take a nap. We have so much equipment to put on to dive—I hate it, although I love the diving part. So do one long dive and you only put your equipment on once.

I am not sure how many other divers do this, but part of my decompression dive planning involves calculating how much gas in my main tanks would be needed to complete a full, safe decompression if my pure oxygen tank were to fail for some reason. This means that I generally am starting up the line from the wreck with a good amount of back gas left. Deeper dives mean I use up my gas faster; they also require longer decompression, so I need to have even more back gas left at the end of the dive. So my deeper dives get even shorter. I think my optimal depth for a 40-minute-or-longer wreck dive is about 110 feet deep to 130 feet. Deeper than that and the dive is annoyingly short—about 25 minutes or so. Digging around in the sand with my shovel or scooter makes me use my air even faster and limits the dive even more.

I suppose I could carry a second pony bottle. If I did that, I might be able to use a bit more of my back gas. So let's see: double back tanks, 40 cf O_2 on one side, another 30 cf on my left, canvas tool bag, scooter, ascent reel. This is already out of hand. I am not bringing another tank underwater!

So I was happy we were doing only 110 feet instead of 125.

I was among the last in the water and descended to the wreck. Visibility was about 30 feet. We were tied in at the large boilers, and I toured with my scooter. Following the flattened plates and ribs brought me to the still-intact bow.

There were a couple of huge goosefish, also known as monkfish. These leftovers from some horror movie lie flat on the bottom like a flounder, but that is the only thing they have in common with the flatfish. Their heads are at least a foot wide, and an immense mouth stretches the whole way across. I annoyed one of these monsters by digging too close to him, and he jumped up, surprising me, showing me all of his long teeth as he threatened me. I got the daylights scared out of me and backed off. I opted against activating the monkfish mincer scooter option reasoning that the fish's head was actually too big to fit through the propeller shield of the scooter anyway. (Just kidding; I would never mince anything in the scooter, except for the occasional other diver.)

The bow of the wreck is still upright and looks like a bow. Going aft, past the boilers and some debris, I went searching for the stern but realized that I had passed it not too far from the boilers. This wreck produced a number of nice lobsters for some of the other divers. I had to be content with the bottom of a china cup I found lying on the sand near the wreck. I poked here and there without finding anything else but had a great time circumnavigating the old ship with the scooter.

Water temps were 46 degrees, and I was back on the boat about 65 minutes after I dropped in the water.

I had felt a bit queasy on the trip out, even with my scopolamine patch. Even in the water I had felt a bit "off." I didn't get seasick, though. I ate enough today, but maybe I have some mild bug or something.

Usually on the *Jeannie II* I bring a cooked rotisserie chicken which I eat cold after the dive. Last night I couldn't find one in the supermarket, so I got an Empire kosher barbequed chicken. When I looked at it today, I realized that it was packed with very messy sauce, and it became a major project trying to open it and eat it without messing up the entire boat. Steve Burke of LIDA took a photo of me eating it like an animal, covered with barbeque sauce and holding the entire messy chicken, pulling off limbs and meat savagely. Janice and Steve did try it in spite of its shark-chummy appearance, and all agreed it was rather tasty.

Another nice day out on the ocean and diving.

P.S. There was no shipboard meeting between Roosevelt, Churchill, and Stalin. It was on terra firma.

A Trip to the Oregon – Saturday, June 25, 2005

One of the reasons I love our local wreck diving is the history. I've been a history buff since childhood, my mind filled with visions of ancient civilizations—the Greeks, the Romans, and all the way up to imperial England and the great sailing ships of the nineteenth century. I'm one of those who can get glued to a book like *Attila: King of the Huns*, and the History Channel. Perhaps some divers go down to a shipwreck and see a lot of junk and a formless mass. I see history. I've got a decent ship-related library filled with books on the steamship age, many of which contain drawings and photos of the massive engines. I've got books about military ships and sailing ships, each loaded with construction details that allow me to see that formless mass of the sunken ship as a still-living and breathing piece of history. Shhhh...if you listen carefully you may still hear the waves breaking against the bow as the 518-foot-long nineteenth-century liner SS *Oregon* cleaves through the seas at 18 knots from England to Sandy Hook, New Jersey in record time. And always, in the background, another prominent sound: the deep, thumping sound and vibration of the massive engines, engines which can hurl this floating city across the Atlantic in seven and three-quarters days.

Usually I try to read something about the shipwreck I am to visit. Lots of information can be found on the Internet. Yesterday, I got a double dose of history. Some was related

Loss of the Cunard Ship Oregon, Picture courtesy Herb Kaasmann,
OREGON, GREYHOUND OF THE ATLANTIC

to the demise of this great liner, the SS *Oregon*, which sank in 1886 off Fire Island after being struck by another ship. The rest of the history had to do with the dive boat I was on.

I was excited about this dive. I would be taking the dive boat RV *Garloo* out of Captree, Long Island. The *Garloo*, owned and captained by Hank Garvin, used to be known as the RV *Wahoo*. It had a long career as a dive boat, and in fact was involved in a 100-year-anniversary commemorative dive on the nineteenth-century *Oregon* wreck in 1986. If you were to mention some of the great local wrecks, such as the USS *San Diego*, the *Andrea Doria*, and others, somehow the *Wahoo* would have been at the center of things. By the time I came on the northeast dive scene in 1999, the *Wahoo* was still the dive boat to take if you had business with some of these shipwrecks. Most weekends, the *Wahoo* would visit the USS *San Diego* one day and the SS *Oregon* the other day. Many serious, hardcore, local wreck-divers and explorers liked to go back to their favorite wreck again and again. Perhaps they were doing ongoing, exploratory penetrations into the *San Diego*, going in a bit farther each dive. Some divers might have had a secret spot on the *Oregon*, a spot they could dig for artifacts. It could take a diver a lot of work, sometimes more than a couple of dives, to get a porthole off the *Oregon*. The boat to take if you were in this diehard group was always the *Wahoo*. In fact, it was on the *Wahoo* that I was first introduced to the USS *San Diego*, one of my favorite wrecks.

One of the crew members that used to captain the boat was Hank Garvin. Hank is now the owner, and the boat is now known as the RV *Garloo*. Hank is a friendly guy and knows this boat inside and out from his years of crewing on it.

You can tell the *Garloo* is unique among local dive boats right from the dock at Captree, before you even board it. Prominent on the afterdeck is a crane/winch that can raise large items from the ocean bottom and onto the boat. Once on the boat, you'll find a large cabin and lots of space for divers to suit up. My favorite feature, though, is this: the boat has 20 bunks. I like to be able to take a nap, either going out to the dive or afterwards, and there is ample space to do this.

While the first scheduled dives for this season were to occur on a July fourth overnighter to Montauk to explore the U-853 German World War II submarine and some other wrecks en-route, Hank was taking the *Garloo* out this weekend to the *San Diego* and *Oregon*. Chris B., an accomplished wreck and cave diver was there too for his first trip on the *Garloo*.

245

As usual, I napped on the way out and was awakened by the slowing down of the engines as we approached the wreck. Seas were an easy-to-handle two-to-four feet, and before I napped, I made sure to catch the rising sun as we headed out through the inlet. Seeing the newly awakened sun is one of the great moments in a day of wreck diving—fingers of golden orange light reaching out across the waters, stretching across the sparkling sea. You have a cup of coffee in hand, the boat is moving fast beneath your feet, and you are off on another adventure!

While I had been to the *Oregon* a number of times, I didn't really understand the big picture yet. My dives had generally been near the boilers, and from time to time I had ventured astern to see the enormous steering quadrant and propeller. Today I had brought my scooter and planned to see the entire wreck, stem to stern. No digging today, just a tour. By the way, the SS *Oregon*—even though she has lain underwater for over a hundred years—is still yielding many artifacts. Some are from the ship and some are items the 800 passengers left behind when they abandoned the ill-fated liner.

My dive—35-minute bottom time, maximum depth of 125 feet—was great, thanks in part to a visibility that was 30 feet or more. There was a large ray with a four-foot "wingspan" lying in the sand near our tie-in point, towards the bow end of the wreck. It stayed there for the entire dive. I scootered the length of the ship. At the stern, I floated for a while near the huge, half-buried prop, gazing up at the steering quadrant that controlled the ship's rudder. This part of the ship, shaped like an enormous wheel, is large enough that a diver can easily swim through it, between the spokes.

I pointed the scooter forward and headed up towards the bow. My depth was about 110 feet, so I could see things below me, could use my air a bit more slowly, and could build up less of a deco obligation. Then I spied it! My artifact for the day! I had to go down to 125 feet to get it. I must have been experiencing the effects of nitrogen narcosis, because I was certain that somehow I would be the lucky finder of a vintage pillowcase from the original linen store of the SS *Oregon*. What a find! How could it have survived so long? I touched it tentatively, in case there was a biting monster under it, and realized that now it looked like nylon—maybe it was a diver's catch bag or an early nylon laundry bag that had been used on an experimental basis aboard the *Oregon*. I scooped it up into my red canvas bag and went up a bit to resume my scootering towards the bow. Now back at 110 feet and with a clearer head, I felt a nagging doubt about what I had placed in my canvas bag. I decided to sort it all out later up on the boat.

I passed the large ray in the sand and continued forward past the ascent line to the bow. The bow is on its side and retains some of the original structure. I scootered around the bow, moving to the other side of the great ship. The wreck becomes a mass of collapsed plates and debris as you head aft from the bow, and I headed across it to expected location of the ascent line. Good: it was there. Check my gas—still some left. I headed back across the wreck to check into something else I had noticed. Yes, here were bricks lying around, bricks that were similar to the kind you would typically find near the boilers farther back in the ship. There, the bricks would be used to line the coal-eating fireboxes under the boilers. These bricks were different, though. The face of one had a porcelain glaze. Perhaps there was a kitchen or galley here aft of the bow, and maybe this brick was related to that. I'll look into that.

I headed up the ascent line, back to the dive boat. At about 60 feet deep, there was a layer of yellow-brown water that had to be passed through. It was about 10 feet thick, and once I was above it, the water changed back to its normal greenish hue.

Back on the boat after being in the water some 68 minutes, I experienced two surprises. I reached into my red canvas bag only to find that my "pillowcase" was in fact a fairly standard, black plastic garbage bag. I was also surprised to hear the other divers talking about all the sharks they had seen. Evidently, when ascending to the dive boat through the yellow-brown layer, the divers had looked up to see six to eight four-foot-long sharks circling around them. Somehow I missed that. I felt a bit disappointed, because I have not seen many sharks locally.

Recommended reading:
Kaasmann, Herb. *OREGON Greyhound of the Atlantic.*

"Cowboy Diving" at the Ponquogue Bridge – Saturday, July 23, 2005
Steve from the Sea Gypsies sounded depressed. "That's what she said: zero vis!" he complained. Steve, having left a few minutes ahead of me, had completed his two-hour drive from New York City and was now reporting live from the Ponquogue Bridge in Hampton Bays at Shinnecock Bay, Long Island.

"Hey," I said, "we can go in anyway. It'll add some adventure." Privately, though, I was disappointed too. I guess *Apollo* would have to stay in the car.

When I arrived at the parking lot, Steve brightened up a bit. "Now she says 'only' eight-foot vis." Whoever was feeding Steve this info was obviously planting it as part of a wider disinformation campaign to keep "outsider" divers from tainting the local dive sites.

Well, I had just freaked out my wife two nights ago. She'd dragged me to the local Home Depot, ostensibly to get a replacement orchid plant. I insisted that she come into the tool corral. I immediately put on a leather apron and work gloves and pretended to assist a non-English-speaking customer. I was obviously ready for anything. Diving with Steve in low eight-foot vis certainly wouldn't the first odd thing I had done this week.

Another friend was there. This would be his first dive with a spear gun. Steve and I agreed that we would stay far away from him, yet would be ready to administer first aid if needed. I had to keep reminding myself that it was not a good idea to pull the spear out of the victim until he was safely in the hospital, assuming that you wanted to prevent him from bleeding to death.

To give us some time to get away from the hunter, we opted to enter the water quite early, in spite of a heavy incoming current. It looked like it was gonna be a "cowboy dive." That's cowboy as in rodeo-bull and bronco riding. Definitely not suggested for you if you are not familiar with the strong tidal currents at the Ponquogue Bridge. Definitely not suggested for new divers. Our plan was simple. We'd go in a good 20 minutes before the tide was supposed to slacken, and we'd then just...go with the flow.

The current snapped us up fast as soon as we let go of the wooden bulkhead at the base of the old bridge. It swirled us out of the shallows and carried us rapidly to the old bridge, a few pilings out. We each grabbed on to a piling. Right before we descended down our particular pilings—legs and arms locked around the piling in an embrace—I could see a group of other divers look at us with concern from the shallowest point under the old bridge. They were basically hanging out on the rocks and waiting for the current to abate. I could just picture the dive master telling his students, "Look at those two divers! They don't know the bridge! They went in too early!"

What they didn't know is that we were, in the time-honored tradition of extreme sports, doing a little bit of cowboy diving. We had a plan. The tide was running into the bay, not out to sea. We had compasses. Stay negative and go with the flow. Emergency? Go due south. I'll take this any day over riding a bull in a rodeo!

We dropped down to the little depression between the pilings; the current is a bit weaker there. If you turn your head 90 degrees to the flow, you risk the regulator being torn out of your mouth. We got our bearings, made sure we were very negative, and let go of the rope we had grabbed down there. The current immediately took us west, but—because we were negatively buoyant and dragging on the bottom—not quite as fast as you might think.

I saw the shadow of the new bridge and its support pylons and knew that now was the time for us to head north towards the wooden wall defining the boat channel. I gave Steve a prearranged signal, he grabbed onto my hip D-ring, and I pointed my scooter north and turned it on. On its highest power setting it had no problem taking us both at a 90 degree angle to the flow; in seconds we were at the big, square, concrete block right before the wooden pilings that define the boat channel. There is a space with lots of nooks and crannies between the block and pilings that is home to all sorts of fish. We saw many circling striped bass and other inhabitants of this tidal bay. We hung around in this area waiting for the current to slow and stop.

We used the scooter here and there; we swam, we explored, and we played with sharp, rusty things. Steve put odd, rare fishhook lures in his BC pocket, collecting them like I collect rocks. (I hope he remembers they are there.) I created billowing clouds of silt digging with the scooter. We scooted in circles. Who knows where we were. Slack tide had arrived, and we had lots of gas. We lay on our backs in the sand, watching our bubbles rise to the surface, clearly visible some 20 feet or so above us.

All good things must end, and so did slack tide. We let the current carry us east. I turned on the scooter, and Steve grabbed on. A slight miscalculation, and suddenly we were in heavy current among the pilings of the old bridge. I swooped to the right, then to the left to avoid the rapidly oncoming pilings. Thump! Steve hit a piling on the turn. I headed north, and Steve hung on for his life as the current whipped us towards another piling. Whack! Uh oh, that was Steve again, missing the turn, centrifugal force hurling him against another piling. Sorry Steve. He weakly gave me the OK sign, nervously looking around to make sure we were clear of the old bridge.

We headed over the crest of the ridge and dropped down into the 33-foot-deep Porgy Patch area. Steve seemed okay. I apologized again. I passed him *Apollo* and watched as he scooted around in this deeper area which was protected from the easterly currents by its western ridge. We played around for about 15 minutes in this area.

Now we each had about 800 lbs of pressure in our tanks, and it was time to leave.

I activated *Apollo*, and Steve grabbed on. I gave him the international diver's signal that I would not go anywhere NEAR the pilings of the old bridge ever again, and we were off. We headed south until, when we reached a depth of 15 feet, the current whacked us hard. I turned the scooter due east, following a ridge of sand. Powered by the *Apollo*, both of us kicking, and with the full force of the current directly behind us, we flew east. I mean FAST! Exhilaratingly fast. Surprised flounder exploded off the bottom. Clumps of seaweed periodically caught in the scooter's prop and changed the constant whir of power into a chunky, coughing sound until I stopped the motor and cleaned out the debris. Finally, as the current began to let us go, we headed south again, dive over.

Our dive was a full 72 minutes. That's quite long for a dive at the Ponquogue Bridge. We went to Tully's Seafood afterwards, right over the bridge on the north side. We had called in our order while putting our gear away, and soon we were enjoying fresh cooked lobsters, Alaskan king crab legs, and cole slaw. What a great way to finish up!

A few hours later, I went back to the bridge at low tide and hunted around the exposed rocks for treasure. I think I found something: a stone axe head. It is now sitting in a vinegar bath for a few days to remove encrustation. It's probably just a rock. But I am having a lot of fun, so humor me!

Thousand Islands, Saint Lawrence River – August 1, 2005

I just came back from a couple of days of great diving in the St. Lawrence River up on the border between New York State and Canada. We dove with an outfit out of Brockville, Canada and had a good time.

The St. Lawrence River is the path that heavily laden freighters and other cargo ships take take to reach the inland Great Lakes from the Atlantic Ocean. It is a very busy river with more than its share of shipwrecks. From its shores, one can watch the freighters make their way. Sometimes daredevils in speedboats or jet skis follow, catching a thrill as they jump the waves of the great ships.

There were two dives on Saturday, two on Sunday, and two on Monday. I skipped the Monday dives, opting to start out early for what ended up being a nine-hour drive home. That means I did four dives. I only saw three of the four wrecks though. Here is what happened to me on that first dive.

Currents in the St. Lawrence River can be quite strong. Typically, the SCUBA diver descends to the shipwreck by following a line down to the wreck from the dive boat. In strong currents, it is critical that you not let go of this descent/ascent line, because it is easy to get caught up in the current and to be taken far away. That can be dangerous, because very large ships traverse the St. Lawrence Seaway. There's heavy recreational boat traffic as well, and you do not want to be a lost diver drifting among the boats.

This was the first dive of the trip, and it was to a depth of 90 feet. That's about as deep as a nine-story apartment building. We were warned that there were substantial currents. Some of the more experienced divers teamed up with a newer diver, and we went in. I was near the top of the line when I looked below the boat and saw another diver, a newer diver, drifting away rapidly under the boat. He was already about 40 feet deep and was sinking fast. He could not make it back to the line and seemed to be rotating slowly in the current and looking up, his arms outstretched towards the line. He was also rapidly getting smaller as he drifted away. I knew this guy was headed for big trouble. This dive was deeper than he usually did, and he only had a single tank of air. I let go of the line and propelled myself down to him. We dropped to the bottom together. As far as I was concerned, his dive was over, and my job was to get this fellow back to the surface safely now.

The wreck and dive boat were nowhere to be found. I signaled for him to grab onto the small rock near us to prevent being carried farther by the currents, and I looked around. We had just jumped in the water, so he probably still had a lot of air. Of course, we were 90 feet deep. At that depth, a diver uses up air about three or four times faster than on the surface. That meant that my companion had, conservatively, about 20 to 30 minutes of air left, assuming his tank had been filled to the max and that he was not breathing faster due to anxiety. I had double air tanks, so I wasn't too worried about myself.

Should we look for the wreck so that we could find the ascent line and get back to the surface safely? I weighed the options but decided to not do that, because it would mean we would have to swim against the current to do the search. That exertion would cause us to use our air much faster, and then we could be in a life-and-death emergency. I had actually practiced for an emergency such as the one I was now in, quite a few times. But now I would have to do this self-rescue for real.

I was clearheaded, but I must admit I was concerned —not so much for myself, but for the less experienced diver that was now my charge. I looked around. There was nothing in the immediate area that was heavy enough to secure us. I spied a large rock. To reach it, we would have to swim hard into the current, but it was not too far. We made it to the rock. I signaled to my buddy to hold onto the rock so that he wouldn't drift away. A couple of times, I caught him letting go and starting to drift. Now was not the time to play with the current. I sternly put his hands back on the rock.

As I've mentioned before, I carry a six-foot-long inflatable sausage, one of the large ones with a eight-inch diameter. I also carry a wreck reel with 240 feet of strong, nylon line on it. The plan would be to attach the sausage to the line and to then inflate the sausage, which would shoot to the surface. I would then cut the line off the reel and tie it to the rock. The dive boat (and other boats, hopefully) would see the bright-orange emergency sausage and know that there was a problem. We could use the line to ascend safely and slowly to the surface, and once there we could await assistance without drifting farther away.

I first made sure I could get the line all the way under the heavy rock, under the center. Once sure I could secure the line to the rock, I detached my inflator hose from my dry suit and connected it to the sausage, taking very good care that nothing would get fouled when I inflated the sausage. The buoyancy of the sausage would easily shoot me to the surface uncontrollably if any of the line caught my gear on the way up.

Not only did the entire operation go perfectly, I was also pleased with how calm and levelheaded I was during this emergency. I attribute that to lots of practice with my gear. I knew exactly what had to be done. I had already done it many times for fun!

When we were about 20 feet below the surface, a diver appeared and asked if we were okay. I gave him the OK sign, and he vanished. It occurred to me later that he must have swum back to the dive boat, indicating that the current on the surface was more manageable than at depth. At the time, I opted to remain with the safety sausage, as I did not know the limitations of the diver I was with. If we had started swimming back and if he had had problems, we would have been adrift, probably heading toward the large ships. With the orange safety sausage anchored to that big rock on the bottom, we were in a relatively safe position. I was not going to take any unnecessary risks now.

Once at the surface, I found I still had to keep an eye on my buddy. He kept letting go of the line until I addressed him rather sternly and told him to put his wrist through a loop so that he would stop drifting off. It is altogether possible that he still does not realize the danger he was in. Assuming that he would have been able to ascend slowly enough to not kill himself, he would have been drifting that whole time. Even as we waited for assistance, a huge ship passed us in the channel, probably an eighth to a quarter of a mile away. Would he have drifted that far? I don't know. I do know that a diver in a black wetsuit would be almost invisible to a boater.

My wife Lynda was on the dive boat and spied my orange sausage. She immediately recognized it as mine from seeing it in the bathroom after numerous dives. She raised the alarm. A swimmer made their way out to us with a life ring, which we grabbed. The boat then pulled us in. I had to cut my line, and it sank 90 feet back to the bottom, still tied to the big rock.

I am not sure how far we were from the dive boat: maybe 100 to 150 feet. I told my buddy not to try to swim for the boat, because the swim would be against the current and it would tire him out. If something else went wrong, he would be exhausted and less able to help himself. "Let them pull us in," I said. They did.

After the dive, many of the divers jokingly expressed their condolences that I had not actually seen the wreck on the river bottom; I had logged only a nine-minute bottom time. But this will be a dive I will never forget. It was a much more challenging dive, and, in spite of its serious nature, it was also much more fun. I felt good that when I was called upon to help another diver I was able to step to the plate and help change what could have been a disaster into just another learning experience for both myself and the other diver.

And that's the story of why I missed one of the of the four shipwrecks on my dive trip to the Thousand Islands this past weekend.

An Unusual Encounter with an Unusual Fish – Saturday, August 15, 2005

It's 10:30 p.m., and I just got home. It was a long day that started with a dive at Ponquogue, followed by lunch at Tully's, a nap on the beach, changing my mom's flat tire and then dinner out east, and the long drive back. But it is the dive today at the Ponquogue Bridge that lingers in my mind. This place, which I have dived so many times, continues to throw new stuff at me and keeps my interest.

I met Ben and Laurie from the Sea Gypsies at the old bridge. We swam under the old bridge to the steel cross that gazes eastward towards Jackson's Marina, the last berth of Ken and Jean's dive boat *Jean Marie*. Ben and Laurie enjoyed rides on *Apollo* for a while, and then we left the familiar area of the old bridge to explore parts unknown. At the end of the dive we spent time in the deeper Porgy Patch, looking at fish as the current passed harmlessly over us. We headed back, and when the current hit us, we allowed it to sweep us east a bit. The three of us then hitched a ride on *Apollo*, continuing towards the still-rising sun and finally heading south again for shore.

It was a great dive, and since I still had a lot of gas left I decided to head back out into the current with my scooter.

I got out to where the current was fairly strong, and there I saw it. Only its strong, thick tail was moving, propelling it into the current. The rest of its body seemed eerily still. It looked like a five-foot-long UFO. I had no idea what it was—some kind of a large round ray, or maybe even a weird shark. Muscles worked beneath the dark and scaleless skin as it cruised about 10 feet above the bottom and 10 feet deep. I had seen a very large ray or something similar lying in the sand near the ascent line during a dive on the *Oregon* recently. At the time, I had thought that it must have been a large goosefish, but this was the same beast—only it was swimming and taking no note of me at all. I revved up *Apollo*, but it continued to ignore me, swimming languidly into the current as if no effort at all were required. I was fascinated. I turned my scooter and followed. The creature allowed me to come alongside, and at one point I could have touched it. I backed off a bit as it occurred to me that having no idea what the beast was meant that I also did not know how big its teeth were or how aggressive it might be. I fell in behind it as it headed west towards the "hill" upon which the old bridge is built. It was amazing how effortlessly it seemed to move. When it got to the sharp slope, it headed up, following the contour of the landscape like a silent stealth aircraft. As it topped the crest of the hill, it was hit by the full force of the current. Without skipping a beat it swooped up and banked to the left just the way you would expect a fighter jet to do. It was beautiful. I had followed it up the hill a bit more slowly, taking care to not ascend too quickly. The last I saw of the creature, it was headed back east with the full current behind it as I too made that hairpin turn when the current hit me.

I stopped by the Hampton Dive Center to get my tank refilled and described the fish to the owner, Randy. He thought for a minute and then said, "Torpedo. Electric torpedo ray, I bet that's what it was." He handed me a book with a picture; he was right! Now I had a name.

"What do you mean, electric?" I asked. Randy explained to me that these members of the ray family grow up to six feet long and can give a shock of up to 220 volts! I admit, I am glad I did not touch the fish. No wonder this member of the shark family wasn't worried about me. Randy recently saw a six-foot torpedo ray on the Panty wreck and added that for some unexplained reason there seems to be a high number of sightings of these unusual fish this year. Well, if anybody lost one, I know where it is. At our very own Ponquogue Bridge.

A Lesson in Running a Line when Penetrating a Wreck: USS San Diego – Sunday, September 8, 2005

My first thoughts when I got to the dive boat this morning at 5:00 a.m. were confused. "Barry's right," I thought. "This does look like a fishing boat. Where's the ladder? There's almost no room for divers on the deck."

Barry had visited the marina and boat a couple of days earlier to just check it out. It was the *Sea Hawk*, and neither of us had ever rode her out to any of the many local shipwrecks off the southern shore of Long Island.

Barry's good like that. New boat, he's gotta get all his facts together and check it out, reconnoitering the situation and reporting back to Central on conditions. So there was a flurry of emails. Barry reported his findings that the *Sea Hawk* looked more like a fishing vessel. No dive ladder and no door in the side for divers to use to jump into the water easily. Randi, at whose invitation we were joining this diving party, wrote back, rather patiently, "Of course it has a ladder! Of course it has a way to get in the water. What are you TALKING about? Of course it's a dive boat!"

Well, here I was. It was not quite 5:15 a.m. and I was now telling myself that we would just have to make do with this poor excuse for a dive boat. Barry arrived. We waited for the other divers to show. We waited for the boat's captain. Then an SUV started to pull into the lot, thought better of it, and pulled out again. We waited some more. Now it was 5:45 a.m., and no one else had shown up. I remember telling Barry, "Do you know what the odds are? Two dive boats at the same marina with the same name? Fuggetaboutit!"

One of us then decided to walk back towards the street and there spotted an SUV with its back open, full of dive gear and parked in the next lot. "Uh oh. I think we're in the wrong place!" In two seconds we are there at the real *Sea Hawk*, which was in the final stages of loading, in preparation to go out to the USS *San Diego*. Activating our superpowers, we got our gear loaded, and shortly thereafter the *Sea Hawk* headed to sea with all parties on board.

We got a little ribbing from the other divers and crew when we told them that there was another boat with the same exact name in the same marina. Randi put it all into one sentence when she asked, "But was it a DIVE BOAT? No? Then you should have known it wasn't the boat!" As is true in many cases with Randi, she had a good point there.

The *Sea Hawk* is a "six-pack-sized boat" optimally sized for about six divers, and was a pleasure to be on. We listened to Captain Frank Persico's tales of local diving history as we rode out into an emerging day which gave no hint of the recent storm, Ophelia. We were all certain that that departed storm would be responsible for lousy visibility on the wreck.

The seas were great, the sun was out, we dove. I had decided not to take my scooter because of the expected poor vis, but once I was in the water I could see the descent line at the bow from my position at the stern of the boat. So I changed my mind and asked someone on the boat to lower me *Apollo*.

I had brought a strobe light along to help me find the ascent line in the expected low vis, and I saw that my method of attaching it to a jon clip was not the way everybody else did it. I made a mental note to attach a brass clip to it the next time I decide to use it.

We were tied in right at the bow of the USS *San Diego*, and I took off with my scooter, heading around the bow to a place in the sand on the debris field or "light side" of the wreck. Once there, I used the scooter's prop wash to excavate a small hole under one of the now-missing forward portholes. Since you can't take anything from this wreck, it doesn't matter what I was looking for. I moved on.

Until today, my penetrations had been very tentative: I'd only entered through the largest openings and had never gone deeper into the ship, never beyond the room I had first entered. I wanted to go inside the wreck a bit more. At the first entrance into the ship that I found, I could see another lone diver exploring inside with his light. I decided not to go in there. I didn't want to disturb the diver's Zen-like experience, so I looked for another opening farther down, around the middle of the ship.

In the future I will not bring my scooter inside the wreck, but now it was with me so I made sure it was neutrally buoyant, floating perfectly next to me, and I went into the wreck through an opening formed by a large, missing metal plate. This time I could see the next opening some distance away, farther towards the stern, and resolved to make my way to that exit opening from inside the wreck. At all times I had visual contact on my original entry point, so I wasn't too worried. If I found I couldn't get to the next exit, I could retrace my way back to this one.

I looked back a few times and was gratified to see that there was little or no evidence I had been this way. I was using the bent-knee style finning position, and my Force Fins were working great. Once outside the wreck again, I scootered to the stern and between the enormous prop shafts that protruded from the end of the sunken naval vessel.

Wriggling Through the San Diego

On previous dives I had swum around inside here at the stern, which was fairly open. In fact, Barry and I had visited here together a few dives ago, worming our way between crumpled steel and sea anemones. I went forward a few feet and found another opening on the dark side of the wreck, and again I went inside the wreck. Here I did not see another exit, but I thought I would go in as long as I could keep the entrance hole in sight.

This area was full of vertically oriented debris and columns and pipes. I made my way between them, following what appeared to be a clear path, going farther and farther in. Suddenly it opened up; it seemed as if I was in a large room. In reality, some of the decks had collapsed here inside the San Diego, forming a large, vertical shaft. I looked down and saw pipes and a confused mass of debris. I thought for a second that I saw torpedoes, but then decided that I was too far forward of the stern area—torpedoes wouldn't have been housed in this part of the ship. I don't even know if there were torpedoes in the stern of the ship.

I drifted down vertically in the shaft about 15 feet to look around some more, then gently rose to begin my exit. Once I regained my "altitude," I could again see the bright green square through which I had entered the ship. But I could not see what I had originally taken to be a direct, simple path to and from that entrance/exit. I looked around and saw that

I could squeeze between two vertical, pipe-like, encrusted things to get out. No problem. I would fit. But it disturbed me how easily I had lost my path even when I could see the exit. When first coming into the wreck here, I had navigated my way in without having to squeeze through or between anything at all, but now I could not see how I had accomplished that. I made my way out easily enough, but I considered it a very serious lesson learned: I will run a reel on all penetrations from now on, and I'll leave my scooter parked outside. I suppose— no one's gonna steal it, right?

My dive had been planned for a 40-minute bottom time or until I was down to 1000 psi in my double tanks. It was now at 35 minutes, and it was time to go. I was still towards the stern and had to get to the bow for the ascent line. I rode *Apollo* there in about 90 seconds. Love that scooter! On the way, I saw something shiny in the sand and dropped down to investigate. I turned *Apollo* around and dug for a few seconds, uncovering what appeared to be a contemporary boat's round barbeque-grill cover. Maybe it was from the *Eagle's Nest* dive boat, I thought. I left it in the sand for someone else to take and continued forward.

My bottom time was 40 minutes, and water temperature at depth was about 55 degrees. I breathed 28% nitrox and decompressed for 16 minutes on 100% oxygen. Additionally, I did a number of deeper stops and used my back gas. The vis might have been 25 feet or more in some places—excellent conditions on a day when we all thought vis might be close to zero.

I surfaced to a bright sunny day, and we were soon heading back to the dock, back from this single-dive outing. There was lots of great food on the barbeque, and more stories too. All in all, a great day.

Barry was ecstatic that he had passed the in-water-skills section of his advanced nitrox class, qualifying him to do 100% oxygen deco. He took the class with Randi Eisen. I also had taken her class. She is one of the New York area's diving legends, and as a teacher she's a tough taskmaster, so I know passing that class means a lot to Barry.

A Dark Dive on the USS San Diego – Sunday, November 5, 2005

It had been too long since my last boat dive. Two dives to the USS *San Diego* cancelled because of high seas and winds. It would be another week before I actually got to the dive boat and we finally headed out, again to the *San Diego*. On the way, the captain redirected to the closer *Iberia*, which sank in 1886 with its cargo of dates en-route to New York City. Hovering over the *Iberia* like a hornet ready to release its divers, the captain decided that the seas were too "snotty"—he was worried we'll all be seasick. No one entered the water. We returned to the dock for a consolation prize—barbequed steaks and other lunch items, a high protein breakfast at 8:00 a.m.

Never give up! I tried calling around to the area's dive boat captains. "Are you going out this weekend?" I asked. A couple have stopped running for the season; another says, "Maybe but I doubt it. Weather doesn't look great." Eventually I reach John Gorman of the dive boat *Lockness*, out of Freeport, Long Island.

"Lockness" Dive Boat

Courtesy Captain John Gorman

"We're gonna try to get out on Saturday to the *San Diego*," he says, before pausing and adding something to the effect of, "It's gonna be a bit choppy." I reassure him that I am willing to get sick this trip—that's how badly I want to get out to the wreck. He laughs, tells me to be at the boat by 5:30 a.m., and hangs up.

I have never been on the *Lockness*. Worried that I will get lost and miss the boat, I allow myself some extra time to get there. I am not too concerned about getting sea sick; I am too psyched up about visiting my favorite local wreck.

After a few years spent using sleep-inducing Dramamine and Bonine for seasickness and still getting sick on rough days, I asked my doctor for a prescription for the scopolamine patch. This little round patch is placed on your skin under your ear. The patch can be kept on for three days as it continues to release its anti-nausea drug into your body. Usually I put it on at about 10 p.m. the night before a dive. As with all these anti-seasickness remedies, the patch must be applied hours before you get on the boat. Once you are seasick, it's too late. The only thing that might help you then—other than getting back to the dock—is a wristwatch-like device that delivers a measured shock every few seconds. (By the way, I also have one of those, and it works—somewhat.) But the patch is not perfect. I have found that I sleep very lightly and fitfully the night before a dive. I blame the scop patch for that. So, for this dive, I applied the patch as soon as I woke, at 3:45 a.m.

The *Lockness* turned out to be no problem. I recognized a couple of divers and felt right at home on this new boat. My gear aboard, I looked around. The boat has a very spacious afterdeck for gearing up, and it boasts an easy-to-climb Christmas-tree-style ladder for access to and from the water. Numerous divers can easily suit up at the same time without getting in each other's way. After watching the sun rise, I followed my usual pattern. I found myself a bunk and fell back asleep to the rhythm and roll of the five-foot waves and swells as we pushed through the chop on our way out to the sunken naval vessel.

We tied into the wreck, and I descended into a gloomy darkness. It was overcast and the light was not penetrating well through the murky seas where the visibility was already not great from the preceding few days of 35 knot wind gusts and higher seas. I got to the base of the ascent line and attached a powerful strobe light to help me find the line later in the darkness. It looked like we were tied into the wreck on one of the two bilge keels, somewhere amidships. Some ship bottoms have a pointy area at the very bottom called the keel. Large ships, particularly ones that are top heavy because of armor and massive gun turrets, have additional keels. These run parallel to the main keel for much of the ship's length. They add stability to the wide vessel and serve as useful landmarks to the diver.

I was not sure where on the 500-foot-long ship I was. It didn't really matter as long as I kept track of where I was relative to the line that went back up to the dive boat. I dropped over the side of the ship and looked for an opening in the ship. There are many openings now in the side of this once-great ship, this vessel which had once been the flagship of the fleet at the beginning of the twentieth century. About halfway down the 25 feet or so to the sand there was a rectangular opening. These openings are generally caused by an entire piece of steel plate falling off the ship. The plate comes off in one clean piece because the rivets are made of a different metal than the plates, and the seawater causes an electrolytic reaction that eats away the rivets. Some of these openings lead to dead ends—maybe a room with a mysterious purpose, or perhaps some of theses spaces are merely the gaps between the outer hull and the useful working part of the ship. Some of these openings lead deeper into the ship.

I turned on my light and was welcomed by some small brown fish. There were no visibility problems here inside the ship. No murkiness. Just pitch-black darkness. Outside, the stirred-up ocean offered only five to 10-foot vis, but in here, protected from the surge and 104 feet below the surface, I could clearly see as far as the light from my lamp could reach. There—right in the middle of the room scrabbling about, a medium-sized lobster. He moved backwards, lobster style, and bumped up against a ridge of metal. He stopped, trapped now, with no escape.

Don't worry, Mr. Lobster. I'm just passing through.

I looked around the small room. The floor on which I stood was actually the ceiling—in the days before this ship sank, flipped, and hit bottom. I moved farther into the room. Towards the back, I found a mass of tangled, collapsed metal. It was hard to

Crew of six-inch gun aboard USS San Diego, circa 1916.
Image courtesy of the US Navy Historical Center.

tell what used to be what. There was a round thing; it looked like a hatch of some kind, now filled with sand. But there was nowhere to go in that direction. I was now in the very back of the room, perhaps 25 feet from the opening I'd come in through. I covered my light with my hand. Total darkness enveloped me. I slowly turned my head towards the opening. It was so dark out there that what would normally have been a bright green light allowing me to see my exit clearly was now only the dimmest hint of light and was not easily visible at all.

So far, I had not silted up this room at all. I'd used my fins with the tiniest motions and had kept myself perfectly balanced, not touching floor or ceiling. But one sloppy kick and the vis would fall to zero. The weak green light from the entrance would become impossible to see. I turned my head back towards the inside of the ship, uncovered my light, and kept exploring. Following the room all the way to the left, I discovered a passage between some twisted pieces of metal back in one corner of the room. I put my head through the gap and saw another room. This next room was also parallel to the hull, and I could just make out another hole, a missing plate and a hint of green light in that room. Although it seemed like an easy swim through the hole and into that next room, I decided to return to my original entrance and tie off some line from my reel, so that if I decided to go deeper in I'd have an easy way out should I mess up the visibility or get lost.

I tied off the line and noted some electrical cables running along the inside of the hull. Must be the wiring for the anti-mine degaussing system, I thought. I couldn't remember where I'd read about the anti-mine system. It used electrical currents to change the ship's magnetic signature. Apparently it didn't work as well as it could have, as evidenced by the probable cause of sinking for the *San Diego*: a mine placed by a German submarine.

My line tied off within arm's reach of the opening, I turned back around and headed back into the dark room. I squeezed through the restrictive gap and into the next room, unreeling my line as I gently flicked my fins, knees bent to keep them away from the floor so as to not raise a cloud of silt.

In the next room, I again covered my light and looked for the glow of the outside world through the hole in the hull up ahead. I looked behind me and found no trace of the first entrance, only my thin nylon umbilical disappearing into the gloom.

I uncovered my light. Something was in this room with me.

Quickly, it swam through the sudden cone of light as I removed my hand. For a second I was certain—it sure looked like a shark! There it was again: two dorsal fins on its back, one some distance behind the other. It swam in and out of my light and then retreated to some dark corner of the room. It was only a few feet long and wouldn't stay still long enough for me to get a good look.

The thought of being alone in a dark room in a shipwreck some 100 feet down with a shark as my companion was not a pleasant one, no matter what the size of the beast. In spite of that, I poked around a bit more, finding some fire bricks and ceramic tile. Maybe this was the galley area? I was not sure. There was also, at the far end of this room, a much tighter path through some entangled debris, and a space beyond. I decided I'd go there next time. I turned around, reeled my line back onto the spool as I negotiated my way back to the first room, nodded to the lobster on the way out, and emerged back into the shadowy green world outside the wreck.

I decided to go along the hull for a while at sand level and, plunging into sudden darkness, I came under the shadow of the great six-inch guns. My, this was all a bit spooky today. Before I knew it, I was close to the stern. I ascended 15 feet, halfway back up the side of the ship. Figuring I had gone far enough, I ascended farther, now to the level of the keels. Oops! Overshot the ascent line, so I headed back down a bit and finally was rewarded by the flash of the strobe beaconing me back to the dive boat above. I still had some quantity of air left (in addition to the amount that I wanted to keep as a safety reserve) so I decided to head across the bottom of the ship to the other side. You really realize just how big this ship is when you cross it in low-vis conditions. Its beam, or width, seems to go on forever. I looked over the other side but was not able to make out much detail due to the poor visibility, so I headed back to the line.

I ascended slowly. For this dive, I had left more reserve gas in my back double tanks than I normally do because of a possible problem with my oxygen deco bottle. On my last dive on the *San Diego*, about a month ago, the bottle had gushed air from the first stage when I turned it on to do my 20-foot O_2 deco. The first stage is where the breathing regulator attaches to the tank. I had to disassemble the equipment underwater to reseat the regulator on the tank, and it worked fine, supplying me pure oxygen as needed for that deco. Unfortunately, if you take this equipment apart underwater, corrosive salt water gets in. That means you absolutely must get the equipment serviced and cleaned out before using it again. I had the setup cleaned, and, last week when I tried it (luckily not underwater), it did not work at all. So I rushed to get it serviced again. This would be the first time using it for real, underwater, again. Actually, on the way down, at the beginning of today's dive, I did test it at about 15 feet deep—it seemed okay.

My deco was uneventful, and, after paying my dues hanging on the anchor line for 15 minutes at 20 feet, I got back on the boat and was greeted by the delectable smell of barbequed steak and other treats. After snacking a bit, it was back to the bunk for me. I got about three more hours of sleep as the other divers did a second dive, and then we headed home. Like an alarm clock, the sound of engines throttling down always wakes me, and it did so now as we passed the jetty and entered the inlet for the dock.

I had a great day on the *Lockness*. She's run by a very friendly crew and captain, and I look forward to diving with them again soon. There are only a few weeks left in the season. Hope I get some more trips to the USS *San Diego*.

Bumped by a Shark During Deco on the USS San Diego – Saturday, November 19, 2005

Evening yesterday, I was at the Long Island Divers Association Annual Film Festival. One of the video clips showed a local wreck. I nudged my wife with my elbow. "That's the *San Diego* wreck—that's where I'm going tomorrow." As it was, I didn't get to bed until a quarter to one, waking up just a few hours later to make the trip to Freeport, Long Island to board the dive boat *Lockness*. I was awakened by my idea of a diving nightmare. I had been on the boat and had forgotten my scopolamine anti-seasickness patch! Awake now, I looked at the clock. It was 4:15 a.m., and I was relieved it had only been a dream. Now it was time to head out into reality.

I head out. The seas are flat calm, and it is a beautiful, sunny day. It is quite cold today, but the boat's cabin warms up soon, and I sleep some more on the way out. What a sight! A boat full of guys in ski jackets, parkas, and other heavy winter clothes, all of them about to jump into the ocean for a dive!

I have a bit of trouble clearing my ears as I descend, so I swim from a depth of 12 feet nearly back to the surface to try again. Finally, I am on my way down the line. It's another darkish dive. Large particulate matter drifts by in the steady current. My eyes adjust, and I see that we're tied in at the very aft section of the bilge keel on the port or "dark" side of the wreck. Right below and a bit forward is a large opening into the old warship. I scout it out to see if it leads deeper in. Two dives ago, I had entered the wreck somewhere in this area without running a line and had become a bit disorientated while exiting. I would use a line for this penetration.

I tie off near the entrance and head in. The inside of the USS *San Diego* is a world of reddish browns and other dark colors. Pale yellow sea anemones and hints of green are visible in the distance where the ocean has broken its agreement with the ship's designers. These green, sharp-edged breaches in the hull can mislead the diver into thinking he can exit via a hole other than the one he used for entry. But there may be no direct path to that hint of green, or it may be too small to squeeze through.

My plan is to exit the same way I entered. If I see another exit, I might check it out and make a note of it for a future dive.

I cover my light with my hand (you should never turn off your light while inside a wreck, because it may not come on again: the biggest stress to the lamp occurs when you first turn it on). After a few seconds, my eyes adjust. Now there are no browns—only darkness broken by patches of dim green light in the distance. I uncover my light again and look around. How can anyone tell what all this stuff used to be? An item from 1918 is now almost totally obscured by nearly a hundred years of marine encrustation. Loose wires still hang, but they now wear a living insulation—a deadly threat waiting to snag the unwary diver.

My way is now blocked by debris. I shine my light straight up, illuminating a big space that stretches to my left. I think for a minute about the heavy machinery and metal plates in the ship that are periodically collapsing as the USS *San Diego* continues its chaotic disintegration into a pile of debris on the ocean bottom. Another 100 years or so and the ever-powerful ocean will fully reclaim this once-great ship of war. Hopefully, none of that heavy collapsing will occur today with me in the ship's center.

I head to the left, keeping my line taut, and make a straight run aft now. Another 40 feet and now the way is blocked again. Careful not to stir up the silt, I wrap my line around a pole, make a right into another space, and then double back through another set of rooms, heading forward on a path that's roughly parallel to my initial aft run. Here and there I can see my own reel line between the posts and girders. I am now about 40 feet forward from the spot where I made the right turn. I'm roughly even with the hole I used to enter the ship, but I'm now on the other side of a wall which is composed of broken beams, flat metal pieces, and dangerous-looking wires. I see something that looks like a shelf and try to move it. It's trapped by a twisted girder, and I can't budge it. Something catches my attention as I shine my hand-held HID light down and to my left. Tiny eyes. Reflecting the lamp light are six pairs of little red eyes. Each with a large shrimp attached to it. I KNEW I was being watched!

It's a bit spooky in here. I check my remaining air. I still have a lot left but decide that I want to go back to the outside of the ship to determine exactly where I came in. Later, at home, I will consult my set of USS *San Diego* plans to see where I was in the ship.

I do a perfect, slow-motion, 360-degree turn without stirring up the room, then I tighten up my reel and start my exit. I head towards the stern again, following my line and reeling it back onto the spool as I go. I make my turn back forward, following my line out through the labyrinth of collapsed debris, and all of a sudden I am stuck. Hmm, didn't see that! I back up a bit and try again. Now I am through the space with nothing more than a rust stain on the back of my gear. A couple of minutes later, I am back outside the ship. I note where the entrance is with respect to the end of the bilge keel and start up for the surface.

My 40-minute time on the bottom requires some decompression time, so I make a stop. Usually, if the current is not too strong and the surface wave action is not great, the time spent hanging on the line to do deco can be restful and almost meditative. You watch the myriads of jellyfish drift by, look up at the beckoning rays of the sun filtering down through the greenish depths, and it and relax. Perhaps you are mentally reviewing the dive you just finished, or thinking about that artifact in your bag. You really want to pull it out and look at it, but you're scared that if you drop it now it will be lost forever in the sand some 80 or 90 feet below you. You check your dive computer. You wait some more. You watch the bubbles from another diver heading for the surface. At first they rise lazily, but they ascend faster and faster as they expand with the decreasing pressure.

Oh, sometimes I think about sharks. I consider how I will respond if I see a larger one while I am doing a decompression stop. I am worried that I will get scared and bolt for the surface. Now that would be a big problem. If I fail to complete my deco, I will certainly end up in the hospital with the bends.

Suddenly I feel something knock into my tanks. I whirl my head around. There is nothing there. The rope is in front of me so I couldn't have knocked into that, yet it felt like my doubles were smacked and hit into my back sharply. Thirty seconds later I feel it again. Maybe my tanks have shifted and have knocked into my back. I wonder. A minute or so later I look up towards the dive boat, some 20 feet above me, to see a shadowy form perfectly silhouetted against the green-and yellow-rippled sunlight from above. It's a shark! For a few seconds it remains balanced in an almost vertical pose, its sinuous body in a gentle 'S' shape. I am looking at the beast from below. It is not moving. It just looks, for a second, frozen in time. It's not taking notice of me. It's looking up at the dark hull of the dive boat.

Now at the moment of truth, confronted by my first decent-sized shark, I feel no fear. Just awe. The lighting is perfectly eerie. It is a beautiful moment made much nicer, I am sure, by the shark's ignorance of me. I recover enough to look around for other sharks, but I see none. And when I look again, the shark is gone. I finish my deco after another 10 minutes and climb back onto the boat. Another great dive.

We had a barbeque, and in retelling my shark story I resisted the urge to expand the shark to eight—or even 12—feet long.

Another diver also saw it, and together we estimated a length of about six feet. Our guess is that it was a blue shark. I don't know. I do know that I do not recall ever feeling something crashing into my tanks before while doing deco. Some of the other divers went in for a second dive. I napped as usual, and before long I was back at the dock unloading my gear.

Once home, I pulled out the general plans for the USS *San Diego*. The ship was first commissioned as the USS *California*, and the plans are dated 1907. It was a real hassle to get these plans from Washington, D.C. The original drawings are seven feet long. I have them on microfiche, from which I have had four-foot copies made.

According to the outboard profile in the general plans, the bilge keel or docking keel is around frame number 85. The hole I entered was a bit forward of that, perhaps near frame number 82. Using that frame as a reference point, I must have entered the ship and arrived in what was left of the engine room. The large, cavernous space was probably the result of a collapse: maybe one of the heavy engines had fallen down through a couple of decks, right through the upside-down armored cruiser. Then I had headed aft for about 40 feet. Depending on which deck we are talking about, I could have been in the blower rooms, magazine rooms, engineer stores or junior officer state rooms.

Because the ship is upside down, things that were on the higher decks when she floated are now on the bottom of the wreck and are covered with stuff from the lower, less-interesting decks. There is still a lot of exploring left to be done in this dangerously collapsing wreck.

I'll be back. sharks or no sharks.

Last Boat Dive of 2005 Season – Saturday, November 26, 2005

I'm going out on the dive boat *Lockness* for its last trip of the season. Last weekend, we had a great dive on the USS *San Diego* wreck—this week's destination as well—and I had a shark encounter. I found out later that there were actually a couple of sharks, one of which came straight at another diver. It turned away at the last second when the diver blew bubbles at it.

Whenever I speak to old timers about SCUBA divers and sharks, they generally shrug and say to not worry. I'd always thought that perhaps there was some secret technique they used that allowed them to relax and forget about the possibility of becoming dinner for one of these human-overpopulation problem solvers. Hmm. But BLOWING BUBBLES? That's the secret weapon? Let me tell you this: if blowing bubbles is the best we can do to protect ourselves against these predators, then we are in trouble! It was reported that one of last weekend's sharks had been wearing a bib which depicted all the different cuts of meat that a diver provides.

I want to make something clear. I do not consider myself brave. When I talk to non-divers about diving, I sometimes get the impression that they think I am either extremely courageous or nuts. But with my diving, I'm always doing risk analysis, deciding that this or that can be done fairly safely with an extra air tank here, redundancy there, etc. I carry a couple of reels, emergency ascent equipment, a couple of lights, and I try to add some element of conservatism to my decompression calculations. Brave? No. Smart, careful, and in control of as many of the variables as possible? Yes.

Now we return to wild animals that cannot be planned for. A species that is so efficient a hunter that its design has changed little in eons. A swimming dive-o-matic that combines elements of a stealth aircraft with those of a Cuisinart food processor.

The only sure way to avoid sharks is to stop diving. Until they evolve little stubby legs and come on to land, I will then be safe. What do you mean that's already happened, that they're called alligators? Anyway—you get my drift.

Last night, the night before my dive, my wife and I stumbled across a show I've seen before. *I Shouldn't Be Alive* is a Discovery Channel series that explores true stories about life-threatening situations, and—wouldn't you know it—this week's episode was about a bunch of shipwrecked folks adrift on a small raft in the Atlantic Ocean. Whether or not they thought they had a population problem, the sharks helped them to solve it. I particularly liked one scene. A man, in the water and hanging on to the raft, yells to another man. "Stop kicking me!" Seconds later, he realizes that he is being bumped by a shark, and is now an unwilling participant in a pre-attack dance choreographed about millions of years ago. He makes it into the raft, but it reminds me of how a shark bumped me the last time I visited the *San Diego*.

My wife was a bit nervous that I'd be going back into Sharkland again in a few hours. The night before a deeper boat dive, there is usually a moment when, lying in bed and trying to fall asleep, I think about all the risks in this sport, and I experience a moment of panic. At those times, I feel like canceling the dive, and I ask myself a question: why the hell do I do this? Maybe I imagine running out of air, getting lost in a wreck, getting entangled, being attacked by another panicked diver who starts a knife fight for my air hose, getting the bends, getting very seasick, or making a rapid ascent ending in an embolism. The list is endless. I always end this negative train of thoughts with a positive statement.

"Well, I think I've planned for that. Hopefully it won't happen, and if it does, I think I can handle it." The thought goes away, and I fall asleep.

After watching that damn show on TV and going over old *Jaws* movies in my mind, I thought about diving with cuts of skirt steak coated with Tabasco sauce, attached to my diving gear as armor. The idea was that the beast would taste and run. Since I might meet a shark that LIKES Tabasco sauce, a shark that puts it on everything it eats, I opted to not do that. I fell asleep.

Right before the alarm goes off, I'm up. I am going diving. I realize that I am really not that worried about sharks, and I'm looking forward to visiting my favorite wreck again. I'd like to continue the penetration I did last Saturday. I am getting very familiar with that area. I make sure my laminated deck plans of the stern area of the USS *San Diego* wreck are in my gear box, and I'm off!

Boy its cold! Air temperatures in the 30s while it's still dark out. My oxygen decompression bottle falls over, and when I turn it on, it's hissing badly from the first stage. I replace the O-ring, reseat the regulator, and it's fine. As we head out to sea, I am lying in a bunk next to a cold window, but one with a great view of the rising sun. The grey horizon gives birth to horizontal streaks of orange and red. The black silhouettes of bare-branched trees asleep for the winter on a spit of land between us and the waking sun completes the painting.

I wait for most of the other divers to go in, and then I'm in the water. Uh-oh. Very bad vis. In addition, it's overcast, so it's going to be another dark dive. As I descend, the vis is so poor that I am startled when my legs brush up against the wreck. I didn't even see it! I attach a flashing strobe to the line to help me find it later.

I have an idea that we are tied in amidships on the starboard or light side, where the debris field is substantial. I want to be on the other side of the massive wreck so that I can continue my internal explorations. I decide I will cross the 30- or 40-foot width of the ship's 500-foot-long bottom to get to the other side. Then I'll follow the bilge keel aft. The hole I want to use to enter the wreck is right around the end of that bilge or docking keel.

I get halfway across the bottom of the ship and start to get worried. Because the vis is SO low—perhaps just a couple of feet—I probably should run a line from my strobe to the wreck. I have over 20 dives on the *San Diego*, and it is very easy to navigate on the outside of the wreck. I have never thought that I should run a reel on the outside of the wreck. So I decide that even though I have two reels, I will go back and stay on the light side of the wreck, near our tie-in point. This may be a short dive anyway with this lousy vis. I go back to my flashing strobe and go over the side, down another 20 feet or so to the sand, and head aft. I can see very little. The water is full of particles, and my light illuminates them, making it almost impossible to see.

I cover my light for a second. Down here, under the big guns, I am in almost total darkness. I look for the opening into the ship, the one I went through a couple of dives ago. I find it, and head in. This is not good. A lot of times when vis is bad outside the wreck, it is fine inside. Today, even the inside vis is really lousy. I think about going farther in and running a line, but I stop. Here's why I have survived so long in this dangerous hobby. Like a speed brake governor on a plummeting elevator, common sense kicks in. Time to end the dive. Let's go home. I can't see anything. There will be other dives.

It occurs to me that if I leave now, I'll have little or no deco and will not be hanging around as bait for that shark any longer than I have to. That clinches it. I'm out of here. I check my shark-o-meter; it agrees with me. A low-vis dive is not worth it. Perhaps if vis was better and if I was having more fun, I'd stay down longer, maybe 40 minutes. For now, my 21 minutes of bottom time is fine. I exit the ship and ascend slowly along the side to the line that will return me to the dive boat.

I am not really too worried about sharks even though the visibility while ascending continues to be lousy. I get to my 20-foot stop and decide to do some pure O_2 deco, even though this has been a short dive and I only need to stay a few minutes here using my 28% oxygen back gas before I can ascend.

I turn on my O_2 bottle and am very startled by an explosive popping sound followed by uncontrollable gushing bubbles from the first stage of the bottle. Aghghh! This bottle has been nothing but trouble on the past few dives. I decide this bottle needs servicing again—no matter that it had just been serviced a couple of weeks ago. I decide to try to reseat the first stage. Doing this underwater means a certain trip for servicing. I remove the first stage and the little O-ring; dislodged from its seat, it floats away into the current. Disgusted, I playfully make believe I am attaching the first stage to the ascent rope as if to breathe off the ascent line instead of the tank. Uh-oh. The diver for whom I put on this little show seems to be asking me if I'm okay. I give him the OK sign and put the first stage away. I thank the powers that be that I did a short dive and really didn't need the oxygen anyway.

The divers above me on the line are now gone. It's just me alone. Or am I really alone? I look around 360 degrees. Nothing. From what I understand, sharks don't need good vis to see their targets. They live in an electric world, navigating with sensitive organs that can pick up electrical signals. I wonder if my still-flashing strobe would attract them. I don't want to turn the strobe off underwater, as it's a twist on/off control. I don't want to risk flooding it. I decide that because I am not doing an oxygen deco, I need to add some extra time, and I settle in for a few more minutes. I stay for eight minutes at 20 feet, in addition to some lower stops, and then head for the surface.

I get a lot of questions about offshore water temperatures this time of year.

Some temperatures for USS *San Diego*, at 105 feet deep, are as follows:

Date	Water Temp	Air Temp
04/30/2005	52	41
09/05/2005	68	52
09/18/2005	77	55
11/05/2005	66	57
11/19/2005	55	57
11/26/2005	45	52

The coldest time is generally early in the season around April, when the boats start going out to the wrecks. In April, temperatures can be in the 40s. Now, in November, deep water temperatures are still fairly warm, often in the 50s.

A last politically correct comment about sharks...

These poor beasts, some of which are being fished to extinction, are merely curious about us divers, temporary visitors to their watery world. I was kidding about the shark that had been reported as wearing a lobster-type bib with a picture of a diver on it. The shark's behavior of bumping its intended victim is nothing more than the primitive animal taking a smell of its dinner, similar to what you or I do when we smell a clam on the half shell before eating it. Most so-called shark attacks are nothing more than the next logical step in this pre-ingestion sensory process for the shark. It represents the end of the smelling process and the beginning of the tasting process. Please remember that the shark has still not committed to actually eating its victim at this point. Medical science has noted a clear relationship between the size of the sample taste and the victim's lifespan. I think more research is sorely needed into discouraging the shark at the smelling stage so that it doesn't need to take a taste.

A Trip to the USS Olympia: a ship of similar vintage as the USS San Diego – Sunday, January 22, 2006

We were inside the ship. Deep inside, and to make things worse, we hadn't run a line. I tried to look behind me in the passageway and found that I couldn't turn around. I couldn't even back up. I pressed forward into the bowels of the hundred-year-old warship. This obscure, rust-lined passageway led forward and provided the firemen that stoked the boilers of this steam-powered naval cruiser access to another set of boilers and fireboxes. With the ship running full steam and forced draft at a powerful 22 knots, this passageway would have been over 125 degrees hot. Those blackened, grimy-faced sailors must have raced through here knowing that to stay too long meant a slow roasting. Pick your way to be cooked. In here? Or up on a higher deck by the heat of battle? We had already passed a vertical pipe it in the last boiler room. The pipe contained a ladder. That would have been the emergency exit. People fleeing a leak of superheated steam or incoming water from a torpedo hit—people running for their lives—would have used that ladder to escape.

We continued on in the claustrophobic space, passing through a square hatch almost like a doorway and clambering through other hatches with gently arching tops. I remembered someone, perhaps Steve, mentioning earlier in the day that this ship had a feature: ammunition-related hatches were rounded on top, while other kinds of hatches were square. He didn't know why. It was just another piece of history, part of the lore of this great ship. The information not found in any books. It was just passed on orally from person to person.

I looked at my knees and forearms, covered with the reddish stains of history from squeezing through these spaces never visited by tourists. So similar to how my dry suit looked after explorations of the USS *San Diego*. But today I was not on the *San Diego*. No, I was with a group of Sea Gypsies who'd been given a unique opportunity to explore a similar warship, the

USS *Olympia*, docked at Philadelphia's Independence Maritime Museum and in no danger of sinking. Or so I thought.

My ruminations were interrupted by a yell. Steve from the club was ahead, in the next room. "There's a leak! I hear water!"

Our guide rushed past to see what Steve was talking about. He paused, listening for a second, then crouched and disappeared through a vertical sliding door into one of the many coal bunkers that were in the space between the boilers and the outer hull of the ship. We were below the waterline. Steve had discovered a leak in the USS *Olympia*—the pressure of the water was causing the incoming water to arc in a graceful parabola across the coal bunker. Our guide's radio could be heard from our station in the boiler room.

"I'll be there in a second!"

Moments later, the footsteps of another *Olympia* staff member reverberated through the passageways as he ran down a catwalk. "Please move back," he said. He reached down into the boiler room to remove a heavy metal floor plate, pulling on a ring that lay in a small indentation in the plate. The wiry fellow, clad in once-tan coveralls, looked up and said, "I'm going in." He vanished under the floor of the boiler room.

The 344-foot-long cruiser USS *Olympia* represented the generation of cruisers built a little over 10 years prior to the USS *San Diego*, and both ships had been built by the Union Iron Works in San Francisco. She saw action in Manila and had a long and noble career as a flagship of the American navy.

The 504-foot-long USS *San Diego* was originally commissioned as the USS *California* and was given the designation ACR6. It was an armored cruiser of the Pennsylvania class. In a time when a visible navy was hugely important to the United States, an emerging sea power then, cruisers represented a new approach to the projection of power. Rather than building many heavily armed battleships that could not move quickly due to their heavy protective armor and bulk, the United States invested in cruisers, which were lightly armored, comparatively speaking, and a little less armed. But they could move fast. They were able to convey messages by rapidly showing up off coastlines, intimidating and threatening. They could maneuver at high speed and usually were the flagships of the fleet. Both the *Olympia* and the *San Diego* have admiral's quarters on board towards the stern.

I had wanted to visit the *Olympia* since famed diver-author Gary Gentile had mentioned her in a Sea Gypsies presentation a few years ago. The tour turned out to be beyond all expectations. I had called on Saturday and mentioned we were coming. I expressed disappointment that the engine spaces were closed. They said they'd see what they could do. When we arrived around noon, we spent a few minutes wandering around the officer's quarters then went down a staircase amidships to the engine room. That is when the miracle occurred. A ghostly apparition, clad in paint-stained dungarees and a cap, appeared. Was this the "Lost Workman" that, in 1892, had fallen into the hold during the *Olympia*'s construction, only to vanish? No, this was Steven Green, history buff and *Olympia* restorer, who'd come to take "the visiting divers from New York" on a most singular tour of the *Olympia*'s innards. He had us walking catwalks, descending ladders, and squeezing through passageways, and he communicated his love of the ship and its history very well to us.

After the *Olympia*, we took a quick look at the *Moshulu*, the largest four-masted sailing ship still afloat. Then it was off into town on foot to locate Jim's Steaks, a well-known Philly cheesesteak joint. The line was so long that I ran to a deli to get us something to munch while we waited on line to eat. The long line gave us a great opportunity to study the man making the sandwiches, whose style and demeanor were obviously based on the Soup Nazi in the Seinfeld episodes. Most of the time he said "next," and the next person on line would order his or her sandwich and toppings in an organized way. There were no questions about toppings or anything. You had to work that out yourself while waiting. I knew there would be problems when one of our crew tried to order a non-steak item. He mustered up all his courage but his voice broke at the critical moment and he said: "I'll have a nurkee with…"

"What was that? Turkey?" The man behind the counter relaxed for a second and enjoyed this, serving my unnamed friend with relish. "You're on the wrong line! Read the sign!"

I was next. I'd have to handle this very carefully. I had seen a Seinfeld episode where Seinfeld had actually tried to engage the Soup Nazi with pleasantries, in order to befriend him. Unfortunately, I had left the TV to get a snack and did not get to see what had happened to Seinfeld. But it seemed like a nice, civilized way to go about ordering my steak. There was no curt "next" for me, though. All I got was a raised eyebrow from the cook. How does he do that? I cannot raise one eyebrow without the other one going up too. He was clearly waiting.

"Hi! How are you today?" I hesitated as he just stared blankly at me; I gave him my order. He slurped some Cheez Whiz onto the bread, and then I made my second mistake. I changed my order. In an effort to catch his attention, I waved my hand at the glass that separated us.

He froze in midair, glowering at me, and in a slow and measured tone said, "Don't do that."

I froze too, like I was turned to stone. The quiet chatter on the line stopped and all the patrons turned to watch what would happen. I slowly lowered my hand and said nothing. He returned to making my sandwich, and everyone relaxed. Then I made my third mistake. "Please leave the peppers off."

He stopped again. "I heard you the first time." I tried to turn on my cloaking device and turn invisible. It didn't work. I took my sandwich, paid, and escaped upstairs to enjoy it.

Bellies full, we headed back for a quick visit to the Seaport Museum, which would only be open another hour. We dropped our coats off in the car and hurried in. Once inside, I discovered that I had left the ticket for the *Olympia* in my coat, back in the car, and I headed out to retrieve it so that we would not have to pay another $40 dollars to get into the museum. When I returned to the museum (the car was parked sooo far away), the lady at the ticket booth said, "Why didn't you say you were with the Sea Gypsies? You don't NEED the ticket. You're the divers that saved the *Olympia* earlier today!"

As usual, the Gypsies were already a legend, this time only hours after entering the City of Brotherly Love. The museum was interesting and worth seeing.

We finished up our day with a dinner at Seabra's Marisqueira Portuguese Seafood restaurant on Madison Street, in the "Ironbound" section of Newark. This is an incredible restaurant with huge portions and delicious dishes and is highly recommended.

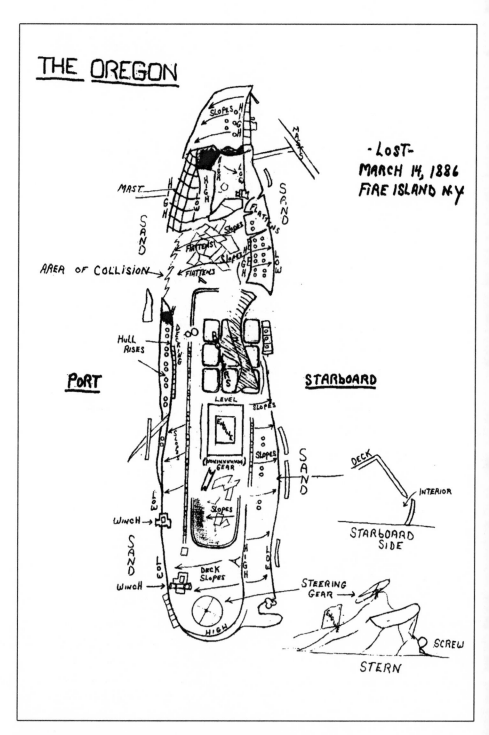

Oregon Drawing by Herb Kaasmann, Circa 1980 , Picture courtesy
Herb Kaasmann, OREGON, GREYHOUND OF THE ATLANTIC

CHAPTER FIVE

The Bald Eagle, Asfalto, Diving Lake Ontario, Historic Mark V Diving Equipment, Entanglement in the USS San Diego, Bottle Diving off New Rochelle

How to Dive the Ponquogue Bridge on Long Island

The following is excerpted from an email I sent a fellow diver when asked how to dive the bridge.

Divers should dive the bridge around high tide, when the current slackens for a period. I find www.noreast.com to be a good source of tide information. For example, on Sunday the 20th of May, 2007, the site shows high tide at 12:10. If I were planning to go diving, I'd plan to be in the water at the end of the bulkhead on the east side of the old bridge by 12:00 p.m. and I'd observe conditions, beginning my dive when the current visibly lessens or stops.

I have gone diving there many times, and I've had great dives of over an hour long without my scooter to help me get back after the current starts up again in the opposite direction.

Head out under the old bridge; go to the end. Check out the memorial plaque for Ken and Jean Marie on the center piling in the last row. They were killed in a tragic auto accident in April 2005. They had operated the popular dive boat Jean Marie out of Jackson's Marina, Hampton Bays. If you continue about 20 feet straight out past the end of the old bridge, you are near the boat channel. (Don't surface!) If you make a left and go west, you should arrive at the supports for the new bridge, which have a lot of fish around them. Wooden pilings under the new bridge mark the boat channel.

After 30 to 45 minutes or so, the tide will start to change. You can check by dropping a mussel shell or some sand and seeing what the current does to it.

Head east when the tide starts to change.

If you get back to the end of the old bridge (as opposed to somewhere closer to shore under the old bridge) you can continue east past the end of the old bridge (about 30 feet or so north of it) and you will see a rise followed by a steep drop off of about 30 feet or so. This is the Porgy Patch. A large pipe runs smack through the middle of the Porgy Patch. The rise shelters you from the outgoing tide, and you can spend time here watching the various inhabitants of the bay that make their home here.

Now, about getting back in.

Do not go back under the old bridge if the current is moving. You will exhaust yourself. It is shallower under the old bridge, as the bridge is built upon a tall pile of dirt/rocks/rubble. Because it's shallower, the current is much stronger here than it is elsewhere. Return to the east side of the embankment which supports the old bridge so that you're partially sheltered from the outgoing tidal current. Keep on the east side of the embankment's base.

Let the air out of your BC and make yourself totally negative, hugging the bottom as you travel. Done this way, coming from the Porgy Patch or the end of the old bridge, you'll continue in a southerly direction. Be prepared for a flurry of seaweed and stuff that may reduce vis or get stuck on your mask. As you proceed, you will encounter a curving ridge heading roughly east/west, and you can see that it will get shallower if you go up the ridge. Go up the ridge a couple of feet. Now relax and let the current take you east. It will sweep you along the ridge, depositing you farther east, and the current will then let go of you. Now proceed south again. You are in the small bay, about 75 yards east of the end of the old bridge. You are in shallow water that rapidly gets shallower as you head south. You will land on the beach right next to the base of the old bridge. Even though this area is not in the boat channel, there can be boats anywhere in this cove east of the Ponquogue Bridge, so avoid surfacing unless you are in shallow water, and even then be aware of the sounds of boats. It's always a good idea to carry an inflatable sausage and let that break the surface first when surfacing in an unknown area. At all times, be aware that boats could be anywhere. When I dive the bridge with a buddy, we agree to NOT surface to look for each other if separated, unless we're under the old bridge.

If you're coming in when there's a current, the biggest problem is getting anxious and swimming furiously and using up your air.

In an emergency, it's okay to just head due south, even if it takes you under the old bridge. Relax and let the current take you east of the old bridge if this occurs. If you are already south enough to be under the old bridge, you will encounter the ridge discussed above and will get in fine anyway.

I have come back in without problems; even when starting with less than 1000 psi, I've had air to spare at the end. You should probably plan to come in when you hit 1500 until you get familiar with diving the current at the Ponquogue Bridge.

This is a great dive with a lot of surprises. I have seen very large fish at this site, including a 10-foot-long stingray, four- or five-foot-long electric torpedo rays, triggerfish, blackfish, and circling gangs of stripers.

A Trip to the Bald Eagle Wreck – Saturday, April, 29 2006

I went out yesterday on the *Wreck Valley* dive boat to visit the Bald Eagle wreck. We had a great day, but it was marred for me by a serious bout of seasickness before the dive. Another diver, unfortunately, was ill for the whole trip. Most of the time, I put on my scopolamine patch the night before. Because it makes my sleep a little restless, this time I decided to put it on when leaving for the boat at 4:30 a.m. I was basically okay until we stopped over the wreck to hook in. A current from one direction combined with wind from another and created a four-foot swell and a "confused sea." Note that sea rhymes with queasy. The patch has worked so well for me over the past few years, but suddenly I felt as if I was not wearing it at all. Oh was I sick! Luckily, because I've been diving for a few years, I was able to keep some presence of mind. I remembered that after a "successful" bout of sickness, I'll often feel perfectly fine again for about 60 seconds. Of course, I'm usually over the rail again within five minutes, but I only need a few of these 60 second periods to finish gearing up.

I geared up while I could and excused myself to run to the rail a second time. The mate on the *Wreck Valley* provided fantastic support and risked his life standing right there in front of me, helping me gear up. After my second trip to the rail, I was ready to dive, and into the water I went. The queasiness was instantly replaced by that serene quietude as I descended. I stopped for a minute or so a few feet down the line to recheck safety stuff—to make sure I had not forgotten some critical thing like my stage bottle in my rush to get off the rocking boat. It was all there, and I descended with decent visibility into the dark world of the 90-foot-deep wreck.

The vis on the wreck was only about five to 10 feet at most, and it was definitely a good idea to run a reel as this wreck is quite large, flat, and confusing. There were bunches of little fish down there. They all seemed to be frowning at me and muttering to themselves something like: "Damn! It's another dive season already?" This wreck is littered with cobblestones, but I'm not sure if they were originally ballast or cargo. It's hard to determine, in part because this wreck may actually be the remains of more than one ship.

I had a wonderful 40-minute bottom time. I spent it with my new HID 13/21-watt focusable Sartek light, teaching myself to hold it while using my reel. On my next dive, I will try using *Apollo* along with the new light. I did extra deco for the cold, 46-degree water,

"Wreck Valley" Charter Dive Boat

Courtesy of Captain Dan Berg

and ended up with a 12-minute oxygen deco after diving with 28% back gas.

Back on the still-rocking boat, I felt fine and enjoyed some barbequed ribs and skirt steak. By now the scopolamine patch had finally kicked in, so I felt much better.

I de-geared and slept while some other divers did a second dive.

A Dive at Ponquogue Bridge – Saturday, May 6, 2006
Almost all SCUBA diving on the southern or Atlantic-Ocean side of Long Island is tide dependant. We dive inlets and bays that fill and empty twice every 24 hours in rhythm with the moon. Most of the time we want to dive at slack tide, usually around high tide or shortly afterwards, when the bay or inlet is full from the incoming tide. The current then stops for some period of time and then reverses to begin emptying that bay to the sea again. The slack period varies by location, is influenced by lunar phase, and is affected by other factors which remain unfathomed by mere mortals. So these dives, at places like Rockaway and Ponquogue, can get interesting for the experienced diver, but they can quickly become frightening and dangerous for the new and unwary diver.

With attention to the gas supply and knowledge of the local features at a dive site, the experienced diver can have very long and fun dives. New divers typically emerge breathless after struggling back against the current at the Ponquogue Bridge. A full 45 minutes later, more-seasoned divers will often emerge from the water. They will have enjoyed a dive that can be up to 70 minutes or longer. Same location, different comfort zone and abilities.

For years I have been using the website www.noreast.com to check my tides and I have found it reliable. This weekend, I noted that high tide would be at 4:29 p.m. on Saturday and made the long drive out to the Hamptons from Forest Hills, New York. I had enough time to get some seafood gumbo soup and chilled lobster at Tully's near the dive site. In another month or so we will need parking permits to dive the Ponquogue Bridge but none was needed today.

Uh oh, I thought. Why were there so few cars in the parking lot?

Two SCUBA divers with spear guns were suiting up. I asked them when high tide was, and they said 3:06 p.m. The spear fishing is often at its best when there's a bit of current, so I understood why they were going in late. I called a local dive shop, and the manager confirmed that I must have misread the tide chart: high tide was definitely at 3:06 p.m., not 4:29 p.m. I HATE when this happens!

The vis looked good. I had my scooter, *Apollo*, with me. I know the dive site very well. I've been just fine at Ponquogue, even in very strong currents. That's it, I thought. I'm going in anyway!

Anticipating a strong easterly current, I entered the water at the boat ramp on the west side of the old bridge, thinking that the old bridge bulkhead would keep me from being swept east too early in the dive. My plan was to head out under the new bridge on a northwest heading into the current, and then to go northeast in order to get to the south side of the channel. Here I would find shelter among the rocks and the large, corrugated-steel-lined base of the bridge support. From that point, the rest of the dive would be like the end of any other dive at the bridge. I am often at that spot for some time after the current switches to the east.

What arrogance! To think that we can make a plan and that nature will follow!

But what do you know. It actually worked out rather well. I got in the 56-degree water and encountered no current. None at all!

Marveling at my good fortune, I scootered along, following my plan, and was surprised when I came across the two spear fishermen. I had thought my course would steer me clear of them, but here they were, farther out than I had expected. I gave them the secret sign so that they would know I was not a large fish and was not to be speared. I realized that my noisy scooter was not helping them stalk the large blackfish that were out today, so I took off.

There seemed to be a lot of blackfish patrolling around the vertical wooden pilings that are the supports for the wooden wall which defines the boat channel. At the west end of this structure are a number of pilings held together with cable— like a bunch of straws held in your hand. The tops of these pilings broach the surface of the water and are tightly packed together, but the bases are spread out and planted into the sand some 25 feet below the surface of the water. These pilings are spread out much like the supporting poles of an Indian teepee would be. There is a large space within them that, on this day, was ruled by a particularly large blackfish. He would come out to see what was going on, and then, when I approached, he would retreat back into his sanctum sanctorum. Around me, spider crabs reached up their claws, inviting me to embrace with them as pairs of horseshoe crabs towed each other around the bay bottom.

The visibility was about 15 feet. The blackfish had left his home, and I could see that a diver could easily squeeze between the pilings and go inside this teepee. But why would a diver want to do that? I do not know, to be honest. Perhaps as a practice wreck penetration. My scooter was clipped off to my left chest D-ring as it always is, and was floating next to me, perfectly neutral. I pushed it into the narrow space between two pilings and followed it in. My plan was to do this carefully and without raising silt at all. Then, once inside, I would be rewarded. I would look out through the pilings and would be able to answer that perennial question asked by divers everywhere: just what does it feel like to be a blackfish? I maneuvered inside and for a second felt a rising sense of claustrophobia, which passed just as quickly.

As I looked out of my little prison, I wondered what the two spearfishing divers would think should they happen upon me. Was I too good a shot to pass up? That would certainly not be very sporting of them to spear me while I was in this wooden prison! Maybe they would release me and count to 10, and then give chase...

Okay. By now I'd been in here too long. Time to leave. I exited the pilings easily and cavorted among the rocks at the base of the bridge support. I watched the smaller fish picking off unseen snacks from the yellow-orange-brown flora which carpeted the sides of the 25-foot-high base of the new bridge support.

I headed to the edge of the channel wall, released some air from my scooter's buoyancy vest, and headed east at full speed, propelled by the now-increasing outbound current. Heading east from under the new bridge, one encounters a six-foot-high ridge running north-south. After going over this ridge, parallel to it, are the remains of the pilings of the Old

Ponquogue Bridge. This two-lane bridge, which was replaced by the new bridge 20 or 30 yards to the west, has been reduced by time and weather to a shadow of its former self: just two fishing piers, connected underwater by the decayed remains of these pilings.

Continuing east with my scooter, I hit another ridge of rocks, the other side of which descends into the 33-foot-deep Porgy Patch. Here is where I usually end my dives, sheltered from the outgoing current by the high ridge. Here is also where the new, foot-thick utility pipe crosses the bay from the mainland to the barrier island.

Hmm, what was this? I could see that the pipe crossed a depressed area and was suspended above the sand some three or four feet above that deeper area. Under the pipe was an electrical cord with a plug on the end of it, coming out of the bottom of the bay. Yup, Looks like a job for El Excavator!

I tugged on the cord. Whatever it was attached to was buried deep in the bay bottom. I turned my scooter around so that its powerful propeller was pointed at the spot where the cord exited the sand. I wrapped the cord around my right hand. It would keep me from being blasted backwards by the force of the scooter as it dug the hole. I turned on the scooter and was instantly enveloped in a dark, swirling cloud. It was night down there all of a sudden. I felt the tugging on my right hand as the cord dug into my dry glove. I turned the scooter off. Because there is always some current even down here in the Porgy Patch, the swirling silt cleared away within a minute, and I could see that I had a two-foot-deep hole. But the electrical cord still vanished into the sand.

Hmmm this thing was deep. I dug again. All of a sudden, the tugging on my right hand slackened. The cord was loose. I waited again for the silt to clear and then looked into the three-foot-deep hole. There it was, my prize: an old, eaten-away black thing. It could have been the base of an ancient television set or a stereo. Who knows? Who cares? The fun was in the digging, in trying to get it out. I poked at a couple of rocks that were now exposed down in the hole, as I'm always seeking the next great Native American artifact, like an arrowhead or an axe head. Nothing.

As I examined again the great pipe which traverses the bay, I recalled a project I did here in Shinnecock Bay a number of years ago when I was spending a lot of time looking at rocks on the bay bottom. I had picked up one of those two-foot-long yard screws which serve as anchors for dog chains. I dove with that a number of times, screwing it into the bay bottom and clipping myself off to it while I worked a 12-foot semicircle in the current searching for things on the bay bottom. You know, that actually worked very well, and I was able to work on the bottom in full current at my leisure.

I looked again at this pipe and realized that the same 12-foot line I keep in my dry-suit pocket could be placed around the pipe and clipped to itself, allowing me to do similar searches in full current. I filed that idea for future use and looked around a bit more.

There were a lot of bricks down there. Why not start building something? I began a cairn using only near-perfect bricks, and I got it five-bricks high. Maybe one of you will find it, there in the Porgy Patch, directly under the pipe.

What a great dive!

The Asfalto Wreck – Sunday, June 18, 2006

I was looking forward to today's dive. Last Saturday in the wee hours I had been sitting in my car near a dive boat that was bound for the *Oregon*. But no one showed, and around 5:30 a.m. I realized that the dive must have been cancelled and that I had not been notified. Today—Father's Day, a week later—I confirmed my trip on the phone instead of through still-unreliable email and was in Sheepshead Bay by 5:30 a.m., loading my gear.

The trip out to the unidentified wreck known as the Asfalto took about an hour, through calm seas. It would be a single dive, and we'd be back at the dock by 12:30 p.m. That meant I'd still have most of this Father's Day to spend with my newly expanded family. In addition to my 22 year old son Matthew, I am now the proud father of beautiful little Sophia born a few weeks ago on May 24. The boat was not crowded, and I suited up to go in early. Usually I wait for everybody else to go in, then I get ready at my annoyingly leisurely pace. But today, because it was a one-tanker and I was planning a long dive, I didn't want to keep everyone waiting to go back to the dock. I was ready a few minutes before we tied into the wreck, so I had to roast in my dry suit for a few minutes. Boy, it was hot in there! Drink lots of water!

Today I brought my Sartek HID light, red canvas bag, and shovel. The last time I visited this wreck (the Asfalto is a wreck comprising one or more garbage barges from the 1930s) I selected a spot, dug a lot, and found some nice bottles. My plan for today was a bit different. I was going to cruise higher up off the bottom if the vis would allow and look over a greater area in search of artifacts lying right on the seafloor. I had decided to use this approach after someone on the dive boat told me this was the first trip of the season to the Asfalto, my reasoning being that winter storms would have exposed many bottles and artifacts. Easy pickings.

As I descended to the wreck, I saw a three-foot-long sand shark. It's funny: until last fall, I had never really seen any sharks, but now I am seeing them a lot. They must have always been there. I wonder what else I am not noticing.

My dry suit was getting awfully compressed and uncomfortable. I pressed the air button to put some air into the suit and nothing happened. I realized that the hose was not seated correctly on the suit and was not working. I would have to remove it and reattach it. My hands were occupied with the descent line and this really needed two hands, so I gritted my teeth and continued to the wreck. I felt like I was being compressed into a small cube about a foot high. I hoped I wouldn't surface back on the boat as a dwarf! At the wreck, I let go of the line and dropped to the sand in the 50-degree water. I disconnected and reconnected my dry-suit hose. A dribble of water came in as I added the air and de-dwarfed myself.

The Asfalto is a large, sprawling wreck. Some think that it's more than one barge, because it looks like there is more than one keel and more than one set of ribs. The keels are at right angles to each other. If a sinking barge can't be cut free, it sometimes drags down other barges and sometimes even the tugboat. I suppose the crew on the tugboat is more worried about cutting themselves free of the sinking barge rather than freeing all the other attached barges...

Because of the easy to follow long lines of the ships, I decided not to run a reel but to pick a piece of the wreck and follow it, always staying to the right. This way I could follow it back easily. From my vantage point eight feet above the bottom and with my powerful light, I found lots of bottles. I went all the way out along one of the sides of the right angle which the two keels form, then came back and went out on the other. One of the bottles looked very interesting and was different from the apothecary-style bottles that are common down there.

I had been down for about 55 minutes and was getting low on air. Time to go up. Did a nice relaxing deco—no sea monsters.

Back on the boat, I reached into my red canvas bag. The first bottle I pulled out was that interesting one. It was a nice one! But now it was broken off at the neck. I disgustedly threw it over the side, back into the water. Five minutes later I was sorry I had tossed it, because there in the bottom of my bag was the cleanly broken-off neck. A bit of Duco cement and I could have fixed it—it would have looked perfect. Oh well. This went over the side too. (There were no divers in the water. In spite of my going in the water first, I was still the last out.)

Anyway, it was a fun start to a great day. I got home, did the official Father's Day nap, and then the relatives came over, and it was off to dinner.

Rockaway Beach 6th Street – Sunday, July 9, 2006

Had a nice dive at Rockaway this morning. We met up at the Sherwood Diner on Rockaway Boulevard near Peninsula Boulevard. Alban wanted to spearfish and has been doing well at the Ponquogue Bridge. I thought I would show him the Atlantic Beach Bridge.

We decided to enter the water at Beach 6th Street at 6:54 a.m. Beach 6th is three blocks closer to the Atlantic Beach Bridge than Beach 9th is, and is also a common dive location. We would ride the last of the incoming tide on the surface over to the bridge and then descend so that Alban could hunt. Then we'd ride my scooter back to Beach 6th on the outgoing tide.

It's always good to have an alternate plan!

The current had already stopped, so we were stuck on the surface and not moving east at all. We went to plan B. Plan B was to use the scooter to pull ourselves to the bridge, underwater—a distance of about three or four blocks. I was mildly concerned, because this would effectively double the scooter's battery drain time. Since in the past I had returned to Beach 6th from the bridge while riding the outbound tide on the surface many times, I decided that the risk of the scooter battery dying was acceptable. We would just go to plan C if that happened.

This would also be my first time operating my scooter while using my new HID light. This light, made by Sartek, is really neat. It's got two power settings—13 watts and 21 watts—and a focusable beam. I got the smaller, two-hour battery, which should work for my normal single-wreck dives. It would even suffice for two-dive outings, the kind of diving I do at Thousand Islands. The light also has a Goodman handle, a square bracket on the light head which is attached by a three-foot power line to the small battery pack, which I have attached to my steel back plate. I have sized the Goodman handle so that my dry-gloved right hand fits snugly and comfortably through it. Once the light is on my hand, I can use the hand more or less normally—the light's head points wherever my hand points. I found that I could grip the scooter's right handle easily and could even operate the push-button throttle while illuminating our path with this very bright light.

I was having trouble reading my compass, which is mounted on the front of the scooter. It works fine there, but my aging eyes were having trouble reading it. I kept stopping to shine the light directly on the compass, and eventually I found that I was not following a straight, easterly course to the bridge as I had intended. Instead I'd been tracing a zigzag course, and it was not doing much to conserve the air we would need once at the bridge. Finally, having no idea where we were, I headed due north to get to shallow water, to surface and get our bearings. We found that we were about 100 yards from the bridge and continued east.

Then we reached the bridge. We were both at about 2000 psi, and so we stayed there around the bridge supports with the scooter turned off, searching rather unsuccessfully for the large striped bass that had circled us and now was nowhere to be found. Because we had less air than originally planned for, I did not want to go too far south under the bridge (that's where more fish are, in the deeper area). That area is also dangerously close to the boat channel. After about 15 minutes, we scootered back to Beach 6th.

Beach 9th Street has a characteristic deeper area right offshore. "The Trench" is about 40 feet deep, and it allows one to be able to tell, when riding the outbound tide, where you need to head north, or "get off," so that you land around your original entry point. Beach 6th also has its signposts: a number of large-diameter poles lying on the bottom of the channel like matchsticks dropped by a giant. When coming back from the bridge underwater, you want to stay fairly north, in the 20- to 23-foot-depth range, parallel to where the beach's white sand slope meets the rockier channel bottom. When you encounter these 18-inch-diameter poles (I fantasize they're old ship masts, but more likely they're construction debris), it's time to make a sharp turn north, and you are back at Beach 6th Street.

All went well, though I felt bad that Alban hadn't caught his dinner. We split up so he could hunt a bit more at the base of the 6th Street jetty, and I headed back out towards the channel, my scooter jumping ahead now that it was only pulling one diver. A few minutes later, I heard the telltale sound of the scooter's engine losing power. The last time I'd heard this sound, I had also been towing another diver, three years ago here at Rockaway  on a frigid winter dive in March. Since then, I've never used the scooter to the point of draining the battery. I turned the scooter off and headed north to the beach.

I had a 65-minute dive and reached a max depth of 34 feet. The water temperature was 64 degrees, and visibility was 10 to 15 feet. Great dive. Of course, we ended up back at the diner for breakfast afterwards.

The Linda Wreck – Sunday, July 16, 2006

The last time I tried to head out for a boat dive, I missed the bedside clock radio alarm. Luckily, seven weeks ago, the little alarm called Sophia was born. So even though I missed the alarm clock the last time I tried to go diving, my wife didn't: she was fully awake, feeding the baby at 4:00 a.m. If she hadn't awakened me, I would have missed that trip to the *Oregon*. I was not going to screw up again, so this time, instead of the gentle buzzer alarm, I set the clock radio to blast News Radio 88 at full volume. A bit inconsiderate of me, if you realize that my wife and baby sleep in the room with me. It went off at 3:45 a.m., and my first thought as I was pulled forcibly from deep sleep was: TURN IT OFF! FAST!

I reached over, still groggy, and found that I couldn't move. Lynda, still half asleep, had grabbed me in terror. I myself was not yet awake enough to realize that the reason I couldn't reach the radio was that my wife had me in a death grip, so I decided that I was having a heart attack and was paralyzed! Seconds later, I wrestled free as News Radio 88 continued to scream news at me and my sleeping family. This little incident did not endear me to my generally very understanding wife. I will have to make it up somehow if I ever wish to dive again!

I had neglected to buy water for the trip, so I had set my alarm to wake me early enough to make it to the little 7-Eleven store to stock up on water and donuts to bring onto the boat. I already had a Ziploc bag full of marinated minky meat (skirt steak), and I arrived at the boat at 5:00 a.m.

Howard Klein, captain of the *Eagle's Nest*, was full of his early-morning good cheer, and we were off promptly at six. The boat was loaded with divers, and I stretched out on the floor in the cabin for a two-hour nap which was occasionally interrupted by Captain Klein, who kicked my legs to clear the way to the engine room, to do whatever tinkering captains do while they are at sea.

Sometimes I wait for everyone else to go in the water first, then I take my time getting ready on an empty deck. On this trip, though, there were so many divers that I decided to be one of the first in the water so that I could take advantage of virgin visibility before it got too messed up.

Descending the line to the wreck, I first saw her when I hit a depth of 95 feet. I stopped to try to memorize as much of the layout as I could before descending more. The unidentified Linda was once a wooden schooner. I am not sure about the length, but I would guess the wreck is at least a couple of hundred feet long. She retains the shape of her hull and is very easy to navigate. There is a large centerboard-type structure in the middle, and she presents about five to eight feet of relief off the bottom. Once, she was famous for being a source of "deadeyes," oval pieces of hardwood containing three holes through which rigging can be run. Now, bereft of artifacts, she provides her visitors with a sense of the majesty of the bygone era of sailing. The top of the sides along her hull are in places punctuated by an 18-inch protrusion every three or four feet. These are what the deadeyes would have been attached to; rigging would have passed through them and from there up to her massive masts. Now, in the place of shrouds, stays and deadeyes, sea anemones gently wave their tentacled flowers with the current. The center of the ship is rather featureless except for a large wooden structure which resembles a great centerboard for a racing yacht. Much of this ship must still remain under the sand if we are only seeing the top few feet of it.

I saw a couple of teardrop-shaped, encrusted "things" lying on the sand and put one in my canvas bag to check out later back on the dive boat.

Instead of cargo, the hold of this sailing ship contains flounder, ling, and scallops. It's a ship that's destined to never sail anywhere again, except deeper into the shifting ocean sands.

The Linda has retained its reputation as a great lobster wreck—there are lots of nooks and crannies for lobsters to hide in. Not being a lobster hunter, I slowly toured around the hull one-and-a half times, cutting back across the 40-foot-wide beam of the ship to return to the ascent line.

As always, if I'm not visited by sharks, decompression is a pleasant, meditative part of the dive experience for me. I used to think it was boring and something to be gotten over as quickly and as possible, but I have worked to change my thinking on this. I did a number of deep stops as per my plan and then extended my 20-foot oxygen stop a few minutes, from 11 to 16 minutes. I attached a jon line to the ascent line, got my buoyancy just right, and then just relaxed, watching the rising bubbles of other divers and the jellyfish that drifted by. It is much more relaxing than going to work!

Back on the boat, as soon as we took off our gear, we were encouraged to clear the dive area. I went upstairs, and the feasting began. It started with a large tray of caesar salad, and then, for the next 90 minutes, trays of delectable barbequed foods were sent up the ladder. Even though the boat was loaded with divers, it was more food than we could eat. And I am not talking hot dogs and hamburgers. Huge amounts of steaks, barbequed ribs, chicken, and delicious sausages, followed by a nice chocolate birthday cake for one of our favorite local divers, Randi. What a feast!

Somehow, after all this, I found an empty bunk and set up shop. I turned on my iPod, and, to an eclectic selection of music ranging from classical to folk, drifted off into a contented sleep. Many other divers did a second dive, and I awoke to the sound of the engines as we headed back to port. I checked that my gear was tightly secured and went back to bed.

A few miles out of the dock, I awoke and had a good laugh with a couple of the other divers as we examined the "artifact" I had stuffed in my bag. Possibly a large piece of coal—but definitely not a deadeye—it went over the side, back to the bottom. It would have an interesting tale to tell the scallops. A tale of a sunny day on a calm ocean with lots of friends and good food.

As for me, it was another great day living the History Channel!

Diving the Holland Tunnel and Lake Ontario – August 28, 2006

I heard it first. A muffled phaboom, almost like a truck backfiring in the distance. Traffic had been stopped in the tunnel for about a minute, leaving me stuck about one third of the way through the Holland Tunnel from the New York side on the first leg of my trip up to Lake Ontario for a weekend of diving. The loud sound was followed by a wave of cars honking, the sound rushing back up the tunnel towards me along with an acrid smell. I could see down the slope to the curve in the tunnel. A roiling cloud of grey-black smoke moved almost in slow motion up the line of trapped cars towards me.

I opened my car door and was horrified to hear the sound of rushing water somewhere below me in the tunnel.

"That sounded like an explosion!" a guy yelled, sticking his head out of a white van in the next lane. I started to say something to him, but now there were people running, out of breath, passing my car to try to escape to the tunnel entrance. Already, I could see a puddle of water advancing in the distance, fast. Very fast.

I had read in a book somewhere that the Holland Tunnel was 93 feet deep and some 8,500 feet long. I was stuck about one third of the way into the tunnel, maybe almost halfway—I was still on the slope of the New York side. So that meant I was probably somewhere like a half mile into the tunnel. That was at least 10 city blocks. If the water kept rising at the same rate,

I would never make it, and even the first people to pass me running were doomed.

I then realized that maybe, just maybe, there was a way! My SCUBA gear was in the back of my large SUV. Two sets of doubles and everything I would need to escape. That's it! I jumped back into my car, remembering to leave the back left window a bit open so that water would fill the car and not seal me in the car, unable to open the door against the water pressure. I had a minute—maybe two minutes—before the water would reach my car's roof, I thought. First, I dug through my blue plastic equipment box and pulled out a mask and one of my regulators. Luckily, it was the reg with the long hose. I attached it to a set of doubles. I could see the water was coming up fast and I'd have to open the door to have enough room to put on my dry suit. I dropped the regulator and quickly opened the door and struggled to get my legs into the dry suit as the water got even with the base of the door. A minute later, with the suit pulled on up to my waist I slammed the door shut again. The water was now lapping against the SUV, about 18 inches beneath the bottom of the window. I was glad that the windows were tinted, worried that one of the passing people would notice my air tanks and kill me for them. But I had little to worry about, as everyone else around me had already left their vehicle and was making a break for it.

The water was streaming into the car now, through every opening it could find and through the partially open window as well. I was surprised that headlights were still working on some of the cars farther down the slope, cars that had already been inundated with water.

I had my mask and my dry suit and a regulator with precious air. I was almost ready. I figured that once the tunnel filled I would have at least an hour or more on this set of doubles, assuming that I was about 60 feet beneath the surface. I would use these tanks to get the rest of my gear on, and then I'd put my other regulator on the other set of doubles and use that rig to escape. I even had my scooter. It was not fully charged, but it would sure help.

Just then my car lights went out. I reached back into my blue box , felt for my my HID light and turned it on...

Okay, so that didn't really happen. I actually was just stuck in traffic in the tunnel, and once we started moving again, I continued my seven-and-a-half-hour journey to Kingston, Ontario for some serious wreck diving in Lake Ontario.

I had left early in the morning and arrived in Kingston at about 3:00 p.m. Some other Sea Gypsies were there, too. We toured historic Fort Henry and had a nice dinner.

Our party was large, so we would split up onto three smallish boats. The first day, Saturday, conditions were less than perfect. Lake Ontario's weather can change fast, and on this day overcast and windy conditions produced a "confused sea" full of three-foot waves that were closely spaced. The nausea quotient was at least equal to four- to five-foot ocean seas, and a number of us were uncomfortable on the small boat. If nothing else, I gained a real respect for weather on the Great Lakes and a sense of how, far from the wooded shores, a ship in trouble would really be on her own in the middle of this large sea.

Saturday's dives were good dives, marred somewhat in the morning by the weather and seas. As fast as the rain started, it ended, and Lake Ontario became as smooth as glass. Wisps of fog lifted up from its surface, forming ethereal fingers of mist which reached up to touch the sun. Quite pretty that whole area is.

Our first dive was the *George T. Davies*, a 177-foot-long composite barge which sank after capsizing in 1945. I reached a depth of 94 feet and found an intact lifeboat lying in the sand next to the ship. A crane and bucket were there too.

The *Glendora* was next. This is a 214-foot-long wooden ship whose main feature is a box situated in the center of the ship. I thought I was looking at a sailing ship for sure, but Internet sites that describe the *Glendora* speak of it as being a steam driven ship. Okay, fine! I sort of had the feeling that all these wrecks were beginning to look alike, and after three trips up to this area it was getting humdrum. I was to change my opinion with the next day's exciting dives.

The evening before, at Fort Henry, we'd found out there was to be a musical event Saturday night. We actually got the last five tickets on sale in all of Kingston, and after our obligatory afternoon naps we assembled to head back to the fort. We bought dinner tickets there, which, to our surprise, also entitled us to great seats and allowed us to skip the whole waiting-on-line thing to get into the event. The show was very entertaining. Top military bands played with skill. The drum majors were fun to watch—little martinets marching here and there around the fort's parade grounds, leading their band and doing various marching tricks, such as having every member turn at the same time, all the time playing music. The Canadian Army then had a contest between two teams that had to disassemble an artillery gun, transport it over a rope bridge (simulating crossing a river or a ravine), and then reassemble it. The first team to fire a blank round from their reassembled two-thousand-pound gun won. Luckily, no one in the crowd was struck by the round.

My best dives happened on Sunday. Any complaints we may have had about the size of the boats vanished on the calm lake surface. It also helped that I did not bring all my extra tanks, so there was room on the boat for divers this time.

Our first dive was the *George A. Marsh*, a three-masted schooner that went down in a "terrible gale" in August of 1917.

Ten of the 13 on board were lost, including the captain's wife and five children. In 1927, Captain John W. Smith confessed on his deathbed that he had survived the wreck and fled to the United States.

This was a great dive. The schooner is in very good shape. Parts of her rigging lay on the deck. Deadeyes were all over the place. I carefully examined a few, particularly the more encrusted ones, to help me better identify such artifacts on future Atlantic Ocean dives. The ship is upright on the lake floor at about 85 feet, and there is a point off her bow where you can look back and see much of the ghostly ship with its intact bowsprit, still being sailed by the doomed crew into the history books. On the deck at the stern, I found iron cauldrons, many more deadeyes, the ship's wheel, and Steve Edelstein perfectly balanced, photographing it all. Oh! Time to go up!

We had all brought our own lunches and snacks, and we munched away as we headed over to the wreck of the *Comet*, a sidewheel steamer that exploded and sank to 80 feet after a collision with the U.S. schooner *Exchange* in 1861. According to the website referenced at the end of this article, the *Comet* was known as a "hard-luck ship" because of her bad accident record. Her sinking had claimed two or three lives, and I could have been her next victim.

As soon as I hit the water, back-rolling off the boat, I felt water entering my dry suit. A lot of water. I realized that I must not have closed my dry-suit zipper all the way. I was wearing the heaviest Weezle underwear available. I had bought it specifically for winter diving, because it was supposed to retain its thermal characteristics even when wet. So I decided to test it and descended to the wreck. I was initially freezing but soon was almost comfortable again after my body warmed up the trapped water in the Weezle.

The *Comet* was a mysterious wreck. The lighting was odd—perhaps shadows cast by the immense side paddlewheel contributed to the very spooky atmosphere on this wreck. Coming down the line, I stopped to orient myself. The wreck lay before me. Or let me say that I *thought* I was orientating myself: apparently I didn't do a good enough job. I drifted through the wreck and around the bow and ran into Eileen and Harry, who were coming the other way. I saw that I could fit in between the large paddles and enter the large wheel, so I did, taking care not to brush against anything and ruin my view. So here I was now inside the wheel, looking to anyone who might have glanced as if I was trapped in a wooden prison. I hovered in the wheel, looking up, down, and all around at my circular enclosure. Very relaxing and eerie.

I slipped back out of the wheel in the dim, green light and found there was a space under the collapsed deck. I could see light on the other side. I slithered through and emerged on the side of the wreck. I checked my air, and it was much lower than I expected. Perhaps the dry suit full of water and the cold had made me use up my air faster than I normally would. I had started this dive with a half-full set of doubles, and my oxygen stage bottle was useless at this depth of 80 feet, unless I wanted to go into convulsions.

I made a left and headed for the line. I should have made a right. I continued and realized that I was about to go off the wreck's stern. The line couldn't be this way. I headed back and arrived at the paddlewheel again. I looked up and saw a diver, Eileen, near the top of the wheel. I headed for her and asked in underwaterese, "Where's the ascent line?"

She pointed in a direction. Unfortunately, there was a piece of the wreck between us and the ascent line, and I thought she was just trying to show me something on the wreck, not understanding me at all. I left her, heading back in the wrong direction to find the line. Now my air was under 400 lbs. So I ascended somewhat to decrease my air consumption rate and then headed back again to the highest point on the wreck.

My plan now was to do a free ascent along the wreck. There were no currents, so I thought I would do it without shooting up a bag and ascending along the line. At this point, I didn't want to waste time doing that. Back at the wreck, there was Eileen again. I asked her again where the ascent line was. This time, noting my confusion, she moved towards the line, and I followed. Ahhh! There it was! I could just see it in the distance. I sprang over to it, ascended a bit, and made sure my O_2 bottle was turned on. I went from 65 feet to 20 feet in two minutes, which was twice as fast as my normal rate of ascent, but I still had the presence of mind not to "shoot up." At 20 feet, I relaxed and switched to my oxygen. Whew! That was close!

When I climbed up the ladder to get onto the boat, my "dry" suit was so full of water that I could barely lift my legs. They were still sore the next morning!

I had to head back Monday morning, and I missed the dive on the wrecks of the *Munson* and the coal-carrying schooner *William Jamieson*, which sank in a storm.

On my drive back home, I looked back at my now-empty SCUBA tanks, thought of my last dive on the *Comet*, and decided to take the George Washington Bridge instead of the Holland Tunnel. Just in case.

Here is a link to one of a number of great websites on shipwrecks of the Great Lakes:

www.boatnerd.com/swayze/shipwreck/

Antique Rockaway Bottle Find – Sunday, August 13, 2006
Well, I was a bit disappointed that I couldn't go out to the Ponquogue Bridge this weekend, due to other obligations. I settled for Rockaway instead.

I got to Beach 8th Street nice and early and checked the vis, which looked fine. My plan was to go in about 20 minutes before slack, while the incoming current was still ripping, do my "ride the current thing," and then come back on my scooter. It was a great dive. Somewhere blocks east of Beach 8th I saw one of those very large rays—at least 10 feet long from nose to tip of tail. I had last seen one of these last year while scootering with Steve Edelstein at the Ponquogue Bridge. They are very cool. This one was moving east fairly quickly in the same direction as the incoming tide, and it passed me fast. I had just started scootering west (against the current), and I did a fast u-turn and followed it for a while. It actually startled me severely when it first appeared. And I do get a bit spooked following these big things: this one was so long that I could only see its four- or five-foot-long tail and the beginning of its massive body in the murky water. I peeled off after a minute or so and turned west again. Now the current was slack, and I went all over the place, stopping to look at various things.

One glint of glass caught my attention, and I soon uncovered the buried object. It was a small bottle, intact, and it looked like it said "Rockaway" on it. Into my red canvas bag it went, and I continued my peregrinations.

There were no life-threatening adventures and no drama, other than the big fish. In addition to that ray, East Rockaway Inlet was teeming with life. Large flounder and blackfish were everywhere, and I roused a few kamikaze blue claw crabs. One of those crazy crabs came at me fast, sideways, up at an angle from his hideaway in the sand, threatening me with his snapping claws.

My 70-minute dive took place in 70-degree water, and I was even rewarded during my safety stop with the sight of a little yellow tropical fish doing a dance among the mussels.

As soon as I surfaced, I reached into my bag and pulled out the bottle I had found. What pristine condition it was in! It was a real keeper and a perfect souvenir. My guess is that it's probably pre-1940s. Embossed in raised letters on the glass were these words:

REGISTERED, D. J. WALSH, FAR ROCKAWAY, N.Y.

When I got home, I was unable to find out anything on the Internet about the D.J. Walsh Company, but if they ever surface looking for a lost bottle, please don't tell them I've got it!

Further research by Mark Smith forwarded to me by past president of the NYC Sea Gypsies Dive Club Bill Cadden indicates that the bottle is probably from the 1920s during Prohibition and was likely to have held soda water or mineral water. Thanks for the help guys!

Diving with the Mark V Diving Helmet and Deep Sea Diving Dress – Saturday, August 19, 2006

This past weekend, we had an out-of-town guest who, knowing my love of diving, brought me a little brass clock shaped like a historic Mark V diving helmet. The clock was set to the time in England, and it continues to show the time for that island country from its prominent position on my desk. The real Mark V diving setup, though, was developed here in the United States in the early part of the twentieth century by the Bureau of Construction and Repair, and it rapidly became the standard diving outfit for military and salvage deep-sea diving. It was used in its various forms up until the 1980s and is the diving dress that comes to most people's minds when they think of deep-sea diving. The heavy suit and helmet can weigh up to 280 pounds, and they force the diver to walk in measured, small steps, almost giving the diver an appearance not unlike that of an alien or monster from a horror movie of some kind.

The very same weekend that my friend gave me the Mark V clock, there was an event supporting Alzheimer's disease research on Long Island. At this event, I would have a once-in-a-lifetime opportunity to put on an actual, historic Mark V diving outfit and do a dive in it.

I felt a bit of apprehension, as all of my technical SCUBA diving is geared towards self-rescue and redundancy in equipment. Here I would be totally dependant on others to both don the equipment and for my surface-supplied air. I had also heard about the extreme weight of the suit and wondered if my recently complaining upper back would refuse to go along with the adventure.

I looked at the equipment—it was antique but well-kept— and asked, "Just how dry will I be in this suit?" Based on the diving tender's answer, I pulled off my jeans so they would stay dry and entered the diving suit through the neck. The suit was rubberized canvas duck and had tight wrist seals. After a liberal application of dish soap, my lubricated hands slid in. I did not notice a neck seal, just an opening in the canvas that was vaguely circular in shape. My feet were then put into heavy, weighted "shoes" which were reminiscent of the new fall line of Inquisitional apparel. As the metal-clad shoes went on and I found that I could barely lift my feet, I realized that I was now totally at the mercy of those who were dressing me. I called out to Bob Rusnak, with the Historical Diving Society, who was now basically responsible for my staying alive.

"Bob? I've never disrespected you or been otherwise nasty to you, have I?"

He hesitated for what I thought was way too long before he said something like, "Nothing I can think of. Now, that is..."

It was a bit overcast, so I did not bake too much in the suit as I went through the time-consuming steps necessary to get me ready to enter the water. There were two people—the diving tenders—getting me suited up, and it took both of them to carry over my weight belt. It was actually a weighted shoulder harness, so the full hundred pounds fell upon my shoulders. I was told that the weight belt was designed like this to prevent air from ballooning the suit right below the helmet, which would, of course, force the helmet above a diver's head and give him a great view of the inside of the chest section of the suit.

No, I thought. That would not be a good thing! I could just picture myself on the bottom of the sea. Damn! Forgot my weight belt! Just then, the helmet pops off my head, still attached to the suit, its weight forcing me—now blind—to stagger along the bottom, flailing my arms in a parody of one of those kid's toys, a Rock 'Em Sock 'Em Robot.

My hands instinctively went to the weight belt to take some of the weight off my shoulders, and there my hands stayed until shortly before I went in the water. A crotch strap was then pulled very tight. Between the heavy weight on my shoulders and now this tight crotch strap, I felt like they were trying to compress me into a little-midget-diver size, maybe to fit through some hatches and narrow passageways aboard a sunken German submarine from which I was to recover the Code Books.

The next item to go on me was the heavy metal collar that would rest on my shoulders and support the even heavier 1943 U.S. Navy Mark V helmet. Bolts on the collar were guided through matching holes in a black rubber seal, and then a number of curved brass pieces were bolted down on top to clamp the collar against the rubber, forming a watertight seal. All that remained was to lower the helmet down on my head.

"Watch your nose!" I was warned. It seemed for a second that the helmet would not fit, but somehow it did. One of the tenders twisted it a bit to lock it into place, and now I was breathing through the tiny three- or four-inch front window of the helmet. They had thoughtfully left this open so I'd have some air until they turned on the air hose.

The helmet had a dump valve on the right, which was designed to be operated by the chin when you wanted to exhaust the suit. I practiced it until I could do it with my eyes closed. I could control the air coming into the suit with an air valve located on my left. A bit different than my DUI dry suit. This was also my air to breathe!

I would have two-way communications at all times, and my designation would be Mark Five Diver One. If I had a problem communicating while the very noisy air valve was open, I could turn my air off to communicate. Don't forget to turn it back on, I was told. Oh, okay. Sounds like a good idea!

Would I even be able to stand up? I could now barely sit up straight. I could not even turn around and look up the boat ramp at my wife Lynda and infant daughter, Sophia, to say goodbye. Two men assisted me in standing up, and I began the walk down the ramp and into the cold, clear waters of Mt. Sinai Harbor. One of my assistants was also wearing a surface-supplied air system, but his employed a modern helmet and wetsuit.

I was glad I had taken my jeans off, because the vintage suit did leak. But I was now in the water with most of the uncomfortable weight off me, and I enjoyed the experience of slowly descending. The water lapped at my faceplate and soon half covered it. And then with another step I was underwater!

"MARK FIVE DIVER ONE. EVERYTHING OK?"

"OH, THIS IS GREAT!" I answered. In spite of the fact that I was walking on the bottom rather than using fins, I could still see the sandy bottom of the marina floor at my feet. A shell. A crab, running sideways across my narrow field of vision. I started to lean backwards to look up the way I would if I were SCUBA diving. Then I realized that all I had to do was tilt my head up and look out through the port on the top of the helmet. I could see the surface some six feet above me.

My buddy gave me the OK signal and I responded in kind. Of course, he could have just asked me over the communications system, but perhaps he thought I might not hear over the constant sound of the air rushing into my suit. I played with my air valve, turning it down to talk and listen.

I wanted to touch the seafloor with my hand, maybe come back with a nice shell that I could put on my bookcase, a souvenir that said loudly that I was here diving in this place and time, capturing this unique moment in my diving experience. I was nervous, though: with the heavy suit, would I be able to lean over and then get back up into a standing position? I asked my buddy whether I would I be able to get back up easily if I kneeled. He said to go ahead, and I dropped down to the floor on both of my knees. Because of the little windows in the helmet, I could not see well. As I groped around for a souvenir, I realized that I had no gloves on. Hope I didn't find broken glass or an irate crab instead!

It was not easy to get up again. I flailed for a second, losing my balance. My partner threw out his hand, and I was back on my feet again. I held the thing I had grabbed off the floor close to the faceplate to examine it. Hmm. Pretty standard-looking clam shell with some attached flora. I dropped it back to the floor and decided I would have to take just my memories of the dive with me.

As we exited the water, I crouched a bit to allow the water to keep the heavy weight off my shoulders. Soon I could crouch no longer. I stood up straight, my back groaning under the 200-plus pounds of equipment. To those watching on shore, perhaps an invasion of aliens from the deep was occurring. I made it back to the bench and kept thinking to myself, wow! Once my faceplate was opened, my partner came up to me and suggested that when trying to stand up from my knees underwater, had I increased the air flow into my suit I would have found the added buoyancy very useful. Live and learn.

This undersea adventure made me feel a great respect for the many military and commercial divers that had used this diving outfit over the three-quarters of a century that it had been in use. During this period the MARK V represented the best technology in existence for this type of diving. It was a heavy suit, had a limited field of view, and required total reliance on my tenders and my buddy. But I was with Captain Nemo, 20,000 leagues under the sea. I was aboard the Sea Wolf. I was gearing up on the deck of a rolling destroyer to do an emergency post-battle inspection. I could palpably feel the roots of the early days of diving; the macho attitudes that characterized early SCUBA must have had their roots in this type of hard-hat diving. The Mark V and the deep-sea diving suit allowed ocean exploration, a type of adventure which, in the beginning, was similar to what space exploration is to us today. This was a day I shall not soon forget.

First Dive on the Refitted Garloo Dive Boat to the Wreck of the Oregon – Saturday, September 9, 2006

Finally, a weekend without gale-force winds and huge seas! I was booked on the dive boat RV *Garloo* out of Captree, Long Island, and I was looking forward to checking out some of the new changes to the boat.

She'd had a complete refit. The old bunk areas were torn out and replaced with individual staterooms. Some have their own bathrooms. There is a total of four heads on the boat. A spiral staircase leads up from the forward area, which has three rooms and two heads, to the main cabin area, which is spacious and has seating around its perimeter. There's also a large table, and a fully equipped galley. From the cabin, you can step down a few stairs, moving aft, to find another head and more sleeping quarters. The fourth head and shower are accessed from the deck of the boat.

The deck of the *Garloo* is dominated by a large, white fiberglass platform, which, on this outing, found use as a convenient sunning and napping deck for a couple of the divers in between dives. Running fore and aft along the starboard and port sides of the platform are long benches built into the platform, which I found to be perfect for donning my equipment. This boat is definitely geared for overnight trips—such as to the *Andrea Doria*—but it also worked great for our trip out to the *Oregon*. Captain Hank also plans to offer local cruises, trips that would be open to non-divers, too.

Seas were almost flat, and the sun shone brightly on us as we tied into the wreck of the ocean liner *Oregon*. I had brought *Apollo*, and was happy to see that someone else had a similar scooter. The battery had died on my Nitek computer, so I brought an old Citizen watch to use as a backup bottom timer, and I dove with my Vyper computer, which doesn't understand pure oxygen decompression. I had my deco tables attached to my wrist and really did not need much more than a bottom timer.

We were tied into the top of the massive engines, and I made the required trip to view the steering quadrant. Here, observant divers will see the remnant bases of immense masts, each of which once supported a sail. Such juxtaposition of technologies was common back in the days predating one-hundred-percent reliance on steam engines. A ship could hit foul weather and end up far from a coaling station. Also, captains were expected to run their ship with great efficiency; some were even charged for unnecessary use of expensive coal.

The *Oregon* is one of my two favorite local wrecks (the USS *San Diego* is the other one), and today I got the chance to explore it at a leisurely pace, exploring, poking, going off the wreck to look back at it from a little distance, and just taking my time. The bow is really neat. It looks like a bow, except it's turned on its side. If you look closely, you can see wood from the deck, bits for hawsers, and miscellaneous machinery that once helped heave lines and anchors.

I hooked up with the other diver who had a scooter, and eventually we came upon a third diver (from another dive boat) who also had a similar scooter. For a couple of minutes we all matched course and speed, cruising together at 120 feet deep and looking to all the world like three characters in a James Bond movie.

What a beautiful dive. Great vis and no drama. Just another opportunity to live out an adventure that combined the best of the National Geographic Channel and the History Channel. I cannot overemphasize how much richer and rewarding my

The Sunken Steamship Oregon, Picture courtesy Herb Kaasmann,
OREGON, GREYHOUND OF THE ATLANTIC

wreck diving became once I started reading about the ships I was exploring. Their history, their construction, their stories.

Always the treasure hunter, towards the end of my 40-minute dive I spied a flat metal plate about three inches wide and two feet long. It had the glint of copper or brass, and I picked it up. I was surprised at how heavy it was. I do tend to find things at depth and may be a bit fogged by nitrogen narcosis from time to time. The plate was heavily encrusted, and I was certain that when I cleaned it off later on the dive boat it would say something like "Saloon" or "SS Oregon." It was heavy enough that it took some maneuvering to begin my ascent. When I got to the top of the engine, near the ascent line, I slid the plate into my red canvas bag. More than half of the plate stuck out the top of the bag. It was ready to fall back into the depths to be lost forever.

I had a long deco to do, and all in all I spent 81 minutes in the water before getting back on board the boat. I clutched my prize through every one of those 40 decompression minutes. Too scared that I would drop it to pull it out and look at it closely, I contented myself with scraping off a bit of the encrustation with my gloved hand. Hmm. Maybe it wasn't copper or brass. Finally I was back on the boat.

Unfortunately, the artifact did not make it to be with me here today. It turned out to be modern stainless steel, which ruled it out as being from the 1886 wreck. It looked suspiciously like a step from a ladder.

Once out of my gear, I heated up a delicious lunch that I had brought and headed back to my comfortable bunk to drift back into a peaceful, post-dive nap. I lay there going over the dive in my mind. The moments gliding around the wreck with the other scooters, the pleasure I felt upon finding a beautiful, large, perfect scallop shell for my daughter. The excitement I felt upon finding my "non-artifact." When I awakened later, I didn't remember my dreams, but I had a growing conviction that somewhere down there on the wreck of the *Oregon* there lies a brass plate, sized just right to fit over a doorway. It says, "Saloon – SS Oregon," and it's waiting for me to find it.

The Oregon had a number of decks yet like an iceberg, only a small amount of it shows above the shifting sands. She will yield her artifacts begrudgingly over many years. It's a good wreck to dive after a storm, maybe another deck will have been uncovered...

I enjoyed my trip on the *Garloo*. It's a great boat, and I look forward to diving with her again soon. Captain Hank and her crew couldn't have been more helpful, friendly, and

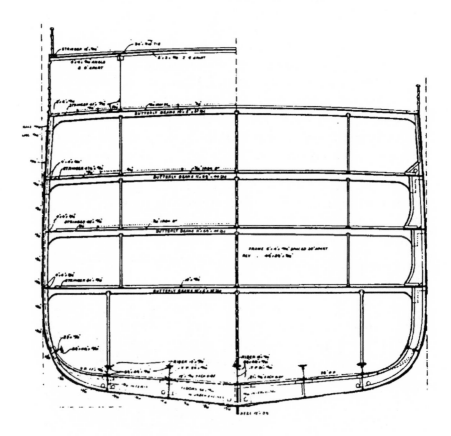

Midship Cross-Section of the Oregon, Picture courtesy Herb Kaasmann, OREGON, GREYHOUND OF THE ATLANTIC

professional. Their schedule can be found on the Internet at www.garlooent.com.

USS San Diego Entanglement – Saturday, October 22, 2006

I'd been out of the water for a month and was excited about today's trip to one of my favorite local wrecks. The USS *San Diego*, a 500-foot-long armored cruiser, sank off of Fire Island in 1918 after striking a German mine. She lies on the ocean bottom upside down, her great artillery guns still pointing out from her sides at some unseen enemy. As long as a 50-story building, she still entices adventurous divers to explore inside her slowly collapsing, narrow, dark corridors and rooms.

I have had a lot of excitement on this shipwreck, ranging from finding a small shark in the room with me to air problems to confusion about how to exit once inside. Today's dive would be added to my list of not-mundane dives on this great warship. I got entangled inside the wreck. Wreck line carried on a reel can be dangerous in the water. On land, if you let go of a rope or line, it falls to the floor. Underwater, it billows in sinuous loops, which are affected even by the little currents you create as you reach for it. No, it does not drop to the floor innocently; it coils like a living snake, waiting to trap the diver.

This morning, I slept through my 4:00 a.m. alarm. I have no idea how that happened. It couldn't have gone off. It would have woken up my wife, and when I checked, it was set correctly. It just did not go off. So when I did wake up at 4:36 a.m., my first thought was that since I have never missed a boat because of oversleeping, perhaps this was an omen and I was supposed to miss this trip. My mouth was bone dry from the scopolamine patch I had put under my ear before going to bed. I stood in the kitchen pouring boiling water to make my coffee as I stupidly stared at the kitchen clock and said to myself, "Just go back to bed—the sea is supposed to be a bit rough anyway."

I made it to the boat about 10 minutes late, but there were no issues, and I loaded my gear. As we locked our gear down on the deck, others were talking about the sea conditions. Someone said the buoy 20 miles out had been showing nine-foot waves last night, but now it was down to four to six feet. Uh-oh!

The ride out was actually fine. We had a "following sea," which meant that we were going exactly the way the waves were going, and it was as if they were pushing us. Not uncomfortable at all. Maneuvering to tie into the wreck, waves began to hit us broadside, and the boat started to roll—things were flying all over, including people who were trying to walk or put their gear on. I looked into the cabin of the boat a few minutes later and saw papers and books scattered over the floor. Soon they were joined by a foam mattress and anything else that was not fastened down. Finally we settled down, the boat turning into the wind like a giant weathervane, and the boat took on a pitching motion. A number of divers, including myself, seriously considered not going in the water because of anticipated difficulties getting back on board—the boat was really rocking. When the first diver returned with a report of at least 20-foot vis, I decided to go in but to leave my scooter behind. The first diver had done a fairly short dive so that he would not have to do more than a three-minute hang on the line decompressing. Remember, as the boat pitches violently, the entire line running down to the wreck 100 or so feet below also jumps like a plucked guitar string. It becomes physically painful to hold on to a rope that's bucking like a bull at a rodeo.

My scopolamine patch was working great, and I suited up and jumped in. There was a current, and by the time I pulled myself along the granny line to the descent line, I was breathing hard. I descended very slowly, trying to catch my breath as I went down.

The descent line was tied in at the aft end of the bilge keel on the dark side of the wreck. Great! I liked this area, and on previous dives I had explored inside this area. I went through a big opening on the side and tied off my reel to a metal pipe overgrown with sea things.

I dive with a 40-cubic-foot oxygen decompression bottle on my side and am loath to take it off and leave it anywhere, as many wreck divers do before they enter a wreck. I have heard too many stories in which the diver had an emergency of one kind or another and could not find—or did not have the time—to go back and get his or her deco bottle. In fact, this happened recently to a diver on a deep wreck. He had to be evacuated by helicopter to a chamber because he set his bottle down somewhere, had to rescue another diver, could not make it back to his deco bottle and ultimately missed his deco on a 180-foot-deep dive. It is also dangerous to wear the deco bottle inside a wreck because it's another entanglement hazard. Thinking it all out I opt to risk the entanglement to ensure I can do my deco no matter what; so I take the bottle with me everywhere underwater. I also carry two reels. Both have 250 feet of line. One is wound with a much heavier line. It's a big reel, and its sole function is to act as an emergency ascent line if needed. That one I keep clipped to a D-ring on my crotch strap, so it dangles a bit as I move around.

Back in the wreck…

A corridor-like space stretched before me as far as my HID light could reach, and I headed forward. Disintegrating walls and what looked like a parallel corridor appeared off to my left. I noticed, in that parallel space, another line—some other diver was apparently heading aft inside the wreck from some other entry point forward of mine. I didn't see the diver, and it occurred that there could be a dead body at the end of that line for all I knew; maybe it was an old line belonging to a diver who had never made it out. My mind returned to the task at hand as I looped my line around a metal thing and continued forward.

The space through which I was moving was big enough for me, but there was not a huge amount of space around me. As delicately as I was moving, I could sometimes see large particles of rust or other particulate matter drifting in slow motion. I could not turn around to look back unless I decided to go vertical, but almost certainly I'd contact the fragile walls and really mess up the vis, so I continued forward.

A lot of times, I like to look back to check my wake and see if I've messed up the vis, but I also do it in order to plant visual cues in my head so that I'll know how to get back if my reel line gets cut or broken. You can tell yourself that you went in a straight line, that you were only following the corridor, but when returning you'll often see that because the walls and rooms are collapsing, a path that was clear from one direction is blocked from the other. For example, another wall for what appears to be another corridor may lie at a certain angle, and when you're returning there may suddenly appear to be two or more corridor choices. Which one did you take to get here? I hope you know, or that you've run a line! One path leads back to the outside and to life; the other may go deeper into the ship.

As I went forward, I continued to occasionally glimpse the other diver's line through breaks in the walls. Finally, I arrived at the other diver's entry point. Here, his line made a 90-degree turn and headed out of the wreck via a large opening. I could just see his stage deco bottle lying on the sand. I locked my line and passed it under his line, then maneuvered my body to cross his line. A second later, I realized I must have snagged on something—either a protuberance on the side of the narrow corridor I was exiting, or on his line itself. My body was now on the forward side of his line, and I was stuck. I looked at my oxygen-bottle valve, and there I saw his line, intertwined with mine, both of them ensnared on the valve of my oxygen bottle and wrapped around the little black plug that you use to seal your first stage when it's not attached to a bottle.

My first thought was that maybe oversleeping WAS an omen. My second thought was to check my air. That would determine how this would be handled.

I looked, and, as I was still near the beginning of my dive, I had lots of air. So we would do plan A, which was to try to disentangle myself for a couple of minutes. If that did not work, I'd try to identify both the other diver's line and my own, and I'd cut mine. If that didn't work, I would cut his line and then tie it back together. Plan B was this: if I had been low on air, I would have just started snipping and hoping for the best, retying his line if there was time. I liked plan A. Given a choice, my unseen friend would also have preferred that too, I am sure.

I examined the lines and realized that they were already so entangled that I did not understand the situation at all. I was not only entangled on my bottle but also somewhere else I couldn't see. I couldn't get any slack on the bottle entanglement—it must have been hooked on something else too. I double checked. My wreck reel was locked. It was not playing out more line; it was somehow wrapped in the other diver's line. I felt for my other reel between my legs and could feel loose line all around the area. Ahh! There was a part of the problem. My regular wreck line also freed up now. I gently let go of my regular reel and let it fall a couple of feet to rest against the debris.

One problem I had during this incident was that my light, which is one of those big HID lights with a battery canister and its own electrical line, was not helping. The handle of the light was itself catching line, and finally I dropped the light. Using my sense of touch, I disconnected the reel from my crotch ring, and immediately that entanglement was fixed—except now there was more loose line in my midst. Undoing the tangle had created slack in the other diver's line, and it billowed now all around me.

I dropped the crotch reel onto what I thought was an easy-to-reach area of the floor and was dismayed to see the expensive reel slide and fall through a hole between pipes down to what looked to be the next deck. I was still stuck, so I was not too concerned about that reel. I found the rubber first-stage plug for the oxygen bottle and ripped it off. That little rubber thing was the secret of the knot I was trapped in. A few more turns counter-clockwise around my oxygen valve, and I was free.

What now? Well, I still had a lot of air. Maybe I could get that reel I dropped. I looked around, but there was no way to get it without another arm, one that was six feet long. I left my wreck reel where it was and exited the wreck, as I was right near the hole through which the other diver had entered. From the outside, I could see that if I went back in and moved a bit to the left and down, I might be able to get the reel. So in I went. No reel. I must have been in the wrong spot. Out again, reevaluate, study. Back in again, wriggle through. Ahhh! There! I had it. Wriggle out again. I placed the big reel in my red canvas bag. Never again will it go on the crotch-strap D-ring.

I reentered the wreck again, picked up my dropped regular wreck line from the floor just inside, and shined my light forward. Ah-ha! The corridor continued. I moved forward until it ended some 50 feet or so later in a tangled debris field. It looked like there was an open space to the left and that I'd be able to get past the debris. As I turned to the left, I shined the light into a room. What struck me about this room was that its walls were intact—it looked like a room. It had just a single entrance. Walls were an overgrown yellowish brown, but there were no holes. There was nothing visible in the room, but I figured it might be worth feeling around on the floor, actually the ceiling in this upside down wreck, a bit. I checked my air and decided that I was at the limit of today's explorations. I stayed there a few minutes and then headed back, reeling in my line. About 30 feet after I passed the other diver's line again, I saw the other diver. He was heading forward as I headed aft. We waved and nodded to each other. I felt good that I had been able to resolve my situation without cutting his line.

I had a great 36-minute bottom time complete with heart-pounding adventure. I did my deco and was back on board for the barbeque soon thereafter. Getting back on the boat was easy. I timed my reach for the ladder with the waves and was almost pushed up the ladder.

I am still not sure how I went from being in control of everything to having an entangled meltdown so fast. When I got back on the boat, someone asked me if I was the guy who had tied a line tied off to a stage bottle in the sand, and then I remembered something I had not paid much attention to earlier. After I had detangled myself and headed out of the wreck at the point where the other diver's line came in, I noticed that his line was tied to his stage bottle, which was lying in the sand next to the wreck. I think what happened was that when I snagged his line with the reel on my crotch strap, it pulled on his line. Now, the end that he was running out in the wreck was looped around something every so often, so when I hit his line he didn't even notice. But the other end of his line was attached to his bottle in the sand right outside the wreck. So when I became tangled in his line, my exertions pulled his bottle a few feet towards the wreck, creating much more slack that coiled and snared me.

Lessons learned? Watch out for dangling stuff, just like they taught me in my first SCUBA class! Also, it's good to loop the line around things often, not just at turns and corners. This will minimize slack, and also, in the event that someone should cut my line, some of my line should stay taut—some of the line will still be attached to objects in the boat, and I should be able make my way out by following what's left. Never attach a wreck penetration line to something that is not going to stay put.

Ammo Shells on the USS San Diego

Two weeks later, I was back on the *Lockness* dive boat, headed to the USS *San Diego* again. This time, seas were calm, but visibility was reduced. The water had been clearer the last time I had been here. We were tied into the wreck a bit farther aft, and a jumble of six-inch artillery shells was visible inside the ship from this location. You don't really want to start playing with these unstable live rounds, but it was pretty neat to be able to see and touch them if you wanted to.

I found the bilge keel, and, using that as a reference point, again went into the ship. It looked totally different this time. I must have gone through another hole in the ship's hull, perhaps a bit deeper. I did not recognize anything once inside. I tied off my reel line.

To avoid entanglement problems, I entered the water this time with the large emergency reel in my red canvas bag and my regular wreck reel on the crotch D-ring. In the wreck, I planned to disconnect the reel from the crotch strap in order to use it, at the same time eliminating it as an entanglement hazard.

Once inside, I headed aft, which was the only direction not blocked by debris. I passed machinery, including large tanks that appeared to be covered by parallel, narrow strips of some material—maybe wood? I remembered seeing these things when we toured the *Olympia*, a similar ship berthed in Philadelphia. Unfortunately, I have no photos of these objects in the *Olympia*'s engine space. I remember thinking, back in January 2006 when we saw these tanks, that the parallel wood strips were likely for protecting crew members from accidentally contacting some very hot pieces of machinery.

There wasn't much space, but I squeezed by, heading farther aft and also a bit deeper into the ship. I was still not totally used to my high-power HID light. The battery pack is attached to the right side of my backplate, and a three-foot-long electrical line emerges from the pack, ending at the light itself. The light is mounted on a U-shaped bracket, a Goodman handle. The handle slides over my gloved right hand, leaving the hand free to do some work, yet allowing me to shine the very bright lamp wherever I point my hand. In theory, it's the ultimate underwater dive lighting system.

But it's different than what I'm used to. In the past, with my less powerful handheld light, I could hold my reel and the light both in my left hand. This left my right hand free to tend to things, including entanglements and other problems. Because I have the new light mounted on the right hand, the Goodman handle catches line, making it difficult to manipulate and correct the line problem. I even had to drop the thing to free myself during my recent entanglement.

Well, I'm not sure how it happened, again on this dive now, but I must have become distracted with my light or something; I dropped the reel somehow. Just like the last time I was here inside the *San Diego*, the reel un-spooled as it dropped down and came to rest on some debris about 10 feet below me on the next deck. Last time, I was able to go outside the wreck and come back in through a different hole to retrieve the reel. But I could see that this time I would not be able to do that. I was deeper inside the wreck this time, and there was no way to reach my reel.

I gently pulled on the line. The reel obliged and un-spooled, creating billowing tentacles of dangerous line. The reel was not locked, so if I wanted to retrieve it by pulling on the line, I would have to let the line un-spool fully before I could pull the reel back up to me. I checked my air and bottom time. Looked to be okay. I tried jerking the line to get the reel to jam. No such luck. This Halcyon reel has never jammed on me yet and it was not about to jam today. I pulled the line off the reel and wound it around my left arm as fast as I could. Finally, with all the line now wrapped around my arm, the reel came up at last. I could see the dim green light of an exit. I headed over there, cut the line, balled it up, and left it tucked between metal plates so that it wouldn't be a hazard to other divers. The other end of the line was still attached to to the ship where I initially entered. No time to remove that on this dive. I'd been down 43 minutes, still had about 1500 psi of air, and was in no rush. But it was time to leave.

I am going to make two changes to my setup. One, I'll put the light on my left so I can keep it in my left hand like I used to. Second, I will attach a lanyard to my reel so that it cannot be dropped and lost again.

Bottle Diving in the Long Island Sound off of New Rochelle – Sunday, January 7, 2007

Someone please tell Al Gore that global warming has at least one positive thing about it. We are having some real nice weather here in the New York area. Temperatures were near 70 on Saturday and a bit lower on Sunday, but clear, sunny skies and not having to get to the boat until 8:00 a.m. made for a great day of diving.

I went out with three other divers on the dive boat *Sea Hawk*, captained by Frank Persico. This winter, his boat—normally berthed on the south shore of Long Island—is on the Long Island Sound, near Port Washington. We took a 30-minute run over flat, calm seas to the entrance to the municipal marina of New Rochelle. Commuting to Westchester was never such fun.

"Sea Hawk" Charter Dive Boat

Courtesy Captain Frank Persico

At our target depth of about seven feet, we were guaranteed a long dive on a single tank as long as we were suitably suited, so to speak, in the 50-degree water. I had an 85-minute dive and was comfortable the whole time. Visibility was fine. At least 10 feet, until you touched the silty bottom. Then the water would instantly turn black, full of swirling clouds that were impenetrable to anything except radar.

I wear dry gloves and have to be a bit careful about jagged-edged glass, so on this dive I brought my little gardener's shovel. Unfortunately, the old rusty shovel was a casualty of the dive. It snapped off at the handle during some particularly rough digging after providing me with years of service.

But soon I realized that there were many bottles visible on the seafloor in the area that I was in—there was no need to dig. Just be observant. I had brought a big, yellow mesh bag in addition to my red canvas bag, and soon it was so full of stuff that it was dragging on the bottom like a prisoner's ball and chain.

The idea here is to KEEP MOVING, to stay ahead of the cloud of silt you are creating by picking up the bottles. Each "surface bottle" is actually embedded in the mud, perhaps showing only a bit of itself. Pulling it out creates a huge mess. There is no delicate way to do it. If you take your time doing it, you just are giving the inevitable cloud more time to envelop you. So pick 'em up, smoothly put 'em in a bag, and KEEP MOVING. Before you touch anything, look around, because if there is a second or a third bottle right there that you want, you need to record its position in your mind so that you can get it when you're blinded by the silt from the first bottle.

I used my own silt cloud as a guide, working in one direction and then back along its edge. Hmm, I thought. What's that over there? Looks like a bloated human hand, severed at the wrist.

I let my imagination run wild as I approached it. It looked like a human hand, distended with decomposition gases. Some poor diver must have lost it on a boat prop or while digging in the muck and encountering a glass guillotine. I gingerly picked it up, shook it politely, and placed it in my bag. Perhaps I would need an extra hand later when cleaning the bottles.

Soon my bag was very heavy. I decided to toss out some of the questionable bottles I had picked up early in the dive. Now I was finding some very old ones. A little while later, I decided that my bag was way too heavy to be dragging around, so I inflated my six-foot Halcyon safety sausage and attached the mesh bag to it. Now I could tow the mesh bag behind me, suspended three feet above the bottom, while putting bottles into it as if it were a shopping cart in a supermarket.

Slowly I made my way back to the *Sea Hawk*, where the others were busy cleaning out their bottles. My bag was almost too heavy to lift onto the boat. When I went through it, I was pleased to find that quite a few of the bottles had writing on them, including dates such as "1908." And I had some with "bulb tops," which indicated that they were quite old. I also found some ceramics ranging from an intact coffee cup to part of a creamer set which was decorated with a colorful pattern. There was also a thing with teeth sticking out of it—I'm not quite sure what THAT is!

A lot of the stuff went back into the water, including the "hand," which turned out to be a mannequin hand or something similar.

We had a great barbeque on board and were back at the dock by 12:45 p.m. Belly full of pork ribs and steak, I was happy. The only thing missing from this dive was my traditional nap on the boat, but I took care of that when I got home. My wife did insist that I put the stinky bottles—which were encrusted with still-living shellfish—on the terrace, and she made me scrub the sink I had used with disinfectant. I pointed out that one of the bottles clearly said "Listerine" (it was probably from the 1930s or so). But I still had to thoroughly clean my mess.

Diving the USS San Diego – Saturday, May 5, 2007

What a great day I had yesterday! My sunburned face is evidence of the clear, sunny skies. My pleasantly aching body gives testimony to the exertions of an underwater explorer. I went out on the *Garloo*—its first trip of the season—and we had an uneventful ride over calm seas to the USS *San Diego*. As usual, on the way out I grabbed a bunk and dozed off listening to my iPod.

The RV *Garloo* has long been a part of local dive history, both now and in her previous incarnation as the RV *Wahoo*, and has always been a favorite of mine. Now reconfigured with cabins for overnight trips, it's different, but I still enjoy going out on her. I wish I could go on one of the weekend trips, but now with one-year-old Sophia at home, I am grateful to be able to get out to the wrecks a couple of times a month on day trips.

The *Garloo*, for now, does not do a barbeque. Diving, diving, and diving is what it's about. So I brought alternative chow. One of my favorite items to bring when there is no barbeque is, oddly enough, a barbequed chicken. Something very primal about doing my dive and then standing at the stern ripping at the poor bird with my bare hands, throwing the bones in the water as I eat. I usually turn to whoever is standing near me—possibly a seasick person—and offer them some chicken. I am quite a sight with barbeque sauce all over my face and hands, talking with a big chunk of chicken in my mouth. Mmmm, want some? The other person usually declines.

Well, the chickens did not look up to my high standards at the local supermarket the night before, so I had to come up with a plan B. The *Garloo* has a full complement of galley equipment, so I brought one of those Korean shrimp kimchi soups that come in the large foam bowls. Just add boiling water and only half of the spice packet and you have a nice, spicy noodle soup. Add the full spice packet and you are in trouble! Very spicy! I also brought a package of large frozen, cooked shrimp that I figured would defrost by about 11 a.m. I would toss them in the soup.

The boat was not crowded, and it was a pleasure suiting up. There were no other dive boats on the wreck. I followed the granny line to the descent line and found that we were tied in on the light side (the upside-down USS *San Diego*'s starboard side) right at the end of the bilge keel, towards the stern of the great ship.

About three weeks ago, I dove the *San Diego* along with my scooter, *Apollo*, and did a lazy survey of the exterior of the wreck, which is as long as a 50-story building is high and as wide as a six- or seven-story building. I looped around her effortlessly with *Apollo*, spying some new openings and finding that the crack in her keel, which runs across her at the other end of the bilge keels towards the bow, had enlarged. Today, though, we were at the stern, and I didn't have my scooter, so I would limit my explorations to local features.

I knew exactly where I wanted to go. Finding the end of the starboard bilge keel, I headed across the bottom of the immense ship to the dark side and descended down along the side of the ship towards the sand. There are openings into the ship here, and last season I had penetrated the wreck in this area many times. My goal for today (not having done any penetrations since last season) was to do an easy one in an already-familiar area, just to warm up on my reel and my "slithering" skills. I entered through an opening I'd used before.

Before I entered the water, I had a conversation with another diver who told me that he never runs a reel inside a wreck, implying that it was dangerous, and that he does "progressive penetration," and learns an area before proceeding. Because of that conversation and the fact that I was going into an area I had been in a number of times before, I decided not to run a reel. There are a couple of ways to do a wreck penetration. One way is to enter spaces through which you will obviously fit easily, and to make sure you have a wide path. If you use this approach, you are a bit limited in terms of how far you can go because of lack of cooperation from the wreck. When I'm using a line, I usually end up wriggling between things and along encrusted equipment, and that is often more challenging. If I turn around to see how I entered a space, it's not at all always clear to me and I am grateful for the line.

By now I was a bit into the wreck. I turned around and saw the green light of the hole through which I'd entered. It wasn't far away, but my exit path was not obvious. I had not gone in far at all, but this disorientation served to remind me that I had promised myself to *always* run a line when going into a wreck. I turned around, easily returned to the entrance, tied off my line, and headed back in.

My biggest enemy when diving is myself. There is a kind of thinking that plagues even advanced divers, perhaps even more than newer divers. It's a kind of thinking that denies that an accident can happen. Not to me, never to me. So critical safety steps are omitted. SCUBA diving is unforgiving, and taking that omitted precaution can one day mean the difference between life and death.

For example, many advanced divers carry an additional small air tank for decompression. I always carry one everywhere with me underwater. Many divers leave the tank outside the wreck if they go in at the base of the ascent line. Their argument is that it could get caught on something when they go inside the wreck; they can easily pick it up again at the base of the ascent line when they're finished with their dive. But what if they get lost in or on the wreck and have to do an emergency ascent? Now they have no deco bottle. It does happen. Or what if they encounter another diver who's low on air, start "buddy breathing" (as people do on an emergency ascent), and cannot go back to get their bottles? That recently happened, resulting in the two divers being airlifted by helicopter to a recompression chamber.

Sometimes, when you talk to the divers who don't carry their bottles with them, they'll scornfully say something like, "If you can't get back to your stage bottle, you shouldn't be diving," implying that an experienced diver would never run low on air or have a problem finding their deco bottle. But the fact is that it DOES happen to the most experienced divers, especially the ones doing more aggressive things like wreck penetration. As I said, SCUBA and the sea are unforgiving, so these divers get seriously hurt or die the first time they are wrong.

That all in mind, I continued my buddy-less penetration of the wreck, heading astern and realizing that this place, which I thought I knew from last season's explorations, had changed, and I did not recognize it inside as well as I would have liked. Just to give me the heebie-jeebies, I covered my light and floated motionless for a minute, letting my eyes adjust to the darkness. This was dark. Not one glimmer of light in any direction. Had I a problem with my light and my backup light, my reel line would have been the only way I would be able to have even a hint of how to get out of here.

These are small spaces inside the wreck. I was somewhere in or around the engine room. With my light uncovered, I could see massive pieces of equipment: the great steam engine's pistons and the arms connected to them, all covered with the same brown growth—hundreds of generations of sea creatures. I continued aft. I shone my light down at what appeared to be a sledgehammer, also encrusted. I could picture the engine-room sailors in the 110-degree heat, two of them using sledgehammers, perhaps to loosen a lever or a huge locked bolt that was stuck. Shirts off, their brows dripping sweat, a cacophony of noise from the massive engines.

The USS *San Diego* sank in 1918. Let's say that some of her crew were as young as 18 at the time. Any still alive would be 107 years old today in 2007. There is probably no one left to tell us if my mental picture of working in the engine room is realistic or not. I bet none of those young crew members ever gave much thought to the idea that she might sink offshore of Fire Island, New York, or that a few brave souls would visit her every year as she slowly disintegrated into the sand.

I looked at my air and realized that even though I could explore the inside for another 10 minutes or so, I was getting chilled in the 43-degree water. I proceeded forward into a wider area so I could easily turn around and head back out. Exiting was a good reminder as to why I run a line. There was absolutely no ambient light. My line ran between vertical poles and debris in such a manner that more than once I said to myself, "This is how I came in?" Trusting my line, I exited without incident and was soon outside the ship again. I rose to the top of the ship. The top of the wreck at this point is about 80 feet beneath the surface. The sand is about 105, perhaps almost 110 in some places. I crossed the broad keel, using the lines of the plates to make sure I was crossing straight across, and decided to stay a bit longer around the massive guns on the light side of the ship.

Inside the wreck, I'd moved slowly, so I got a bit chilled. Here, I was moving faster and felt more comfortable. I swam out to the end of the enormous gun barrel and again had that "wow" feeling, just like on the National Geographic Channel! I just love my hobby, diving history! You know, as big as these guns are, they are not the largest on the ship. These fired six-inch shells. The big ones were mounted on turrets on the deck and fired eight-inch shells. The heavy main guns must have been a factor in the capsizing of the ship after she struck a mine placed by a German U-boat. Those guns were so heavy that, once the ship rolled over, they probably ripped out of their turrets and preceded the ship to the sand below, the inverted ship slamming down on top of them. Live artillery rounds are still to be found on the USS *San Diego*, so if you see something that looks like an artillery shell, don't play with it!

Back on board, I enjoyed my delicious shrimp kimchi soup and a bottle of Gatorade, and then slept until the slowing of the engines as we entered Fire Island Inlet.

Author's Note

*In Europe, the 'Stone Age' ended thousands of years ago. The Stone Age in North America though, only ended with the arrival of Europeans **hundreds** of years ago. There are uncountable rocks underwater along our shores suggestive of those early stone age technologies...*

To the new diver, my experiences may sound exciting and like I am at the leading edge of advanced diving. I am not. There is no shortage of 'North-East Technical Divers' that do bolder things and go further into dangerous wrecks like the San Diego. They stay down longer, go to greater depths and generally push the envelope more than I. To these divers I hope my stories give them a nostalgic feel remembering their first few years diving and their first dives on wrecks like the Oregon and San Diego. The next time you are on a dive boat, listen well to their stories.

The stories in this book were usually written the evening of the dive or the next day while the memories were vivid and fresh in my mind. I couldn't believe I was actually experiencing these things! I kept thinking it's like 'Living the History Channel'. I still have that feeling on almost every dive. My mom tells me that when very young I wanted to be an 'underwater scientist'. I certainly am no scientist but my fascination with the mystery

of the sea continues. I didn't know that one day I would collect my tales into the anthology you have just read. I thought I was writing for myself; for that day in the distant future when I would be too feeble to enjoy this demanding sport. As time went on I found that many in the Long Island/New York area did not realize there was fantastic local diving and so many historical shipwrecks. This book then takes on another purpose, to inspire these other divers and non-divers to try our local waters.

This book seemed to me, to end abruptly. In fact though, the story continues. I am still diving every chance I get. Look out to sea and cup the wind to your ear. If you listen carefully you can hear the sound of the dive boat's engines slowing down as the sunken ship comes into view on the sonar. A splash of the crew and we are tied into the wreck. Another few minutes and it's your turn.... You silently slip beneath the waves into a cold dark world filled with history and the souls of a thousand lost ships.

David Rosenthal
Long Island, New York ,
January 2008

USS San Diego Survey Equipment

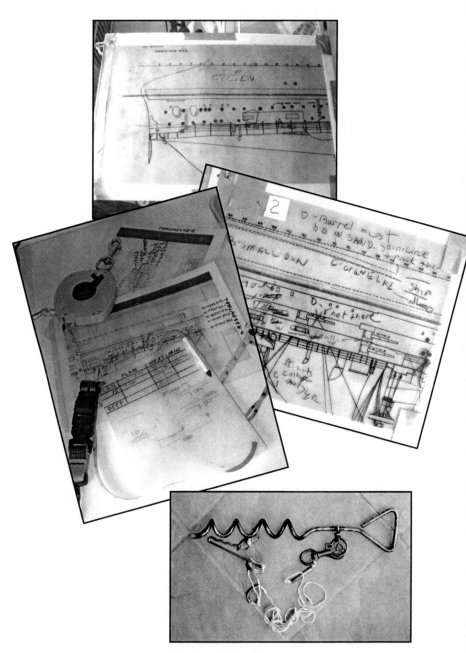

Ponquogue Bay Screw

STORY INDEX
How to use this index:

The page numbers referenced in this index do not reference the page number that a term appears on but rather the page number that a story starts on that contains the selected term. This will allow the reader to easily find all stories where the selected term played a major part. Note that page '1' is the Introduction which was the first mention of many of the indexed terms. Let's say you want to read all the stories where an underwater scooter plays a major role. Look up 'Scooter' and then read the referenced stories. Or perhaps you are diving the wreck of the Oregon for the first time. Look up 'Oregon' under Wrecks and you will be directed to the four stories about her in chronological order.

Dive Boats

Dive Sites (see Wrecks and Dive Sites)

258, 263, 270, 290, 323, 332, 335

Rescue
25, 50, 56, 145, 228, 252, 258, 305, 323

Scooter
1, 56, 66, 81, 83, 101, 119, 123, 139, 145, 150, 151, 174, 202, 208, 218, 220, 223, 228, 235, 240, 243, 248, 252, 256, 258, 291, 299, 318

Seasick
25, 109, 111, 114, 159, 174, 176, 240, 263, 290

Shark
1, 243, 263, 270, 275, 296

Shore
1, 17, 56, 81, 83, 87, 91, 98, 119, 128, 131, 150, 155, 287,313, 343

Technical
1, 19, 37, 43, 50, 56, 62, 69, 91, 119, 135, 139, 145, 162, 179, 184, 198, 228, 252, 270, 296, 299, 305, 323, 332, 335

Techniques
1, 19, 37, 43, 50, 56, 62, 69, 81, 91, 111, 119, 135, 139, 145, 162, 170, 184, 205, 208, 220, 248, 258, 270, 287, 291, 296, 313, 335

Wildlife
1, 69, 81, 83, 87, 124, 139, 150, 151, 198, 223, 235, 240, 243, 248, 256, 263, 270, 275, 291, 296, 299, 311

Wrecks And Dive Sites

Printed in the United States
201498BV00003B/55-75/P